Writing from the Core

A Guide for Writing

Writing from the Core

A Guide for Writing

Dona J. Young

Writing from the Core: A Guide for Writing
Dona J. Young

Cover designed by Caroline Baty-Barr
www.baty-barr.com

Apple illustrated by Katherine Orr
www.katorriginal.com

ISBN: 978-0-9815742-0-2

Printed in the United States

Writer's Toolkit Publishing LLC
109 Ogden Road
Ogden Dunes, IN 46368
877-933-0910
www.wtkpublishing.com

The authors and editors have used their best efforts to insure that the information presented herein is accurate at the time of publication.

To Charley

Brief Contents

Part 4 Editing for Clarity 187

Part 5 More Mechanics 253

Introduction

Writing depends on structure for sense and credibility and, at the same time, structure can interfere with writing. For example, when you stop composing to struggle over correct grammar or punctuation, you do so at the expense of losing your ideas.

Writing involves critical thinking, bringing higher levels of understanding to unique topics or problems. In contrast, structure is about syntax: how words string together for different effects. Structure, for the most part, involves applying finite rules; in contrast, writing entails creativity, curiosity, and inquiry.

Writing is a complex problem-solving activity, and learning about structure adds another layer of complicated information to an already challenging pursuit. That is because elements of structure are linked: to understand one principle, you must also understand a myriad of other concepts, making it easy to become confused. So why even discuss structure?

One reason is that using correct and effective structure adds clarity and credibility to writing. Another is that as you mull over how to make your words string together in more effective ways, you are likely to gain more insight into your topic.

Writing from the Core simplifies essential topics and orders them so that one concept builds to the next. Complex principles become easier to understand because you review foundational principles first.

Writing from the Core takes you step-by-step on a path that leads to correct, clear, and concise writing. As you learn each new principle, your editing and revising skills will improve, and thus the quality of your writing will also improve—as long as you apply what you are learning.

By the time that you finish this book, you will have significantly improved your writing skills—or more specifically, your revising and editing skills. Good luck on your journey, and remember that practice makes progress: *Now go for it!*

Dona Young

About This Book

Writing from the Core untangles structure, easing you into complex concepts by first covering foundational principles. This book applies the method of *principle and practice*: as you learn each principle, practice it until you integrate it into your writing.

Part 1, Foundations, reviews core principles for writing and revising. In Chapter 1, you learn about the writing process; in Chapter 2, you review the sentence core; and in Chapter 3, you learn how to structure cohesive, coherent paragraphs.

The sentence core is where structure and writing cross paths: controlling the sentence core is key to producing correct and reader-friendly sentences. Once you understand the sentence core, issues of style such as using the active voice, applying parallel structure, and being concise become easy.

Part 2, Mechanics for Writing, presents comma and semicolon rules, taking the guessing out of punctuating and reinforcing the sentence core.

Part 3, Grammar for Writing, covers the basics of verbs, pronouns, and modifiers, other core elements of structure.

Part 4, Editing for Clarity, presents principles that lead to a clear and concise writing style.

To achieve excellent results, do the exercises in the prescribed manner. Improving writing skills is a bit tricky: the more you write, the stronger your skills will become; but first, stop the habit of editing and revising as you compose:

Compose freely and then edit ruthlessly.

Once you start working on Part 3, Grammar for Writing, this book helps you identify the difference between local language patterns and Standard English (also referred to as Edited English).

As you may know, everyone speaks a local language to one degree or another. In fact, no geographical location exists in the United States (or anywhere in the world, for that matter) where Standard English is spoken "purely." In every location, people have their own particular way of using English that varies slightly in terms of grammar, word usage, and pronunciation.

Since no one speaks or writes English perfectly, perfection is not your goal. Instead, focus on improving your skills until you become competent and confident; you then have more options for how you use language in formal situations.

This book helps you improve your writing skills because it helps you become an expert editor. Start the process by taking the pretest at the end of Chapter 1. Your score will give you a starting point from which you can gauge your current skills and track your development.

Work through each chapter and do the activities as prescribed. To give yourself immediate reinforcement for your practice, refer to the keys to the exercises. You will find the keys to the Practice exercises, the Skills Workshops, and the Editing Workshops at the back of the book in **Keys to Activities**, starting on page 407.

Learning involves change, and change is challenging, even painful at times. That is why you must commit yourself to the learning process as well as the writing process. If you commit yourself, you will become an expert editor by the time that you finish this book. In fact, you may even become an *incurable editor*! Good luck on your journey.

A Note to Teachers

Writing from the Core is a supplemental handbook for any class that requires writing. *Writing from the Core* covers similar content as other handbooks while sequencing principles from the simple to the complex and using a narrative style to engage learners.

Writing is a core activity in education as well as the professions. Even those who are challenged by writing must learn to write effectively or be seriously limited in their career options. Professionals in all fields communicate in writing: e-communication has sealed the importance of writing—if not for eternity, at least for the present.

A traditional approach to improving writing skills has been to work with learners individually, giving them feedback and coaching. This approach is powerful, yet it also consumes time while keeping significant accountability in the hands of the teacher rather than in the hands of the learner.

As an alternative, *Writing from the Core* quickly gives learners a set of principles on which to base writing decisions. Learners also acquire a common vocabulary to discuss editing, making peer editing activities productive and even fun. *Writing from the Core* easily allows you to:

- Present chapters in workshop format.
- Encourage learners to work on specific learning activities on their own or with a peer, using the keys at the back of the book.

Writing from the Core charts an instructional design that is in tune with the Taxonomy of Educational Objectives. As a result, learners readily fill knowledge gaps that may have gone undiagnosed. For example, the Taxonomy reveals why learners have a more difficult time with higher-order principles of writing if they do not first understand lower-order principles. The Taxonomy also gives insight into how a graduate student can write an insightful analysis of a complex theory but still have difficulty with run-on sentences or subject-verb agreement.

Once learners understand the sentence core, they are on the path to understanding structure, working from the simple to the complex. Sentence fragments and run-ons are no longer mysteries, and advanced principles such as parallel structure and consistent viewpoint become easily achievable. Even the graduate student who analyzes complex theories gains more credibility by presenting ideas in a style that is engaging as well as correct.

Writing from the Core also provides teachers and learners with a common vocabulary for punctuation. The "shortcuts" this approach includes makes it easier to learn the rules and to provide feedback efficiently. The methodology also integrates principles of structure with principles of style so that a learner's writing becomes correct as well as clearer and more concise.

Experiment using individual chapters as workshops; or instead, incorporate more activity-based learning by having learners read a chapter and then teach the principles to each other in small groups.

For additional pre- and posttests as well as other supplemental materials, please contact me at www.wtkpublishing.com. Additional worksheets are also located at www.commasrule.com. I look forward to hearing from you.

All the best,

Dona Young

About the Author

Dona Young is a teacher and facilitator. In addition to teaching writing at Indiana University Northwest, she facilitates writing and communication programs for corporations.

Young holds a B.A. from Northern Illinois University and an M.A. from The University of Chicago. Young considers herself a lifelong learner, believing that who we become is a result of what we learn. Young is also the author the following books.

Which Comes First, the Comma or the Pause?
A Practical Guide to Writing
Writer's Toolkit Publishing, 2009

The Mechanics of Writing
Writer's Toolkit Publishing, 2008

Business English: Writing for the Global Workplace
McGraw-Hill Higher Education, 2008

Foundations of Business Communication: An Integrative Approach
McGraw-Hill/Irwin, 2006

And on the lighter side:

The Princess and Her Gift
A Tale on the Practical Magic of Learning
Writer's Toolkit Publishing, 2009

The Little Prince Who Taught a Village to Sing
(with *Andrew's Story*)
Writer's Toolkit Publishing, 2009

Contents

Part 2 Mechanics for Writing 73

Part 4 Editing for Clarity

PART 1: FOUNDATIONS

Chapter 1: The Writing Process

Chapter 2: The Sentence

Chapter 3: Paragraphs and Transitions

Even though writing and structure can be at odds with each other, you have a way out of this quandary. Here is how:

- First, manage the writing process effectively: learn to compose freely.
- Second, diligently build your editing and revising skills.

While you compose, you are creating: you are putting original thoughts on paper. While you edit and revise, you are analyzing, evaluating, and re-working structure on many levels; but you are also gaining new insight into your topic.

Composing is a process, and Chapter 1 gives you basic tools for managing the writing process. However, do not underestimate the discipline it takes to apply what you learn. Composing is the most difficult part of writing because you are *thinking on paper*, and each new insight takes energy and effort.

Revising is also a process. You start your journey to build editing and revising skills by working on the sentence core, the power base of every sentence. The sentence core teaches you structure, opening the door for understanding grammar for writing and for applying principles of editing.

Once you understand structure, issues of style, such as using the active voice, applying parallel structure, and being concise become easy. These principles are covered in Part 3: Grammar for Writing and Part 4: Editing for Clarity.

Here is what you will learn in **Part 1: Foundations:**

Chapter 1, The Writing Process: you learn how to manage the writing process, separating composing from editing. You also learn about pre-writing and revising as well as about audience, purpose, and voice.

Chapter 2, The Sentence: you learn how to control the sentence core, the starting point for gaining control of structure. Once you understand structure, verbs, pronouns, and modifiers become easy to understand; in addition, principles of editing, such as active voice, become easy to apply.

Chapter 3, Paragraphs and Transitions: you learn how to develop cohesive, coherent paragraphs. Effective paragraphs contribute to reader-friendly writing.

By the time you finish this book, you may find that you are an incurable editor; but that will happen only if you apply what you are learning to your own writing. As you work through each chapter, write on a daily basis; writing in a journal loosens up your composing skills. However, to develop your thinking skills, you need to use writing to solve problems.

When you get to Part 3, Grammar for Writing, you learn that grammar is more than a set of rules—grammar is alive. Every time that you shift the way that you speak, you are actually shifting your grammar. Part 3 helps you gain control of your various voices, showing you how to use your local language as a springboard for improving your Edited English.

Use this book to expand your language skills and gain control of how you speak and write: the stronger your skills, the more academic and professional options that you have.

1

The Writing Process

When you write, what are you trying to achieve? Are you more concerned about your grade or what you will learn?

Focusing on the *writing process* rather than *final product* aids you in achieving an important aim of writing, which is *to learn*. Writing develops your thinking skills, partly because writing itself is a problem-solving activity. As you write, you gain insight that leads you to deeper levels of understanding. Writing forces you to clarify your thinking.

Even so, when writing is difficult for you, none of that matters. You want to get your writing tasks finished as quickly as possible so that you can bring your "suffering" to an end. That way of thinking leads to the **first and final draft** approach to writing: you force yourself to get your words down right as you compose. As you try to get your words down "right," your ideas evaporate before they hit the page. Being stuck . . . well, that is downright frustrating.

The fact is, trying to make too many decisions all at the same time is one reason why you get stuck. First and final draft writing is a habit that results from anxiety about the final product, a habit that also makes writing much more difficult than it needs to be. Therefore, here is the most important principle to learn about the writing process:

Compose *or* edit, but do not do both at the same time.

To compose freely, you must not only understand the writing process but also embrace the process. Dropping the first and final draft mentality is a huge first step, even if you think the first and final draft approach works for you. You see, even if you get good grades, the first and final draft approach robs you of long-term learning.

In this chapter, you learn composing techniques and tools as well as more about each phase of the writing process. Then in the following chapters, you learn how to make effective editing decisions to improve your final product.

Though improving your writing skills may seem like an ominous task right now, realize that writing is a skill. Like all skills, writing improves with practice. So let's get started learning how to manage the process so that you gain control of your writing.

Process to Product

The best papers look as if they were easy to write: the words flow and the ideas link together logically. Yet behind every beautiful, finished piece of writing lies uncertainty and hard work. Even the best writers question themselves and their ability as they write. While writing *Grapes of Wrath*, John Steinbeck wrote in his journal,

> I'm not a writer. I've been fooling myself and other people. I wish I were. My work is not good, I think—I'm desperately upset about it. Have no discipline any more . . . [1]

Part of the reason writers—including you—become so discouraged is that they become concerned about the final product while in the midst of creating it. Uncertainty never feels good. Therefore, one challenge all writers have is immersing themselves in uncertainty as they work toward deeper understanding.

Once you start writing, you gain deeper insight into your topic, even when you are not consciously thinking about it. Writing forces you to make progress, even when it feels painful: putting critical thoughts on paper takes energy and courage because you are forced to think clearly.

Writing is a creative process, so you cannot depend on formulas to produce good writing. However, embracing the process allows you to take your attention off of the product and instead to focus your energies to get the best results.

The writing process consists of distinct phases, for example: [2]

- **Composing**:   creating, inventing, exploring, solving problems
- **Proofreading**: correcting grammar, punctuation, and spelling
- **Editing**:   improving the quality and structure of sentences
- **Revising**:   changing, rearranging, and reinventing

Though the above phases are not sequential, they are cyclical. Thus, when you write, move back and forth between compositing activities and editing activities, but stay focused on one type of activity or the other.

Think of composing as a right-brain activity and editing as a left-brain activity. When you compose, you are drawing from your creative side; when you edit, you are drawing on your analytical skills. That is one reason why you can quickly get stuck when you edit as you compose.

Until you are able to compose freely, writing is much more difficult for you than it needs to be. When you stop editing as you compose, and composing still feels excruciatingly difficult, you may not yet understand your topic. When that is the case, focus on *the thinking behind the writing*. In fact, you may be confusing the difficulty of writing with the difficulty of clearly understanding your topic.

So let's add one more phase to the writing process: **pre-writing**. You see, the writing process actually begins *before* you start to compose.

Pre-Writing and Composing

Have you ever started writing and found yourself stuck? Trying to compose before you are ready contributes to **writer's block**.

Writing is a process because learning is a process. By focusing on pre-writing activities, you develop your understanding of your topic in a more gentle, natural way and have a better chance for good results. So if you find yourself avoiding a writing task, do some pre-writing activities:

- **Pre-writing**:   reading, thinking, discussing, summarizing

Reading is a form of meditation or reflection, and some of your best ideas bubble up as you read. Activities such as walking or discussing your project with a friend also allow you to reflect on your topic. Reflective thinking gives you insights when you least expect them; so when you feel blocked, change activities but stay engaged.

As you read and discuss, jot down insights and questions and put concepts in your own words. Keep a notebook or note cards handy so that you can collect your insights as you experience them.

However, do not make the mistake of thinking that you need to understand your topic completely before you start writing:

Write to learn.

Write yourself clear-headed: as you write, your understanding becomes clearer. Go back and forth between pre-writing and composing: when you feel stuck, read more and then discuss your ideas with a peer. After you read and take notes, summarize what you have learned *in your own words*. (Cut and paste plagiarism will hold you back and destroy your confidence.)

Set a time to write, and then show up and trust the process:

Start early and write often,
even when you do not feel like writing.

As soon as you take action, you will feel better and have something to show for your efforts. Getting your ideas on the page, even when your thinking is "messy," is a hurdle you must overcome. You need to get your rough draft thinking on the page before your best insights appear.

Write about what you know first. Start with the body, developing your core ideas. The body will lead you to your conclusion. Once you have written your conclusion, you will have a clear idea about how to write your introduction, posing the questions you have already answered.

At some point, you must come to terms with your purpose for writing. You see, without clarifying your purpose, you cannot be sure that you understand your mission. Here are two mistakes writers make:

1. Trying to understand their purpose fully *before* they start writing.

2. Thinking their project is complete *without* defining their purpose.

Whether you define your purpose before you start writing or whether you jump right into a task to see where it leads depends partly on your learning style.[3] For example:

- **Global learners** tend to be spontaneous, jumping right into a task to see where it will lead.

- **Analytic learners** plan and organize, focusing on the details.

Can you tell by the above descriptions which type of learner you are? If not, you can go to the Internet to research *learning styles*. Knowing your learning style validates your unique approach and aids you in making effective choices, especially about the planning elements of writing.

Though global learners might want to jump right in and start writing, analytical learners are likely to prefer putting down more details before they start writing. So let's look at some elements of planning next.

Problem, Purpose, and Plan

Gertrude Stein, an early 20th century writer, once said, "What is the question? If there is no question, then there is no answer."[4]

As a writer, you may be drawn to developing your response immediately, sometimes at the peril of not understanding the question that is at the root of your problem.

You see, on some level, all writing involves solving a problem, even though the problem may not always be obvious. Focus on understanding the problem, and eventually your purpose will become clear.

Articulating your purpose not only helps you understand your mission more clearly, it also helps you convey it to your audience more effectively. Once you understand your purpose, your purpose will drive the writing process.

To define your purpose, start by defining your problem:

- What is my core question?

Next, turn your question into a **thesis statement**:[5]

- A thesis statement is a one- or two-sentence summary of the problem along with a general overview of the writer's response.

For example, let's say your task is to write about pollution and the environment. Start by stating the problem as a question:

Thesis Question: How does pollution affect the environment?

Next, turn your question into statement:

Pollution affects the environment by . . .

Finally, once you understand some of the broader implications of your question, draft a statement that reflects your broad response:

Thesis Statement: Pollution affects the environment by destroying specific aspects of it, such as nature and wildlife.

As you write about your purpose, avoid using the word *purpose*. For example, your first draft might include a statement such as the following:

The purpose of this paper is to discuss how pollution affects the environment.

When you revise your purpose statement, remove the word "purpose":

Pollution destroys the environment, especially wildlife and their natural habitats.

Let's turn one more problem into a thesis statement. For example, here is how you could work through the topic *finding a job*:

Thesis Question: What does finding a job entail?

Thesis Statement: Finding a job requires skill and know-how.

The thesis statement typically occurs somewhere in the first paragraph; the first paragraph develops the thesis and gives an overview of the paper. (For more on paragraphs, see Chapter 3: Paragraphs and Transitions.)

Regardless of when you define your purpose, your purpose is likely to change as your thinking becomes deeper and clearer: your writing evolves as your thinking evolves.

Though analytic learners might prefer to write an outline first, global learners are more inclined to use less structured planning tools such as the ones discussed below.

Planning Tools

The planning tools discussed here assist with composing. For example, a tool such as mind mapping focuses attention and ignites critical and creative thinking.

If you do not now think of yourself as being creative, ask yourself if you are good at solving problems. Creativity entails solving problems. *Creativity is listening to the obvious and responding effectively.* Focus on solving the problem, and your writing will flow.

Mind mapping. This form of brainstorming, also called clustering, allows you to get your ideas down in a quick, spontaneous way. First, choose your topic. Next, write your topic in the middle of the page, circling it. Finally, free associate ideas, as in the mind map below which is in response to the question, "What is my dream job?"

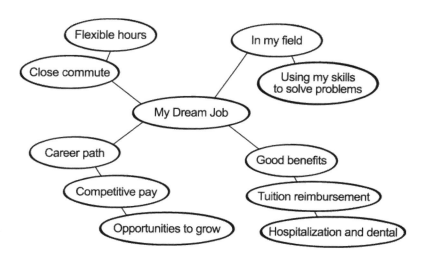

Mind mapping is an alternative to writing a formal outline. If you have great ideas but cannot seem to get them on the page before they dissolve, mind mapping is one part of your solution.

Also use mind mapping as a way to plan your day or to plan an important phone call. Select a topic and work on it for 3 minutes.

Scratch outline. Rather than using the cluster technique of mind mapping, simply make a list of your ideas. Keep a notepad close at hand so that you collect your insights as they come to you.

Freewriting. Get your words on the page in a free-flow, stream-of-consciousness way: pick up a pen and start writing. As you freewrite, you build your ability to compose freely while blocking out your compulsion to correct your writing.

If you have never tried freewriting, simply set the clock for 10 minutes and start writing. Since writing is a problem-solving activity, you may find yourself actively working on solving problems that now drain your energy. Freewriting helps clear your head, allowing you to focus and renew your energy.

Focused writing. Choose a topic and write about only that topic for about 10 to 15 minutes or 3 pages.

Focused writing can help you make good use of small amounts of time that would otherwise be lost. Focused writing can also help you jump-start a project that you have been avoiding.

Page mapping. Put the key points from your scratch outline or mind map along the side of a blank page. Then fill in the details by using each key point as the topic for a focused-writing activity.

This technique helps eliminate one of the biggest fears of any writing task: starting with a blank page. For example, let's say that you did a mind map on "finding a job"; the following could be your side headings:

Finding a Job

Introduction

    Thesis Statement: Finding a job requires skill and know-how.

Networking

    Associations

    Local Organizations

    Online

Portfolio

    Résumés

    Letters of Reference

    Work Samples

Pay and Benefits

    Medical and Dental

    Tuition Reimbursement

    Training

Once you have your page map, write about what you know first. When you get stuck, do more research.

Fishbone Diagramming. A fishbone diagram is also known as a *root-cause diagram* because it forces you to probe deeply into a problem. First, identify the problem. Next, identify major components of your problem. For each component, ask *why* five times.

For example, let's say you have difficulty completing a writing task. Start by turning your problem into a statement and then work through it by asking the question *why* five times.

Problem statement: I am having difficulty with this writing task.

Why?	I am having trouble getting started.
Why?	I am feeling as if it is out of my control.
Why?	I don't understand the topic well enough.
Why?	I haven't done my research.
Why?	I haven't taken the time to find resources.

Once you have gained insight into your problem, here is an additional step to add to your fishbone diagram process:

Next Step: Do research today from 3 to 4 p.m.

Answering Journalist's Questions. Journalists focus on the *who*, *what*, *when*, *where*, *why*, and *how* of an event. When you find yourself stuck, use these questions to tease out the dynamics of your problem.

- **Who?** Who is involved or affected? What are their attitudes and beliefs?

- **What?** What problems need to be resolved? What are the desired outcomes? Which details are important, which irrelevant?

- **When?** When did the event happen? What is the timeline? Is the time frame relevant?

- **Where?** Is a specific location involved? Is the location significant? What is unique about the location?

- **How?** How did the events occur or the situation evolve? Who did what?

- **Why?** Why did this happen? Why is this important? Why is my solution the best?

In addition to using these questions to identify purpose, you may also adapt these questions to plan your task:

- **Who?** Who is my reader? What does my reader expect?

- **What?** What am I trying to achieve? What outcomes can I expect?

- **When?** What is my time frame? When is this project due? What internal due dates do I need to set?

- **How?** How will I complete this task? How can others assist me?

- **Why?** Why is this issue important?

See beyond your own point of view by putting yourself in your readers' "shoes," seeing the problem from various angles. If you are arguing a point or trying to persuade your audience, include the opposing argument and then show how your points are superior.

Now let's look at how to proofread and edit effectively.

Proofreading and Editing

Many people suffer as much from **editor's block** as they do from writer's block: they do not know what to look for to improve the quality of their writing, so they hold their breath, turn in their work, and hope for the best.

The only real solution to editor's block is to develop proofreading and editing skills. Proofreading and editing are distinct activities:

- When you proofread, you are correcting grammar, punctuation, and spelling (but you are not changing the wording).

- When you edit, you are upgrading the quality of writing by improving its readability.

The best time to proofread a document is after you have edited it. Since editing is about making changes, you defeat your purpose if you proofread your writing to perfection before your words are in final form. Often a deadline will put a natural end to editing—but if you do not leave enough time to proofread after you edit, your document will contain errors.

Here are some **proofreading techniques**:

1. Establish proofreading as the final part of your writing process.

2. Set an internal deadline before your project is due so that you have time to correct your work.

3. Read your document sentence by sentence to make sure each is correct, clear, and complete.

4. Print out a copy of your final draft—you will see errors on a hard copy that you will not see on the computer screen.

5. Use revision symbols to mark drafts (see page 15).

6. Keep a log of the types of errors you consistently make along with examples of how to correct them.

Here are some **editing techniques**:

1. Throughout your writing process, go back and forth between composing and editing or revising.

2. Remove or re-write sentences that do not make sense.

3. Edit important documents with a peer.

4. Have someone read your paper out loud to you.

5. Leave as much time as you can between your final draft and your final edit, also allowing sufficient time to revise your document.

6. As you go through each chapter in this book, develop an editing checklist.

Take a moment now to review the revision symbols on the next page. Only the most commonly used symbols are listed, with many more revision symbols being available for professional editors.

Revision symbols provide a common language for writers so that they can edit and proofread efficiently. Practice using these revision symbols until you become comfortable with them, even applying them when you edit your own work.

Can you think of an instance when someone edited your work and you did not understand certain symbols? Or can you think of a time when you saw a symbol but glanced over it because you did not understand it?

While proofreading and editing ensure that a document is correct and written in a reader-friendly style, revising brings your work to its highest level of quality. So let's take a look at revising next.

Revision Symbols

Symbol	Meaning	Example
∧	Insert a letter or word	I nee^d to go to ^{the} store now.
⊥	Add a space	at our$^\#$next meeting
ℓ	Delete a letter or word	most of the ^{ℓ}the times
⊂	Delete a space	Too ⌒ many spaces
∪∖	Transpose letters or words	I believe you that said
⊡	Indent	⊡ In the next chapter,
≡	Capitalize	chicago, illinois
⊐⊏	Center	⊐Title⊏
/	Lowercase a letter	While You were out
⋯	Do not change: Stet	at 5 p.m. on May 15 and 16
⊂⊃	Spell out	We will arrive at your apt on Fri
♂	Move as shown	President Janet Sims
DS⊏	Double-space	DS The next presentation will reveal the changes that are being made.
SS⊏	Single-space	SS Bring your laptop to the meeting next week.
‖	Align vertically	‖ Please let me know by Friday.
⊙	Insert a period	The date is near ⊙
¶	New paragraph	The project has been completed. ¶ The new budget is not ready.

Revising

When you revise, your goal is to evaluate your content, not to change the way your words flow. Your revisions reflect your deeper understanding of your topic and your purpose.

Revising is a *re-visioning* process. Revising requires that you see your material with fresh eyes and an open mind. You are ready to revise once you know your topic at a deeper level than when you first started writing about it.

Change is inherent in the thinking process, and answers change as your thinking evolves. As you revise, you are likely to find that you must shed some of your original thinking, which can be painful. You are also likely to find that you must shed some of your well-constructed sentences and paragraphs, which can also be difficult.

To revise, you must step back and evaluate your document and its purpose. Here are some qualities of the **revising process**:

- **Re-visioning.** Has your vision shifted? Does your purpose statement or thesis still reflect the essence of your document? What are your main points?

- **Questioning.** Are there gaps in your thinking? Have you developed your thinking beyond first responses or superficial ones? Are you overly attached to an answer that may not be complete? Are you trying to make answers fit where they do not fit?

- **Identifying Critical Issues.** Can your reader easily identify your main points? Have you presented critical information first? Do you need to reorganize information or eliminate empty information?

- **Rewriting.** Do you need to rewrite some parts because you have reached a new perspective?

First drafts are the most difficult because the content is unfamiliar. Once the topic becomes familiar, ideas flow and writing becomes easier.

Writing, specifically revising, is a *recursive activity*: *recursive* means that it is a process that can repeat itself indefinitely. Each time you go into a piece of writing to revise it, your new vision reflects your deeper understanding. And, at some point, you also need to say to yourself, "This piece is finished—it's time to move on!"

Voice and Audience

Voice is an elusive element of writing that speaks to a reader, engaging the person as well as the intellect. Voice is the connective tissue of all types of writing, not just creative or personal writing, but professional writing as well. Whenever writing does not engage readers, they have difficulty connecting with the topic at hand.

Developing your voice is as important as understanding your audience. In fact, the first step in adapting to your audience is writing in a reader-friendly style. Simple, clear, concise writing meets the needs of any audience more effectively than does complicated, artificial writing. Therefore, before you worry too much about your audience, focus on developing your voice, your style.

If your writing is more complicated than your speech, keep the following mind:

If you would not say it that way, do not write it that way.

Right now, you may be going out of your way to make your writing sound more formal, using words such as *utilization* instead of *use*. Or perhaps you use canned phrases such as "per your request." Would you ever sit across the table with someone at lunch and say, "Per our previous discussion, . . . "?

Readers do not connect with writing unless it is alive and in the moment. To change your writing style, let go of artificial, canned constructions and instead begin to say what you mean in a clear, direct voice. As you write more, this kind of simple writing will come natural to you. By the way, to avoid using "per," simply say, "as we discussed."

Getting past the stage of complicated writing may seem challenging at first. The only solution is to write freely and frequently until you bring your writing to a higher level of skill and comfort.

However, complicated writing may not be your issue. Could it be that your writing sounds too informal and your grammar needs repair? If that is the case,

**Just because you would say it that way
does not mean that you should write it that way.**

At face value, this saying seems to contradict the previous. However, different writers have different issues. Regardless of the issue that interferes with your writing, your solution is the same: write freely and frequently.

Finding your voice is not a one-time event. *Voice* is a process in which you reconnect with yourself, your topic, and your readers every time you sit down to write. Connecting with yourself and others is what makes writing challenging and also what turns writing into a powerful learning tool. As you gain insight, you grow personally and have the opportunity to make important changes.

If you have not yet found your voice, stay committed to the process. As discussed, the first step involves writing until you feel as comfortable writing as you do speaking. The next step is learning how to connect with any topic until you learn it well enough to write freely about it. The final step entails editing and revising your writing until it meets the needs of your audience.

On the path to finding your voice, ask yourself:

- Who is my audience? What do my readers need to know?
- What are my insights, my personal truths?
- What can I teach my readers so that they gain value?

Writing in a journal daily is one step in the process of finding your voice: you are writing not only about topics that are close to your heart but also about topics that you know by heart, which allows you to compose freely. As you write honestly about a topic, you have the opportunity to develop yourself more fully, if that is one of your objectives.

When you compose, do not worry about your voice. Once you are able to write freely, your voice will appear. First get your ideas, your insights, your reflections on the page.

Others may still not hear your voice until after you edit your work. Right now, your voice may be buried under unnecessary and complicated words and the passive voice. Writing from an effective and consistent point of view may also feel out of reach. As you learn to edit, you also learn how to cut and reshape your words so that they connect with your readers.

After a while, you will know whether or not you are speaking from your voice as you compose. Even then, you will need to edit out the clutter so that your voice becomes strong and clear. You see, finding your voice may be about composing, but clarifying your voice is more about editing. Adapting your writing for your audience is as much about editing as it is about composing. Does that surprise you?

The Critic

As you write, you may find that you are critical of yourself. Be aware that you may be hyper-sensitive when it comes to expressing your creativity. When you criticize yourself, you drain your energy and motivation.

Shut down your critics.

Shutting down your inner critic is more difficult than dealing with criticism from others. In fact, the worst part of criticism from others is that it triggers self-criticism, those automatic negative thoughts that drain your energy and self-confidence.

When you feel especially critical of yourself, write about it. Writing about your fears and your feelings processes them so that you do not get stuck feeling helpless. Write until you talk yourself back into feeling strong and secure.

By showing your writing to others when you feel confident, you are more likely to accept their feedback graciously. If your objective is to learn how to improve, you are likely to gain knowledge that spurs you on. However, if your objective is to impress someone, you are likely to be disappointed. Hence, just as you want to shut down your critics, also take your ego out of your writing.

When your ego is overly invested, what you interpret as negative words can shut you down. You have reached an important point in your skill development when you can turn "negative comments" into feedback that spurs you on to higher levels.

An unconscious fear of criticism is worse than criticism itself. That is because once you hear the actual words, you can regroup and emerge stronger. In contrast, fear is paralyzing, and the only way to combat fear is to take action. Start writing, even if you are writing about your own fears.

Fear of criticism goes hand in hand with an unwitting expectation of perfection. When you are disappointed with yourself for not being perfect, you are setting yourself up:

Perfect writing does not exist.

Perfection exists only in the mind, so do not beat yourself up for being human. Instead, expect mistakes, knowing they are the doorway to growth. Each time you embrace a mistake, you have an opportunity to do more than correct the error, you have an opportunity to build your own character.

As Colin Powell once said, "There are no secrets to success. It is the result of preparation, hard work, and learning from failure." Once you learn to embrace your mistakes as learning opportunities, not simply accept them, you have learned a critical life lesson as well.

In Chapter 2, you will review the sentence and learn more about the sentence core, which is the most important element of editing—in fact, the sentence core is the powerhouse of every sentence that you write.

Before going to the next chapter, do the activities at the end of this chapter.

Recap

Learning how to edit helps you make effective writing decisions with more confidence and less effort. However, the only way to become a better writer is to write more, using writing as a problem-solving tool.

Remember, the more you write, the better your skills become, with or without a writing coach.

Here are some of the key points stressed in this chapter:

> Compose freely without looking for the right word or the right wording: *Compose fearlessly and edit ruthlessly!*

> Respond to writing anxiety by working on your task.

> Go back and forth between composing and editing as you work through your project.

> Allow time to revise your work by setting an internal deadline that is earlier than your actual due date.

> Proofread your document as your last step.

> Reach your audience by simplifying your writing.

> Shut down all critics, including yourself, so that you stay energized and focused.

> Use pre-writing and planning tools such as mind mapping, scratch outlines, focused writing, and page maps.

> Follow the plan outlined in this book—no excuses and no shortcuts.

As you write, you are tapping into your creativity and gaining insight. You are also building critical thinking skills and improving your ability to make writing decisions, which improves your career opportunities.

Writing Workshop

Activity 1: What Is Difficult about Writing?

Write a short paper discussing your history as a writer.

1. What is it about writing that challenges you? What causes you to want to give up and walk away?

2. What do you think about your ability to write? What kinds of experiences have shaped your feelings about writing?

3. Have you ever received feedback that made you question your ability to succeed?

4. Finally, what is good about writing? What do you like about writing? How can writing help you grow?

Start by mind mapping the question or by completing a scratch outline. Next do a focused writing: sit down and write. Do not edit your writing as you compose—just get your ideas on the page.

Writing about your experiences as a writer opens the process so that you can make substantial progress. By honestly revisiting some experiences, you can let go of them as well as the unproductive ways of thinking that linger in the background holding you back.

Activity 2: Journaling

Writing daily in a journal is a potent form of self-reflection. The clarity that journaling brings can lead to freedom from the past, giving you more options in the present and in the future. In fact, writing is a discovery process that aids you in understanding your own story more deeply.

Pour your heart into your journal. In fact, may people write their memoir by journaling about one experience at a time. As you journal, you may find that you gain insight into who you are, what motivates you, and how to make important changes. As an ancient saying tells us, "If you hold it in, it will destroy you; if you let it out, it will free you."

Start your journal, and follow the 2 x 4 method: 2 pages, 4 times a week.

1. Get a notebook so that you stay organized.

2. Sit down and write for 10 minutes or 2 pages, pouring whatever is on your mind onto the pages of your journal.

3. Write in your journal 4 times each week.

When you journal, do not worry about grammar, punctuation, or spelling: *just write!*

Journaling will help you connect with yourself and help you find your voice as you gain the experience of using writing as a problem-solving tool. See the example of a journal on the next page.

Sample Journal

The holidays are just getting started, and I'm looking forward to celebrating with my family. I'm writing this journal in the cafeteria while I wait for my friends to meet me. It's kind of weird, I mean at the beginning of the semester I hated writing journals and never knew what to write about. Now I can't say that I love to write journals, but it's not as hard to write about things anymore. The ideas just come to me now. In the beginning, I would sit for 10 or 20 minutes just trying to think of something to write about. Now it's like 5 seconds and I say to myself, "Oh yeah, that will be easy to write about."

Sometimes I write about how I am feeling, and other times I write about what I am learning in my classes or what is going on in my life. Although it still feels weird sitting here in the cafeteria with everyone around me, I don't really care all that much. I can sit here and write about whatever I want, and that feels good.

Skills Workshop

Pre-Assessment

Spend a maximum of 15 minutes completing the assessment on pages 24 and 25.

It's not about the test: It's about what you learn. Once you take the pre-assessment, refrain from reviewing it until you complete the book. If you turn back and forth between the test and the new principles that you are learning, your final score will not be a valid assessment of your improvement. Trust the process: you will improve!

Note: For additional assessments, go to www.commasrule.com or contact the publisher at www.wtkpublishing.com.

Part A: Grammar

Instructions: In each of the sentences below, identify the error and make the correction. If there is no error, write OK at the end of the sentence.

1. The attendant asked Joe and yourself for the information.

2. Keep the meeting between Charles and I confidential.

3. Her and her manager brought the equipment we needed.

4. Sylvia is the account representative that made the sale.

5. If you have more time than myself, complete the project on your own.

6. Ms. Adamchek insisted the account be given to you and I.

7. If you need a new client, call Jim or myself for referrals.

8. Him and his entire team went to lunch at Yogi's.

9. If Bob, yourself, and Jim were on my team, we would win.

10. They assigned the project before Reggie and yourself could respond.

11. The new budget will be froze until further notice.

12. Their customer enclose the check with the application.

13. Has your supervisor ever spoke about that policy?

14. If Martin was you, he would have made the same decision.

15. If the game had went better, we could have won conference.

16. Ms. Donata done a good job as a presenter.

17. After the team has went to the conference, the answers will be clear.

18. You should of sent the invoice directly to the distributor.

19. Our budget don't have an unlimited amount of funds.

20. Martin, along with his team, are going to the meeting.

21. Alice felt badly about the situation and wanted a change.

22. Next week is the most busiest time of our entire year.

23. To get the job, you need to take their policies more serious.

24. Your team performed good on the evaluation.

25. Don't give no one the information about our project.

Part B: Punctuation

Instructions: Insert commas and semicolons where needed in the following sentences.

1. They listed the product on August 15 2007 in their online catalog.

2. Rose Bob and Charley agreed to the new contract.

3. Before you send in your application get the exact address.

4. Our old location was closed last April therefore you should have been using our new address.

5. Juan Marquez human resources director will be in Denver Colorado on August 10.

6. Fortunately my résumé is up-to-date and ready to mail.

7. Ms. Patlan please assist me with this issue when you have time.

8. The applicant's portfolio arrived on September 4 and we promptly scheduled an appointment.

9. Ken finished the project however the company sent him another one.

10. My project ended two weeks ago all reviews were excellent.

11. Any merger therefore requires trust from all parties involved.

12. Mrs. Fleming thank you for supporting our charitable projects.

Part C: Word Usage

Instructions:

For the following sentences, make corrections in word usage as needed.

1. Your principle and interest have remained the same for two years.

2. A company won't change it's policy just because you don't like it.

3. Mike ensured his team that he would finish the project promptly.

4. The changes will effect everyone in our branch office.

5. If the bank will loan you the capital that you need, you are lucky.

Note: For the key to the pretest, see pages 407 to 408 in the **Keys to Activities**. However, wait to score the pretest until *after* you work through all the chapters of this book and take the posttest. In that way, you will have an accurate assessment of how much your score improves based on skill development (rather than by becoming test savvy).

Endnotes

1. John Steinbeck quoted from Nancy Hathaway, "Unleash Your Creativity," *New Woman*, November 1991, p. 48.

2. Peter Elbow, *Writing with Power, Techniques for Mastering the Writing Process,* Oxford University Press, Inc., New York, 1981. *Note*: Peter Elbow is an excellent source for learning about the writing process in depth.

3. Science Education Resource Center at Carlton College, <http://serc.carleton.edu/NAGTWorkshops/earlycareer/teaching/learningstyles.html>, accessed May 29, 2009.

4. Gertrude Stein, last words, according to Elizabeth Sprungge, *Gertrude Stein, Her Life and Work*, 1967, page 265.

5. Indiana University, Writing Tutorial Services, <http://www.indiana.edu/~wts/pamphlets/thesis_statement.shtml>, accessed June 2009.

2

The Sentence

To improve your writing skills, you need to write more; but to improve your final product, you need to edit effectively. Editing involves applying principles that shape writing so that it is correct, clear, and concise. So always keep in mind, good writing depends as much on effective editing as it does on "good writers."

The baseline of editing is the sentence. This chapter starts you on your process to understanding principles of reader-friendly sentences, a key to good writing. In addition to reviewing sentence elements such as subjects and verbs, you also learn about phrases and fragments and how to turn fragments into complete sentences.

This chapter provides a foundation for editing. One principle builds upon another, so do not take any shortcuts: start from the beginning and expect some surprises.

What Is a Sentence?

Think for a moment: *What is a sentence?* You write sentences every day, but can you define what a sentence is?

On the line below, define what a sentence is *or* jot down the words or ideas about sentences that pop into your mind:

Once you can define what a sentence is off of the top of your head, you will have reached the critical starting point of understanding grammar for writing. Understanding sentence structure enables you to fix common yet serious writing errors such as sentence fragments and run-on sentences. So enjoy the review.

Here is the definition of a sentence:

> A **sentence** consists of a <u>subject</u> and a <u>verb</u> and expresses a <u>complete</u> <u>thought</u>.

Even if your definition does not match the above definition exactly, it can still be correct. For example:

- Some people use the word *noun* instead of *subject*.

- Some use the word *predicate* instead of *verb*.

- Some use the phrase "can stand on its own," rather than "complete thought."

Another term for sentence is **independent clause**. The word *clause* refers to *a group of words that has a subject and verb*. When a clause cannot stand on its own, it is a **dependent clause**.

Here is a recap:

- **Independent Clause**: a group of words that has a subject and a verb and expresses a complete thought; an independent clause is a complete sentence.

- **Dependent Clause**: a group of words that has a subject and a verb but does not express a complete thought; a dependent clause cannot stand on its own.

When a sentence consists of an independent clause and a dependent clause, the independent clause is the **main clause**.

What Is the Sentence Core?

Together the subject and verb form the **sentence core**. The sentence core is the critical link between grammar and writing style because it is the hub or powerhouse of every sentence. As a result, being able to control the core improves your grammar as well as your writing style.

Here are few points about subjects and verbs:

- In sentences, the subject almost always precedes the verb.
- The verb determines the subject of the sentence.
- The verb also determines the object, if there is one.

Since the first step in analyzing sentences is identifying the core, let's look at basic sentence structure. Statements are generally structured as follows:

S   V   O

subject – verb – object

In the following examples, the <u>verbs</u> are underlined twice; the <u>subjects</u>, once; and the **objects** are in bold typeface; for example:

<u>Marcus</u> <u>attended</u> the **conference**.

S   V   O

While all sentences have a subject and verb, not all sentences have an object:

The <u>train</u> <u>arrived</u>.

S   V

For questions, the subject and verb are partially inverted and a helper is needed:

<u>Did</u> the <u>train</u> <u>arrive</u>?

V   S   V

<u>Has</u> <u>Marcus</u> <u>attended</u> the **conference**?

V   S   V   O

It is easier to identify the subject and verb of a question if you first invert it back to a statement; for example:

Did the train arrive?   The train did arrive.

In practice exercises, identify the verb first and then its subject:

1. The verb is usually easier to identify than the subject.

2. The verb of a sentence determines its subject.

After you identify the verb, work backward in the sentence to find its subject.

Now let's look at subjects in more detail. To start, are you aware that the *grammatical subject* of a sentence may not be its *real subject*?

What Is a Subject?

Ideally, the subject of a sentence drives the action of the verb and answers the question of "who" or "what" performs the action of the verb.

As Karen Gordon explains in *The Deluxe Transitive Vampire*, "the subject is that part of a sentence about which something is divulged; it is what the sentence's other words are gossiping about."[1]

The subject of a sentence usually comes in the form of a **noun** or **pronoun** or **noun phrase**:

- A noun is a person, place, or thing, but it can also be an intangible item that cannot be seen or felt, such as *joy* or *wind* or *integrity*.

- A pronoun is a word that can be used in place of a noun, such as *I*, *you*, *he*, *she*, *it*, *we*, *they*, *who*, and *someone*, among others.

- A phrase is a group of related words that does not have a subject and predicate and cannot stand alone; a noun phrase consists of a noun and modifiers.

Though knowing how to identify whether a subject is a noun or pronoun or phrase is valuable, another type of analysis is even more important. For example, did you realize that the *real subject* of a sentence could be different from its *grammatical subject*? When you can identify the difference between the real subject and the grammatical subject, you will gain more control of your writing style.

Let's learn more about grammatical subjects and real subjects.

What Is a Grammatical Subject?

Every sentence has a **grammatical subject,** defined as *the simple subject that precedes the verb in a statement.* The grammatical subject is simply referred to as "the subject." Being able to recognize the grammatical subject is important; however, it is not always stated in the sentence.

A **complete subject** consists of the **simple subject** and all the words that modify it. For writing purposes, the simple subject is important for a few reasons, but primarily because a subject must agree with its verb. In the following, the simple subject of each sentence is underlined once:

The new <u>manager</u> will chair the committee.

All <u>members</u> of the task force are in the conference room.

<u>They</u> are working diligently.

Her <u>honesty</u> is admirable.

When the grammatical subject is not stated, it becomes an **implied subject.** Implied subjects come in the form of "you understood" or "I understood."

Here is a recap:

- A grammatical subject precedes its verb in a statement.

- When the grammatical subject is not present in the sentence, it becomes an implied subject.

- Implied subjects come in the form of *you understood* or *I understood.*

- *You understood* is displayed as follows: (You)

- *I understood* is displayed as follows: (I)

In each of the following examples, the implied subject is in parentheses and the verb is double underscored:

(You)   Please <u>take</u> your seat in the front of the room.

(You)   <u>Feel</u> free to call me if you have a question.

(I)   <u>Thank</u> you for your assistance.

The subjects discussed so far—grammatical subjects that are complete, simple, and implied—all relate to structure. The type of subject that more directly relates to writing style is the *real subject*.

What Is a Real Subject?

The real subject of a sentence and the grammatical subject are sometimes the same, but sometimes different. Since the real subject is a critical element of writing style, it merits attention.

You may be feeling a little confused right now because you were not aware that the *grammatical subject* (the subject that precedes the verb) of a sentence was not necessarily its *real subject*. In fact, the term "real subject" may be unfamiliar.

The real subject drives the action of the verb; in other words, the real subject is the "who" or "what" that performs the action of the verb. Here is an example of a sentence in which the real subject and grammatical subject are one and the same:

Billy <u>threw</u> the ball.

In the following sentence, the grammatical subject is ball; the real subject is "Billy," the person performing the action. However, "Billy" is in the object position.

The <u>ball</u> <u>was thrown</u> by Billy.

When the person or thing performing the action is not the grammatical subject, a sentence is considered **passive**. When the person or thing performing the action is the grammatical subject, the sentence is considered **active** (for more information, see Chapter 9, Active Voice).

Here is a recap:

- The grammatical subject precedes the verb.
- The real subject drives the action of the verb.

When the real subject and the grammatical subject are one and the same, sentences are more clear, concise, and effective.

You will gain more practice with real subjects in Chapter 9, Active Voice. Now let's learn a few details about verbs, but just enough to help you recognize them.

What Is a Verb?

The verb is the central force of every sentence, determining the subject and the object, if there is one.

In English, the verb is also the central way to indicate time. In other words, the verb tense tells you whether an event *happened* yesterday, *is happening* now, or *will happen* tomorrow. In fact, the verb is the only part of speech that changes time—that is why verbs have tenses.

Here is some basic information about verbs:

- All verbs have a **base form**; *to* plus the base form of a verb is its **infinitive**: *to go, to see, to be*.
- All verbs have a **gerund form**: a gerund consists of *ing* plus the base form of the verb: *going, walking, being*.
- Verbs often string together, most often showing up in pairs, as in *will go* or *does know*.
- Common helping verbs are *to be* (is, are, was, were), *to have* (has, have, had), and *to do* (do, did, done).

Here are some hints to help you recognize the verb of a sentence:

1. Look for a word that expresses action, such as *speak, implement,* or *recognize*.
2. Look for a word that tells time and in doing so changes form, such as *speak, spoke, spoken,* and so on.

3. Look for the words *not* and *will*:

   a. You will generally find a verb after the word *will*, such as *will implement, will speak, will recognize, will find*, and so on.

   b. You will generally find a verb before and after the word *not*, such as *did* not *go*, *has* not *recognized*, and *has* not *spoken*. (The word *not* does not function as a verb but instead modifies a verb and negates it.)

Here are a few more examples:

Expressing Action:

Michael *finishes* his projects on time.

The committee *meets* every Friday.

I *complete* the inventory monthly.

Changing Time:

Michael *finished* his projects on time.

The committee *met* every Friday.

I *will complete* the inventory.

Preceding/Following *Not* or *Will*:

Michael *will finish* his projects on time.

The committee *did* not *meet* every Friday.

I *will* not *complete* the inventory.

In the following, the verb of each sentence is underlined twice, the subject once:

Alexander <u>watched</u> the PowerPoint presentation.

My new <u>manager</u> <u>will apply</u> the policy to everyone in our department.

The <u>meeting</u> <u>is</u> not <u>scheduled</u> for May 29.

<u>He</u> <u>discovers</u> errors in our reports every week.

At times, a verb will need a helper, which is also known as an **auxiliary**. When you see a helper verb, look for another verb to follow it.

Here are common helping verbs and their various forms:

Infinitive	**Verb Forms**
to be	is, are, was, were, being
to have	have, has, had, having
to do	do, did, done, doing

In the following examples, verbs are underlined twice and subjects once:

Marc had offered to prepare the agenda.

The meeting was cancelled.

The change did not affect our schedules.

Take a few minutes to complete the exercise below.

Practice 2.1

Sentence Core

Instructions: Identify the sentence core in the following sentences: identify the verb first and underline it twice, then the subject once.

1. The order contained too many unnecessary products.

2. I thanked the new engineer for fixing the electrical problem.

3. Thank you for asking that question.

4. Our new program will begin in one month.

5. Examine the order carefully before sending it out.

Note: See page 409 for the key to the above exercise.

What Is a Compound Subject?

A compound subject consists or two or more words or phrases:

> <u>Alice</u> and <u>Joyce</u> <u>attended</u> the reunion.

> Your <u>brother</u> and <u>sister</u> <u>can assist</u> you with the family reunion.

> The <u>committee</u> and its <u>chairperson</u> <u>will decide</u> the dress code.

At times, compound subjects are redundant, for example:

> My <u>thoughts</u> and <u>ideas</u> <u>are</u> clearer today then they were yesterday.

> The <u>issues</u> and <u>concerns</u> <u>were discussed</u> at the last meeting.

Why not simply say:

> My <u>thoughts</u> <u>are</u> clearer today then they were yesterday.

> The <u>issues</u> <u>were discussed</u> at the last meeting.

Edit your writing closely so that you cut redundant subjects.

Practice 2.2

Redundant Subjects

Instructions: First identify the sentence core by underlining the verb twice and the subject once; then cut the redundant subject.

Weak: My <u>plan</u> and <u>strategy</u> for the campaign <u>caught</u> their interest.

Revised: My <u>strategy</u> for the campaign <u>caught</u> their interest.

1. My friends and associates tell me now is a good time to buy gold.
2. The details and specifics about the project were fascinating.
3. Visitors and guests should sign in at the front desk.
4. My goals and objectives reflect my dreams.
5. The results and outcomes reflect our success.

Note: See page 409 for the key to the above exercise.

What Is a Compound Verb?

A compound verb consists of two or more main verbs along with their helpers, as in the following:

> My associate had called and asked me for a favor.

> Hard work causes me to apply myself and focuses my attention.

> Jogging improves my health, motivates me, and encourages me to eat less.

As subjects can be redundant at times, so can verbs:

> I read and analyzed the report.

> The assistant listened to their responses and recorded them.

Why not simply say:

> I analyzed the report.

> The assistant recorded their responses.

Be sure that when you use compound verbs, each verb has a reason to be in the sentence. Of course, a sentence can have a compound subject and a compound verb, for example:

> Margie and Seth opened the invitation and expressed their surprise.

Work on the Practice below before reviewing compound sentences.

Practice 2.3

Compound Verbs

Instructions: First, identify the sentence core by underlining the verb twice and the subject once; next, cut verbs that are redundant.

Weak: Mary identified and requested the rooms for the conference.

Revised: Mary requested the rooms for the conference.

1. Milton's decision uncovers and reveals his true motives.

2. Mark's actions surprised me and caught me off guard.

3. We started the project and worked on it for two hours.

4. I understand and appreciate your commitment to our mission.

5. Melanie greeted us and welcomed us to the banquet.

Note: See page 409 for the key to the above exercise.

What Is a Compound Sentence?

A compound sentence contains two main clauses, as in the following:

Joe <u>called</u> about the opening in marketing, and <u>he</u> <u>expressed</u> an interest.

The new <u>ad</u> <u>will</u> <u>run</u> for two weeks, but then <u>we</u> <u>will</u> <u>need</u> a new one.

My <u>manager</u> <u>asked</u> me to include the details, so <u>I</u> <u>presented</u> the entire report.

When writing a compound sentence, make sure that you are not randomly connecting ideas, for example:

Joe called about the opening in accounting, and we need to run a new ad.

What is the above sentence leading to? How are these two ideas linked? Disjointed ideas are fine if you are speaking with someone face to face; however, when you write, limit your sentences to **one controlling idea**.

In fact, the ideas in the above sentence might not be disjointed. One idea may be related to the other, but the relationship between the ideas is not shown because of the way that the sentence is written. What if the above sentence were written as follows:

Because we have an opening in accounting, Joe suggested that we run a new ad.

When you learn about conjunctions later in this chapter and in the next, you will see how to use conjunctions to show relationships among ideas.

What Is a Phrase?

A phrase is a group of related words that does not have a subject *and* predicate and thus cannot stand alone. Here are two important types of phrases and their definitions:

- **Infinitive phrase:** an infinitive along with its object or compliment and modifiers. (An infinitive is the word *to* plus the base form of a verb, as in *to go, to walk*, and *to speak.*)

- **Gerund phrase:** a gerund along with its object or compliment and modifiers. (A gerund is formed by adding *ing* to the base form of a verb, as in *going*, *walking*, and *speaking*.)

Infinitive phrases:	Gerund phrases:
to go to the store	going to the store
to buy what you need	buying what you need
to attend class daily	attending class daily
to inform the staff	informing the staff

In addition to gerund and infinitive phrases, you are probably somewhat familiar with prepositional phrases. Here is a brief reminder of how to identify a prepositional phrase:

- **Prepositional phrase:** a preposition along with a noun and its modifiers. Some common prepositions are *between, from, to, on, under, with, by,* and *along.*

Prepositional phrases:

on the table	*behind* the desk
to the store	*by* the bookcase
after the meeting	*between* the two of us

Though prepositional phrases can give writers challenges, the most challenging types of phrases for writers are gerund and infinitive phrases.

For example, writers need to use gerund and infinitive phrases consistently within a sentence or in a list. In the examples below, notice how the inconsistent phrases become reader friendly when they are presented as gerund or infinitive phrases:

Inconsistent list:

1. Maintenance of client list.

2. Expense accounts calculated.

3. Travel arrangements made.

Gerund Phrases:

1. *Maintaining* client lists.

2. *Calculating* expense accounts.

3. *Making* travel arrangements.

Infinitive Phrases:

1. *To Maintain* client lists.

2. *To Calculate* expense accounts.

3. *To Make* travel arrangements.

By removing "to" from the above list of infinitive phrases, each item would start with a verb. (See Chapter 10, Parallel Structure).

When you list items, remain consistent in form to ensure that you achieve **parallel construction**: representing words and phrases in the same grammatical form. (Once again, see Chapter 10, Parallel Structure.)

Practice 2.4

Instructions: Use gerund or infinitive phrases to make the following lists parallel.

List 1:

1. Office supplies need to be ordered

2. Appointment scheduling

3. Certificate renewal

List 2:

1. Coordination of schedules
2. Supplies distributed
3. Phoning clients

List 3:

1. Staff training
2. The development of policy
3. Profit and loss reconciliation

Note: See pages 409-410 for the key to the above exercise.

What Is a Dependent Clause?

A **dependent clause** is a group of words that has a subject and verb but does not express a complete thought; a dependent clause cannot stand on its own.

In general, a clause becomes dependent because it begins with a **subordinating conjunction**. Therefore, to understand what a dependent clause is, you first need to understand what a subordinating conjunction is.

- **Subordinating conjunctions** show relationships between ideas and, in the process, make one idea dependent on the other; subordinating conjunctions appear as single words or short phrases.

Here is a list of common subordinating conjunctions:

after	because	since	until
although	before	so that	when
as	even though	though	whereas
as soon as	if	unless	while

The above list is not a complete list; you can test whether a word or phrase is a subordinating conjunction by placing it at the beginning of a complete sentence. If the complete sentence no longer sounds complete, the word is probably a subordinating conjunction (SC). For example:

| **Complete sentence:** | Bob walked to the store. |
| **SC added:** | *If* Bob walked to the store . . . what? |

| **Complete sentence:** | The office manager arrived late. |
| **SC added:** | *Since* the office manager arrived late . . . what? |

| **Complete sentence:** | The sale begins tomorrow. |
| **SC added:** | *Even though* the sale begins tomorrow . . . what? |

Subordinating conjunctions do what their name implies: "to subordinate" means "to make less than." In the examples above, you have seen that when you place a subordinating conjunction at the beginning of a complete sentence, the sentence becomes a dependent clause. Here is another set of examples:

| **Complete sentence:** | The attendant game me a receipt. |
| **Dependent clause:** | *When* the attendant gave me a receipt . . . what? |

| **Complete sentence:** | Our car is in the parking lot. |
| **Dependent clause:** | *Although* our car is in the parking lot . . . what? |

| **Complete sentence:** | Their committee meets on Friday. |
| **Dependent clause:** | *After* their committee meets on Friday . . . what? |

Punctuating a dependent clause as if it is a complete sentence results in a **fragment**; a fragment is a common error, but a serious one.

Write two sentences below, and then go back and place a subordinating conjunction at the beginning of each of your sentences, as shown in the previous set of examples.

1. _____

2. _____

Do you see how a subordinating conjunction can turn a complete sentence into a fragment?

Now let's take a look at fragments, a serious grammatical error.

How Do You Correct a Fragment?

A **fragment** is an incomplete statement that is punctuated as if it were a complete sentence. Most often, fragments come in the form of gerund phrases, infinitive phrases, or dependent clauses.

The following are some examples of fragments broken down by type:

Gerund Phrases:	Walking slowly to the beach on a sunny day
	Following a list of directions precisely as given
Infinitive Phrases:	To walk slowly to the beach on a sunny day
	To follow a list of directions precisely as given
Dependent clauses:	*When* I walk slowly to the beach on a sunny day
	After Bob followed the list of directions that you gave him

Notice that gerund and infinitive phrases do not contain a subject and a verb. However, when a gerund or infinitive phrase is long, it can give the illusion that it is a complete sentence.

How you correct a fragment depends on the type of fragment you are dealing with. Let's take a look at how to use simple solutions to correct this serious grammatical error.

To correct fragments consisting of gerund and infinitive phrases, use the phrase as the <u>subject</u>, add a <u>verb</u>, and then finish your thought, as follows:

<u>Walking slowly to the beach on a sunny day</u> <u>makes</u> most people feel good.

<u>To walk slowly to the beach on a sunny day</u> <u>is</u> highly recommended.

Another way to correct a fragment that consists of a gerund or infinitive phrase would be to use the fragment as the **object** of your sentence, adding a <u>subject</u> and a <u>verb</u>, as follows:

George's favorite <u>activity</u> <u>is</u> **walking slowly to the beach on a sunny day**.

<u>I</u> <u>prefer</u> **to walk slowly to the beach on a sunny day**.

Here is now to correct a fragment resulting from a dependent clause:

1. Use the dependent clause before a main clause to introduce the main clause,

2. Use the dependent clause after a main clause as a finishing thought, or

3. Remove the subordinating conjunction at the beginning of the clause.

In the sentences below, each dependent clause is italicized:

When I walk slowly to the beach on a sunny day, my mind always wanders.

I left work early *because I finished the list of directions precisely as given.*

When the subordinating conjunction is removed, a dependent clause may become a complete sentence; for example:

~~When~~ I walk slowly to the beach on a sunny day.

~~Because~~ I finished the list of directions precisely as given.

Practice turning fragments into sentences by doing the exercise below.

Practice 2.5

Instructions: Use your creativity to turn the following fragments into complete sentences.

Incorrect: Finding enough time to complete the report.

Revised: <u>Finding enough time to complete the report</u> <u>was</u> a challenge.

Or: My <u>challenge</u> <u>was</u> finding enough time to complete the report.

1. Making the right decision at the right time.
2. Because he finished the project earlier than anyone expected.
3. After I made the decision to reclaim my spot on the team.
4. To show interest in a project that no longer has merit.
5. Going slower than planned but staying under budget.

Note: See page 410 for the key to the above exercise.

Now, let's look at why the sentence core is so important when it comes to structure and style.

Why Is the Sentence Core Important?

The sentence core consists of the subject and verb: together the subject and verb convey meaning. One without the other, and meaning is incomplete. In fact, readers become confused if the sentence core is presented ineffectively.

Let's start with an example:

> My associate Jane Culver, who has worked with me
> on several projects in the last few months and who has
> a great deal of expertise in the field of writing as well
> as consulting, will be our keynote speaker.

Does the above sound wordy and confusing?

Now read the following:

> My associate Jane Culver will be our keynote speaker.
> By the way, Jane has worked with me on several
> projects in the last few months and has a great deal of
> expertise in the field of writing as well as consulting.

Is the second example easier to understand? The difference between the two is that the second example broke the information into smaller chunks and used the sentence core effectively:

<u>Jane Culver</u> <u>will be</u> . . .   <u>Jane</u> <u>has worked</u> . . .

In general, the closer the subject and verb are to each other, the easier it is for a reader to understand meaning. Here are some editing tips on how to present the sentence core effectively:

1. Keep the subject and verb close to each other.
2. Keep the sentence core close to the beginning of the sentence.

To further enhance the sentence core, focus on using **real subjects** and **strong verbs**. While most verbs are action verbs, the following verbs are considered weak verbs: *make*, *give*, and *take* as well as the *to be* verbs: *is*, *are*, *was*, and *were*; for example:

Weak: Al *will give* you the information about the change.

Revised: Al *will inform* you about the change.

Weak: *Take* that into consideration when you apply.

Revised: *Consider* that when you apply.

Subjects can also be weak. For example, avoid using *it* or *there* as a subject:

Weak: It is time for change.

Revised: The time for change is now.

Weak: There are many decisions pending.

Revised: Many decisions are pending.

Consider the above points as an introduction to the sentence core. When you work on Chapter 4, Comma Rules, you once again work with the sentence core. When you work on Chapter 9, Active Voice, you focus on developing a strong sentence core.

Do the following exercise to gain more control of the sentence core.

Practice 2.6

Real Subjects and Strong Verbs

Instructions: Edit the following sentences by changing the sentence core so that it consists of a real subject and strong verb.

Weak: It was a decision that Mr. James regrets.

Revised: Mr. James regrets the decision.

1. There are five orders that need to be filled by customer service.
2. It is an electrical problem on the fifth floor that caused the outage.
3. Randy will make a revision of the document today.
4. There is a new report that arrived earlier today.
5. You can make a decision tomorrow.

Note: See page 410 for the key to the above exercise.

Does Sentence Length Affect Readability?

Have you ever read a sentence that you had difficulty understanding? If so, was it an unusually long sentence? The average reader finds it easier to retain information when a sentence contains fewer than 25 words.

Here is an editing tip that you can apply at once to improve your writing:

Limit your sentences to 25 words or fewer.

For example:

> Sentences that are much longer than 25 words have a tendency to confuse readers because by the time that they get to the end of a long sentence, many readers have already forgotten what the beginning of the sentence was about and need to go back to the beginning and reread it again, which can be very tedious. (57 words) *What do you think?*

Writing shorter sentences gives you more control. When sentences are long, writing decisions become more difficult; and writers more easily make mistakes with grammar and punctuation. Simple, clear, and concise writing is reader-friendly writing. So use the following as your guideline:

Less is more.

When you write sentences that are long or complicated, count the number of words. If a sentence is longer than 25 words, cut words or break the information into shorter sentences. At times, you will need to do both.

What Is Information Flow?

Information flow is about how you order information for your reader. To start, information is broken into two types: familiar ideas and unfamiliar ideas.

When a sentence starts with a familiar idea as a lead-in to an unfamiliar idea, readers have an easier time making connections. Think of familiar information as "old information," and think of unfamiliar information as "new information."

For example, suppose you are describing the topic of your next paper. As you compose, you may start with the new information.

New to *Old*:   Changes in consumer spending habits during an economic downturn will be *the topic of my next paper.*

When you edit, switch the order so that the sentence begins with the familiar, old information, which would be *the topic of my next paper* or simply, *my next paper*, for example:

Old to **New:**   *My next paper* will discuss changes in consumer spending habits during an economic downturn.

By beginning the sentence with the familiar concept (*my next paper*), you ease your readers into the unfamiliar information. Here is another example in which "our first team meeting" is familiar information:

New to Old: A set of ground rules and a membership survey needs to be developed at *our first team meeting*.

Old to **New:**   *At our first team meeting*, we need to develop a set of ground rules and a membership survey.

In the next chapter, you will learn more about information flow as well as how to develop cohesive and coherent paragraphs.

Practice 2.7

Information Flow

Instructions: In the following sentences, adjust the information flow so that the familiar information precedes the unfamiliar information.

New to Old: An abrupt change in consumer spending habits is one reason why the economy has shifted.

Old to **New:**   *One reason that the economy has shifted* is that consumers have changed their spending habits.

1. Too many unnecessary and costly items are not being bought by consumers at this time.
2. Buying good used items at a reduced price is how many consumers are choosing to spend their money.

3. The rapidly increasing cost of gasoline has contributed to a change in consumer attitudes.

4. Outsourcing jobs to third-world countries is a topic you might consider for your next paper.

5. Please consider the cost as well as the time required to make the revisions as you complete your report.

Note: See pages 410 - 411 for the key to the above exercise.

Before going on to Chapter 3, Paragraphs and Transitions, work on the exercises at the end of this chapter.

Recap

This chapter has focused on sentence structure and the sentence core. The sentence core is where structure and style cross paths: gain control of the sentence core, and you gain control of your writing.

➢ To identify the sentence core, identify the verb first and then work backward to find its subject.

➢ To identify a verb, look for a word that expresses action and that changes form when it changes time (past, present, or future).

➢ Subjects can be implied or understood, such as *I understood* (I) or *You understood* (You): (I) <u>Thank</u> you for your help or (You) <u>Take</u> your time.

➢ Write sentences in which the grammatical subject and real subject are one and the same.

➢ Avoid writing sentences that begin with "it is" or "there are"; instead write sentences that have a real subject and a strong verb.

➢ When you write a sentence that has a compound subject or verb, check for redundancy.

Writing Workshop

Activity A. Writing Practice

Instructions: Identify a specific goal and develop an action plan.

Do you have a goal that you want to achieve? For example, would you like to lose weight, improve your diet, get rid of clutter, get organized, improve your finances, or enhance your relationships?

Describe your goal in detail. Then identify specific steps you plan to take to achieve your goal. Finally, add a time frame to each step. By adding a date to each step in your process, you are creating an *action plan.*

Optional: Find a magazine article or Web article that relates to your goal, and summarize key points from that article. (Refer to the Quick Guide to Citations at the back of this book to cite your sources.)

Activity B. Journal

Instructions: What are your dreams, goals, and aspirations?

What do you want out of life and why? Dream a little, but be realistic. You are working hard to improve your skills—what is it that motivates you to do your best?

What changes would you like to see in your life in *six months* from now? . . . *one year?* . . . *five years?*

Skills Workshop

Worksheet 1: Removing Redundancy

Instructions: In each of the following sentences, remove the subjects and verbs that are redundant as well as any other unnecessary words; to gain more practice with identifying the sentence core, underline verbs twice and subjects once. (*Note:* See page 411 for the key to this exercise.)

Weak: We know and understand how much you value this project.

Revised: We ~~know and~~ understand how much you value this project.

1. We appreciate and value your efforts on the project.
2. The instructions and directions were clear, but our task was confusing and puzzling at times.
3. We hope and trust that you are interested in working on another project.
4. If you need and want a part-time job, I know someone for you to contact.
5. Your first and initial contact with him should be professional and positive.
6. If you prepare for the interview and are ready, you will make a good and lasting impression.
7. If this is good for you and it works out, you can refer and recommend your friends also.
8. My friends will arrive and be here shortly.
9. Everyone will notice and appreciate the help that you give them.
10. Make a note and mark your calendar for April 15; attend this event with a friend or associate.
11. First and foremost, we thank you for and appreciate your business.
12. Make sure that the materials are here and that they have arrived in time for the meeting.

Editing Workshop

Instructions: Edit the following e-mail for redundancy and fragments.

Dear Mr. Jones,

I am eager and interested in applying for the job you that you have open and that you posted with our college placement office.

My résumé is attached. After you examine and review it, I am sure that you will find that I have the skills and abilities that you need and are seeking for this position.

You can reach me at your convenience on my cell at 312-555-1212, on my home phone at 219-555-1212, or you can send me an e-mail at roger@e-mail.com.

Looking forward to hearing from you and speaking with you about this position.

Best regards,

Roger Di Nicolo

Cell: 312-555-1212

Phone: 219-555-1212

Note: See page 412 for the key to the above exercise.

Endnotes

1. Karen Elizabeth Gordon, *The Deluxe Transitive Vampire*, Pantheon Books, New York, 1993, page 3.

2. Jim W. Corder and John J. Ruskiewicz, *Handbook of Current English*, HarperCollins, 1989, p. 29.

3

Paragraphs and Transitions

Paragraphs play a vital role in making ideas easily accessible to readers: paragraphs break text into manageable chunks, helping readers digest information. In fact, readers dread seeing one long paragraph that seems to go on forever. If you have not yet focused on how you create paragraph breaks, now you can.

While you cannot depend on a recipe to write a paragraph, you can rely on a few guidelines. For example, a paragraph can be as short as a sentence or two or as long as seven or eight sentences. However, not all paragraphs are equal. For instance, when you make paragraphing decisions for a paper or essay, you have different considerations from when you make paragraphing decisions for an e-mail. (One difference is that e-mail is more conversational and paragraphs tend to be short.)

If you do not now insert paragraph breaks naturally as you compose, put them in when you edit and revise. Read your writing out loud or have someone read it to you. When you hear a new topic, start a new paragraph.

Once you have enough experience writing, you will make paragraph breaks as a natural part of composing. When you edit, you will structure the content to make your paragraphs cohesive and coherent:

- **Cohesive** paragraphs develop only *one main idea*.

- **Coherent** paragraphs develop the main idea in a *logical way*.

Let's review principles that are critical to editing and revising paragraphs, including how to develop flow and make transitions.

Cohesive and Coherent Paragraphs

Two important qualities of effective paragraphs are *cohesiveness* and *coherency*.

- **Cohesive** paragraphs develop only *one topic*, demonstrating a *connectedness* among ideas that support that topic. Adequate details support the main idea so that the reader understands the main point.

- **Coherent** paragraphs develop the main idea through a logical *flow of ideas*: one point leads to another.

As you compose, get your ideas on the page without concerning yourself about paragraphing, otherwise you are likely to lose your thoughts.

The first step in editing a paragraph so that it is cohesive is to identify its **topic sentence**. The next step is ensuring that each sentence in the paragraph develops the topic, creating a **topic string**.

- A **topic sentence** gives an overview of the paragraph; a topic sentence is broad and general.

- A **topic string** is a series of sentences that develop the main idea of the topic sentence. Each sentence extends the controlling idea, giving specifics that illustrate the main idea of the topic sentence.

As you compose, do not be concerned about writing a topic sentence or building a topic string. However, do not be surprised if one of the last sentences that you write ends up being the best candidate for the topic sentence.

Here is a step-by-step process for editing paragraphs:

1. Identify your topic sentence. Select the sentence that best captures the broader, more general topic that the rest of the paragraph develops through specifics.

2. Bring your topic sentence to the beginning of the paragraph as the first or second sentence of the paragraph.

3. Screen each the remainder of sentences in the paragraph to make sure that it develops some element of the topic sentence.

4. Cut sentences that do not fit, or use them to start a new paragraph.

Many writers are able to insert paragraph breaks as they compose. However, if you do not naturally make paragraph breaks as you compose, work on them when you edit. Eventually, you will hear when a new topic springs from your writing.

Read the draft paragraph below, which seems to ramble because it changes topics. As you read the paragraph, ask yourself the following questions:

- Which sentence or sentences seem to capture a main topic?

- Which sentences seem off topic?

- Which sentences seem to belong in a different paragraph?

Draft:

I believe editing is important, and I even knew an editor once. But I never knew how to edit before, and I was always confused about how to improve my writing. Before I didn't take the time to edit, now I do because I know how to make corrections and how to how to revise a document. When you edit, correct errors in grammar and punctuation and try to improve the flow of the writing. Editing also involves putting the purpose up front and then cutting what doesn't belong. When I read papers that are not edited well, I can tell because the writer jumps from one topic to another. Editing can turn a mediocre paper into a good one. Poorly written documents also seem to ramble on and on without paragraph breaks, so add paragraph breaks where they are needed. Take time to edit, and you will see an improvement in your final document.

Edited Version 1

The following version focuses on how to edit but leaves out the writer's own experience:

> Editing can turn a mediocre paper into a good one. When you edit, correct errors in grammar and punctuation and improve the flow of the writing. Put purpose up front and then cut what doesn't belong. Also, add paragraph breaks where they are needed. If you take time to edit, you will see an improvement in your final document.

Edited Version 2

Version 2 takes the writer's point of view. Notice how the voice shifts to the *I* viewpoint:

> Editing is important. Before I didn't take the time to edit, but now I do because I know how to correct and revise a document. When I edit, I correct errors in grammar and punctuation and try to improve the flow of the writing. I also put the purpose up front and then cut what doesn't belong. When I take time to edit, I see an improvement in my final document.

For a paragraph to be coherent, ideas must flow logically. In other words, writing should not seem chaotic and full of disjointed ideas. However, as you compose, disjointed ideas seem to make sense. To correct disjointed writing, step away from your work for a while so that you can evaluate your writing objectively.

If you are writing on a computer, the way that your writing sounds when you read it on the screen is different from the way that it will sound when you read it from hard copy.

Here are some steps to take to revise your paragraphs:

- Print out a copy so that you can see final changes that you need to make.

- Have a peer read it, and ask for specific changes that you can make to upgrade the quality of your writing.

- Keep an open mind: others will be able to see things that you cannot; expand your perspective by trying on new ideas, even if they feel uncomfortable at first. You can always toss them out after you have given them a chance to expand your thinking.

Principles of information flow can also assist you in understanding how to adjust your writing so that it is reader friendly.

Information Flow

As you learned in the last chapter, information flow orders ideas so that readers have an easier time connecting how one idea relates to another. Information flow can create smooth transitions between ideas that would otherwise sound disjointed.

Let's review what you learned in Chapter 2 and then add another layer of understanding to it.

- **Old Information**: familiar information, something the reader already knows.

- **New Information**: unfamiliar information, something the reader does not know.

However, information flow is not complete without one more category of information, and that is *irrelevant information*. Here is the third and final category of information flow:

- **Empty Information**: information that is irrelevant to the topic at hand.

On the following page are three versions of a paragraph about listening. As you read the first paragraph, identify the empty information.

Can you identify the empty information in the paragraph below?

> Listening is an important part of communicating. If you take the time to listen to them, most people will tell you about their lives. As you listen, ask questions, and most people will reveal more about themselves. I once had a job in retail sales, and a big part of the job was listening. I didn't do well when I first started because I wasn't a good listener. Once you become a better listener, you will understand people, even if they think differently from the way that you think.

Here is how the paragraph sounds without the empty information:

> Listening is an important part of communicating. If you take the time to listen to them, most people will tell you about their lives. As you listen, ask questions, and most people will reveal more about themselves. Once you become a better listener, you will understand people, even if they think differently from the way that you think.

Once the irrelevant, empty information is removed, the paragraph flows more effectively. Now, let's look at the same paragraph, but this time reversing the information flow: new information appears at the beginning of each sentence and the consistent, old topic "listening" appears at end:

> An important part of communicating is listening. Most people will take the time to tell you about their lives if you listen. Ask questions, and most people will reveal more about themselves as long as you take the time to listen. You will understand people, even if they think differently from the way that you think, once you become a better listener.

Do you hear how choppy the above paragraph sounds? By putting new information first, the reader must work harder to find meaning.

As you compose, you may naturally put new information on the page first and then connect it to your topic (or old information). As you edit, reverse the flow of any sentences that go from new to old information.

Let's take the same paragraph one more time, putting the topic sentence at the end:

> If you take the time to listen to them, most people will tell you about their lives. As you listen, ask questions, and most people will reveal more about themselves. Once you become a better listener, you will understand people, even if they think differently from the way that you do. Listening is an important part of communicating.

Apply the principles of information flow in the Practice below.

Practice 3.1

Paragraphs and Information Flow

Instructions: In the following paragraph, adjust the information flow by:

1. Identifying the topic sentence and bringing it to the beginning of the paragraph.

2. Adjusting information flow so that sentences begin with old information and end with new information.

3. Cutting empty information.

> Writing can be hard and frustrating because sometimes I can't decide on what to write or what to say. Allow yourself to write freely and make mistakes as you compose. Good writing is about composing and editing. Identify the mistakes that you have made and correct them when you edit. A paper should have a beginning, a middle, and an end. Good writing becomes easy to produce once you understand how to manage the writing process.

Note: See page 412 for a suggested revision.

Paragraphs and Viewpoint

Another component of an effective paragraph is consistent viewpoint, which partly depends on the way that you use pronouns. Though you will work with pronouns in detail in Chapter 7, Pronouns, here is an introduction to *pronoun viewpoint* or *point of view.*

A viewpoint can be described as "the eyes through which writing is being portrayed." Pronoun viewpoint, or point of view, can emanate from first, second, or third person, singular or plural.

	Singular	**Plural**
First or person:	I	We
Second person:	You	You
Third person:	He, She, It	They
	One	One

The third person viewpoint, "it/they," could represent the topic about which you are writing. For example, if you were writing a summary about "nutrition," you would not necessarily speak from your own point of view, for example:

> Good nutrition leads to good health. Highly nutritional foods include fruits and vegetables as well as legumes and grains. These foods are high in vitamins and fiber, which is good for the digestive system.

Once you establish a point of view for a particular piece of writing, remain consistent with that point of view within individual sentences and paragraphs and even entire documents.

The following sentences highlight how to stay consistent with viewpoint:

First person singular viewpoint:

> Listening is a skill which *I* would like to improve. When *I* listen, *I* sometimes hear things that change *my* life.

Shifting viewpoint:

Incorrect: Listening is a skill which *we* should all improve. When *I* listen, *you* sometimes hear things that change *your* life.

Correct: Listening is a skill which *we* should all improve. When *we* listen, *we* sometimes hear things that change *our* lives.

Or: Listening is a skill which *all* can improve. When *people* listen, *they* sometimes hear things that change *their* lives.

Here is a sentence written from each of the various viewpoints:

When *I* write, *I* must pay attention to every detail.

When *you* write, *you* must pay attention to every detail.

When a *person* writes, *he/she* must pay attention to every detail.

When *we* write, *we* must pay attention to every detail.

When *people* write, *they* must pay attention to every detail.

When *one* writes, *one* must pay attention to every detail.

For the pronoun *one*, the only appropriate antecedent is *one*; in other words, *he* and *she* are not antecedents for *one*.

Practice 3.2

Pronoun Point of View and Consistency

Instructions: Edit the following short paragraphs by correcting for pronoun consistency.

1. I usually work late on Thursdays because you can get a lot done at the end of the week. When you work late, I usually see other people working late also. Having your boss notice that you are putting in extra time always makes me feel good.

2. Good nutrition leads to good health. When we eat well, you are likely to feel better. People do not find it easy to eat in a healthful way, though. I usually prefer to eat fast food at the end of the day when you are tired.

Note: See page 412 for the key to the above exercise.

Transitional Sentences

Transitional sentences and transitional paragraphs are also elements of information flow, making broad connections between old information and new information.

Transitional sentences provide logical connections between paragraphs. The transitional sentence glances forward and links the topic of one paragraph with the main idea of the next, for example:

> In the next section, our analysis demonstrates the strengths and weaknesses of the model that we applied in our study.

> Next we discuss how good communication leads to success.

> Although production waste has economic implications, waste also has an impact on the environment.

Transitional sentences prepare the reader to understand the content of the next paragraph by seeding the purpose of the new paragraph. By the time the reader reaches the new paragraph, key ideas are already familiar.

Transitional Paragraphs

In addition to transitional sentences, **transitional paragraphs** play an important role for readers, achieving the following:

- Summarizing the key ideas of the current section.
- Indicating how the major theme of the document will be developed in the next section.

Here is a transitional paragraph that summarizes the key ideas of a current section:

> This chapter discusses several of Deming's famous 14 points, known as the Deming Management Method. As they relate to workforce diversity and managing change, the following topics are discussed: poorly implemented management systems, disrespectful and fearful work environments, interdepartmental antagonism, and weak leadership.

Here is a transitional paragraph that glances forward to a next section:

> The educational reform process enabled the faculty to make effective curriculum changes. The evolving curriculum also brought faculty closer to achieving the aims of general education within the stated mission, which is discussed in the next section.

Next, let's look at using conjunctions to make transitions.

Connectors as Transitions

As you have seen, old to new information flow helps create smooth transitions between ideas. Another way to create smooth transitions and facilitate understanding is to use conjunctions.

Do you remember the Sesame Street song, *Conjunction Junction*: "Conjunction Junction, what's your function?" If you remember the song, you may begin to smile as the tune sets in.

Here are the three types of conjunctions:

- Coordinating
- Subordinating
- Adverbial

On face value, conjunctions do not seem to be a vital part of speech, when in fact conjunctions play a critical role in writing.

Along with subjects and verbs, conjunctions play a critical role in grammar, punctuation, and writing style:

- Conjunctions show relationships and bridge ideas, adding smooth transitions to choppy writing.

- Conjunctions pull the reader's thinking along with the writer's intention.

As you use conjunctions more effectively, your writing style also improves. By pulling the reader's thinking along with yours, you help the reader connect ideas and draw conclusions. Conjunctions focus the reader on key points, making writing clearer and easier to understand.

In addition, conjunctions play a key role in punctuation because they signal where to place commas and semicolons. Therefore, realize that the work that you are doing now with conjunctions will make your work in the next chapter with commas that much easier.

Understand how conjunctions *function*, and you will be a big step closer to using them effectively in your writing. Though the terms themselves might put you off, realize that it only take a bit of practice to use the terms *coordinating*, *subordinating*, and *adverbial* with ease. Now let's get to work on conjunctions.

Coordinating Conjunctions

Coordinating conjunctions connect equal grammatical parts. There are only seven of them, and they are as follows:

and   but   or   for   nor   so   yet

Together they spell the acronym F A N B O Y S: *for, and, nor, but, or, yet, so*. The most commonly used coordinating conjunctions are *and, but,* and *or*. The *equal grammatical parts* that conjunctions connect are *sentences*, *words*, and *phrases*, which Chapter 4, Comma Rules, covers in more detail.

Though using a coordinating conjunction as the first word of a sentence is acceptable, it is not preferred and should be used sparingly. But when you do start a sentence with a coordinating conjunction, you are likely to get the reader's attention. In general, the adverbial conjunction *however* is a good substitute for *but*.

Subordinating Conjunctions

In Chapter 2, you learned that putting a subordinating conjunction at the beginning of a complete sentence turned the sentence into a dependent clause.

Subordinating conjunctions show relationships between ideas and, in the process, make one idea dependent on the other; they appear as single words or short phrases. Here is a list of some common subordinating conjunctions:

after	because	since	until
although	before	so that	when
as	even though	though	whereas
as soon as	if	unless	while

Next, let's take a look at adverbial conjunctions.

Adverbial Conjunctions

Adverbial conjunctions bridge ideas, and they are known as *transition* words.

Here are some examples of common adverbial conjunctions:

as a result	for example	in conclusion	otherwise
finally	hence	in general	therefore
generally	however	in other words	thus

Adverbial conjunctions help pull the reader's thinking along with the writer's intention. Use adverbial conjunctions at the beginning of a sentence to *introduce* it, in the middle of a sentence to *interrupt* the flow of thought, or between two sentences as a *bridge*.

Here are examples of adverbial conjunctions and the roles they play:

Introducing: *Therefore*, I will not be able to attend the conference.

Interrupting: The Jones Corporation, *however*, is not our vendor of choice.

Bridging: George will attend the conference in my place; *as a result,* I will be able to assist you on the new project.

Here are some adverbial conjunctions and the kinds of transitions that they make:

Compare or contrast:	however, in contrast, on the other hand, on the contrary, conversely, nevertheless, otherwise,
Summarize:	in summary, in conclusion, as a result, thus, therefore, hence
Illustrate:	for example, for instance, hence, in general, thus, mostly
Add information:	in addition, additionally, also, furthermore, moreover, too
Show results:	fortunately, unfortunately, consequently, as usual, of course
Sequence or show time:	first, second, third, finally, meanwhile, in the meantime, to begin with
Conclude:	finally, in summary, in conclusion

You will notice that adverbial conjunctions appear as single words or short phrases. As a reader, use these transition words to identify key points. As a writer, use these transition words in a conscious way to pull your reader's thinking along with yours.

Besides being bridges and connectors, conjunctions are also comma signals. In the next two chapters, you will see how conjunctions signal where to place a comma or a semicolon.

Practice 3.3

Conjunctions as Connectors

Instructions: Revise the following paragraph by adding conjunctions, thereby improving its flow. (See page 413 for the key to this exercise.)

> The construction for the 9th floor conference room was extended two more weeks. We were not informed until Friday. Our meetings for the following week needed to be reassigned to different rooms. None were available. Jane Simmons agreed to let us use her office. Several serious conflicts were avoided.

As you work on Chapter 4, Comma Rules, apply what you learned about the sentence core and conjunctions. First, however, complete the exercises at the end of this chapter.

Recap

In this chapter, you have worked on paragraphing; you have also reviewed the three types of conjunctions and how they function as connectors and transition words.

➢ Paragraphs break up information into manageable chunks for the reader.

➢ Every paragraph contains a topic sentence, which is then developed into a topic string.

➢ Cohesive paragraphs focus on one topic.

➢ Coherent paragraphs have a logical flow of ideas, which you create as you edit and revise your work.

➢ A consistent viewpoint helps ensure that a paragraph is coherent as well as grammatically correct.

➢ Conjunctions build bridges between ideas and provide cues about a writer's key points.

> As a review, here are the three types of conjunctions and examples:

Coordinating conjunctions:	and, but, or, for, nor, so, yet
Subordinating conjunctions:	if, since, although, because, before, after, while
Adverbial conjunctions:	however, therefore, for example, consequently

In the next chapter, you learn about the role that conjunctions play in comma usage.

Writing Workshop

Activity A: What is on your mind?

Instructions: Start this activity by completing the following sentences. Next, select two or three of your sentences. Use each as a starting point, developing a topic string that radiates from it. Finally, revise each paragraph so that it is cohesive and coherent.

My passion in life . . .

If I were you . . .

I wish that I were able to . . .

When my best friend says . . .

If I could have any job in the world . . .

The best advice anyone ever gave me . . .

The favorite room in my house . . .

When I was a child . . .

Pay special attention to using a consistent viewpoint and using effective connectors.

Activity B. Journal

Instructions: Are you journaling on a regular basis? Write two pages at least four times a week, and your skills will become stronger. As you journal, *compose freely.*

Skills Workshop

Worksheet 1: Conjunctions as Transitions

Instructions: In the following exercise, use coordinating, subordinating, and adverbial conjunctions as connectors. Choose from the following:

Coordinating conjunctions: and, but, or, for, nor, so, yet

Subordinating conjunctions: while, although, because, even though, since

Adverbial conjunctions: however, therefore, thus, hence

Because you did not yet cover commas and semicolons, simply insert the connector without trying to punctuate the message correctly.

Tom:

In your last message, you requested 10 sets of materials. I do have some materials to send you. I will also have a meeting with my staff next week. I cannot send you all of the materials that I have available. I would not have enough for my meeting.

I do not have enough binders. I can send you only 7 complete sets. You can have as many revised policy manuals and new product flyers as you need. You will only need to purchase 3 binders from your office supplier.

Bart

Note: See page 413 for the key to this exercise.

Editing Workshop

Instructions:

Edit the following paragraph by doing some or all of the following:

1. Identify a topic sentence and then develop an effective topic string.
2. Cut empty information.
3. Edit sentences for information flow.
4. Use a consistent point of view.

I believe when you proofread you check a manuscript for errors in grammar and spelling and correcting them. I used to know a proofreader, and I thought she must have been very smart. I never really found out. At least one would have to be very alert. I do occasionally find spelling errors in articles or books that I read, and I am always surprised when I do. I wonder how the error escaped the attention of the proofreader. Apparently proofreaders are human too and subject to errors. When you proofread, I also look for errors in punctuation, capitalization, and number usage. When you proofread, I try to identify and correct run-on sentences and incomplete thoughts. Proofreading makes a document correct and therefore makes it professional and credible. The mistakes I find are usually understandable. They are usually small words and very similar to the correct word.

Note: See page 414 for the key to the above exercise.

Endnote

Just for fun, check out *Conjunction Junction* on this You Tube video: http://www.youtube.com/watch?v=7TQByv_xkuc

PART 2: MECHANICS FOR WRITING

Chapter 4: Comma Rules
Chapter 5: Semicolon Rules

Punctuation is the glue that holds language together. Without punctuation, language lacks meaning because it lacks order. Punctuation provides clarity, but it does more than that. Punctuation communicates with the reader, adding energy and excitement as it packages words into logical bundles that make sense to the reader.

Some of the mechanics of writing, such as commas and semicolons, are key to understanding structure. That is because these two punctuation marks help define structure, and working on them reinforces what a sentence is. As a result, once you understand how to use commas and semicolons, you can eliminate fragments and run-ons from your writing.

Commas are only tiny little scratches on the page, yet they wield great power when you do not know the correct way to use them. With only a little practice, you will use commas and semicolons correctly and, in the process, you will gain sense of confidence. Here is what you will learn in Part 2, Mechanics for Writing:

Chapter 4, Comma Rules: you learn how to place commas based on rules rather than *pauses*. This chapter reinforces your understanding of the sentence core. Also, by having a consistent set of comma rules, you begin to base writing decisions on principles rather than guesses.

Chapter 5, Semicolon Rules: you learn how to use semicolons, which solidifies your understanding of the difference between a sentence and a fragment. This chapter is brief but important; you will further develop your understanding of the sentence core.

You will learn more mechanics for writing when you work on Part 5, More Mechanics. In that part, you will learn about colons, dashes, ellipses, quotation marks, hyphens, and more. Feel free to skip ahead and read about those marks after you have finished these next two chapters.

Each time you learn solid principles on which to base your writing decisions, you are taking the guessing out of how to produce quality writing. As your skills improve, so should your confidence. Now go have some fun as you learn about commas.

4

Comma Rules

What is your main reason for placing a comma in a sentence? Think for a moment. What word popped into your mind?

If you suddenly thought of the word "pause," you are not alone. That is what most people say. Another common response is "take a breath." You may be surprised to learn that neither of these responses provides a valid reason to use a comma.

As a result of placing commas based on pauses, have you ever read the same sentence several times—each time pausing at different places? The pause approach turns punctuating into a guessing game, even though guessing should never be involved.

Part of the problem lies in the fact that there is some truth to the "pause rule." As you have seen, grammar creates natural breaks in structure, and those breaks generally occur between clauses. Now that you have worked on independent and dependent clauses, identifying those natural breaks should seem easy for you, but do not rely on them.

Instead, let go of everything that you thought that you knew about commas. Start fresh, keeping the following in mind:

When in doubt, leave the comma out.

In other words, if you do not know the rule that corresponds with the comma, do not use the comma. If you do the work, this method of learning commas is foolproof.

Here is a strategy to tackle this chapter:

1. Go through this entire chapter quickly—within one or two sittings—and do the exercises.

2. Then, for the next few days, every time that you use a comma, state the rule that corresponds with its use.

3. If you do not know the rule, do not use the comma.

Though comma rules vary slightly from source to source, the rules presented here are consistent with other sources. However, this approach instructs you on how to use commas without going into detail about the exceptions. As a result, these rules may appear less detailed than some other sources.

If you find yourself writing a complicated sentence, consider simplifying your sentence by breaking down the information into more than one sentence. Simplicity is key to reader-friendly writing, which these comma rules help you achieve.

Rule 1: The Sentence Core Rules

Do not separate a subject and verb with only one comma.

Though this is somewhat of a rogue rule in that it does not indicate where you need to place a comma, this rule keeps you from making serious errors. As you already know, the sentence core is the critical point at which grammar and writing cross paths. The sentence core is the most powerful element of any sentence.

As you work through these comma rules, you find that setting off information with a pair of commas is acceptable. However, if you find yourself putting one comma between a subject and verb, take out the comma *or* see if you need to add a second comma!

Now let's review the remainder of the 12 comma rules, all of which give you guidance on where you should place commas.

Rule 2: Conjunction (CONJ)

Put a comma before a coordinating conjunction (such as *and*, *but*, *or*, *for*, *nor*, *so*, and *yet*) when it connects two independent clauses.

By far, the two most common coordinating conjunctions are *and* and *but*. Though some writers automatically put a comma before *and*, a comma is *not* always needed. Therefore, pay special attention about how you use punctuation with these coordinating conjunctions.

As you read the examples below, identify each independent clause. The subject of each clause is underlined once, and the verb twice (making the sentence core apparent at a glance):

Bill stayed late, *and* he worked on the proposal.

The book was left at the front desk, *but* George did not pick it up.

Be careful *not* to add a comma before a coordinating conjunction when only the second part of a compound verb follows it, for example:

Incorrect: Bob worked on the proposal, *and* sent it to my attorney.

Correct: Bob worked on the proposal *and* sent it to my attorney.

However, place a comma before a coordinating conjunction when an independent clause precedes it and follows it, for example:

Incorrect: The idea to implement the project was good *so* we plan to start next week.

Correct: The idea to implement the project was good, *so* we plan to start next week.

The sentence above marked "incorrect" is an example of a **run-on sentence**: *two or more sentences coming together without sufficient punctuation.*

After working on the Practice that follows, you will learn another comma rule that is also based on the use of coordinating conjunctions, Rule 3: Comma Series.

Practice 4.1

Rule 2: Conjunction (CONJ)

Instructions: Place commas where needed in the following sentences. For each main clause, underline the subject once and the verb twice, for example:

Incorrect: Jodie assisted with the last project so Christopher will help us with this one.

Corrected: <u>Jodie</u> <u>assisted</u> with the last project, so <u>Christopher</u> <u>will</u> <u>help</u> us with this one.

1. Mark Mallory is the new district manager and he starts on Monday.

2. Mark will be an inspiration to our staff and an excellent spokesperson for our product.

3. You can leave him a message but he will not be able to reply until next week.

4. The office in St. Louis also has a new manager and her name is Alicia Rivera.

5. You can mail your information now and expect a reply within the next week.

Note: See page 414 for the answer key to the above sentences.

REVIEW POINT Always remember to identify the verb first and then the subject, which precedes the verb in statements. Also do not forget that at times a sentence will have an *understood* or *implied* subject, for example:

(You) Give your information to Lucile.

(I) Thank you for your help.

When you have difficulty identifying a subject that precedes the verb, ask yourself if the subject could be an implied subject such as *you understood* (You) or *I understood* (I).

Rule 3: Series (SER)

Put a comma between items in a series.

A series consists of at least three items, and you may have learned that the comma before the conjunction is not required. That is true. Although the comma before the conjunction *and* is not required, it is preferred, for example:

> I <u>brought</u> potatoes, peas, *and* carrots to the pot luck.

> The <u>estate</u> <u>was</u> <u>left</u> to Robert, Rose, Charles, *and* Sophie.

> My favorite activities are walking, doing yoga, *and* swimming.

In the first example, would you prepare the "potatoes, peas, and carrots" separately or mixed? What if the comma were missing after *peas*, as in "potatoes, peas and carrots"? Would you prepare them separately or mixed?

In the second example, would the estate necessarily be split the same way if the comma after Charles were missing? For example:

> The estate was left to Robert, Rose, Charles *and* Sophie.

In fact, the above sentence is open for debate. Some could argue that the estate should be split only three ways, with Charles and Sophie splitting a third. For clarity, separate each entity (or separate individual) with a comma.

Another mistake that writers make is place a comma before *and* when it connects *only two items*, especially when the items are long phrases (shown in italics below):

| **Incorrect:** | The <u>assistant</u> <u>provided</u> *a series of examples*, and *a good recap of the meeting.* |
| **Correct:** | The <u>assistant</u> <u>provided</u> *a series of examples* and a *good   recap of the meeting.* |

After you complete the Practice, work on Rule 4: Introductory, which involves subordinating and adverbial conjunctions.

Practice 4.2

Rule 3: Series (SER)

Instructions: Place commas where needed in the following sentences. For each main clause, underline the subject once and the verb twice, for example:

Incorrect: Jerry asked for squash peas and carrots.

Corrected: Jerry asked for squash, peas, and carrots.

1. We were assigned Conference Rooms A and B on the first floor.

2. Make sure that you bring your laptop cell phone and client list to the meeting.

3. You should arrange the meeting call your manager and submit your proposal.

4. Mitchell Helen and Sally conducted the workshop on culinary science.

5. They gave a workshop for Elaine Arlene Donald and Joanne on preparing cutting and storing vegetables.

Note: See pages 414 - 415 for the answer key to the above sentences.

REVIEW POINT As a refresher, here are the three types of conjunctions that play a role in punctuation, along with a few examples of each:

Coordinating conjunctions:	and, but, or, nor, so, yet
Subordinating conjunctions:	if, after, while, when, as, although, because, as soon as
Adverbial conjunctions:	however, therefore, thus, for example, in conclusion

Conjunctions also play a role in creating a reader-friendly writing style because they cue the reader to the meaning you are conveying.

Rule 4: Introductory (INTRO)

Put a comma after a *word*, *phrase*, or *dependent clause* that introduces an independent clause.

Since this rule is a bit complicated, let's break it down into the various parts: *word*, *phrase*, and *dependent clause*.

- **Word:** in general, *word* refers to an adverbial conjunction such as *therefore*, *however*, and *consequently*, among others.

     However, I <u>was</u> not able to attend the conference.

     Therefore, <u>we</u> <u>will convene</u> the meeting in Boston.

- **Phrase:** in general, *phrase* refers to a prepositional phrase, gerund phrase, or infinitive phrase.

     During that time, he spoke about the plan in detail.

     Leaving my bags at the airport, I took a taxi into the city.

     To arrive earlier, Michael rearranged his entire schedule.

- **Dependent clause:** a dependent clause begins with a subordinating conjunction, such as *since*, *because*, *although*, *while*, *if*, and so on.

     Although my <u>calendar</u> <u>is</u> full, <u>we</u> <u>can meet</u> this Friday.

     Before <u>you</u> <u>arrive</u> at my office, <u>(you)</u> <u>call</u> my assistant.

     Until <u>I</u> <u>am</u> available, <u>you</u> <u>can work</u> in an extra office.

Placing a comma after a subordinating conjunction is a common mistake, for example:

Incorrect: *Although*, the information is timely, we cannot use it.

Correct: *Although* the information is timely, we cannot use it.

Place the comma after the dependent clause, *not* after the subordinating conjunction!

After you complete the Practice that follows, you learn that some commas come in sets, as with Rule 5: Nonrestrictive.

Practice 4.3

Rule 4: Introductory (INTRO)

Instructions: Place commas where needed in the following sentences. For each main clause, underline the subject once and the verb twice:

Incorrect: Although Mary flew to Boston she arrived a day late.

Corrected: Although <u>Mary</u> <u>flew</u> to Boston, <u>she</u> <u>arrived</u> late.

1.   Because the letter arrived late we were not able to respond on time.

2.   However we were given an extension.

3.   Although the extra time helped us we still felt pressured for time.

4.   To get another extension George called their office.

5.   Fortunately the office manager was agreeable to our request.

Note: See page 415 for the answer key to the sentences above.

Rule 5: Nonrestrictive (NR)

Use commas to set off explanations that are nonessential to the meaning of the sentence.

The key to understanding this rule lies in the difference between the meaning of the words *restrictive* and *nonrestrictive*.

- **Restrictive information** is *essential* and should not be set off with commas.

- **Nonrestrictive information** is *not essential* and can be set off with commas.

Whenever you set off information between two commas, you are implying that the information can be removed without disturbing the structure or meaning of the sentence. Nonrestrictive elements often come in the form of *who* or *which* clauses.

The two examples below illustrate this rule (*who* clauses are italicized):

Alice Walker, *who is a prestigious author*, will be the keynote speaker.

The woman *who is a prestigious author* will be the keynote speaker.

In the first example above, you would still know who the keynote speaker would be even if the *who* clause were removed:

Alice Walker will be the keynote speaker.

However, in the second example, the meaning of the sentence would be unclear if the *who* clause were removed:

The woman will be the keynote speaker. *Which woman?*

In fact, all commas that come in sets imply that the information set off by the commas can be removed; so here is another reminder of how to use commas with *essential* and *nonessential* elements:

- Essential information is restrictive and should not be set off with commas.

- Nonessential information is nonrestrictive and can be set off with commas.

Complete the following Practice to test your understanding.

Practice 4.4

Rule 5: Nonrestrictive (NR)

Instructions: Place commas where needed in the following sentences. For each main clause, underline the subject once and the verb twice. The essential and nonessential clauses are shown in italics, for example:

Incorrect: The artist *who designed our brochure* lives in New Orleans.

Corrected: The artist *who designed our brochure* lives in New Orleans. (no commas needed)

1. Our manager *who specializes in project grants* will assist you with this issue.

2. Tomas Phillips *who works only on weekends* will call you soon.

3. The paralegal *who researched this lawsuit* is not available.

4. Nick Richards *who is in a meeting until 3 p.m.* can answer your question.

5. Your new contract *which we mailed yesterday* should arrive by Friday.

Note: See page 415 for the answer key to the above sentences.

Rule 6: Parenthetical (PAR)

Use commas to set off a word or expression that interrupts the flow of a sentence.

This rule applies to adverbial conjunctions or other short phrases interjected into a sentence. By interrupting the flow of the sentence, a parenthetical expression places stress on the words immediately preceding it or following it.

Parenthetical expressions should be set off with commas because they are nonessential and can be removed, as in the following three examples.

Mr. Connors, *however*, arrived after the opening ceremony.

You can, *therefore*, place your order after 5 p.m. today.

The project, *in my opinion*, needs improvement.

Can you see how each adverbial conjunction (shown in italics) could be removed, leaving the sentence complete and clear in meaning?

A common mistake occurs when a writer uses a semicolon in place of one of the commas, for example:

Incorrect: Ms. Philippe; in fact, approved the request last week.

Correct: Ms. Philippe, in fact, approved the request last week.

When a semicolon precedes an adverbial conjunction, generally two sentences are involved: the adverbial conjunction functions as a bridge or a transition rather than an interrupter. (See Chapter 5, Semicolons.)

Another common mistake occurs when a writer uses only one comma rather than a set of commas, for example:

Incorrect: Our sales <u>representative</u>, therefore <u>will</u> <u>assist</u> you at your convenience

Correct: Our sales <u>representative</u>, therefore, <u>will</u> <u>assist</u> you at your convenience.

Incorrect: <u>Mr. Jones</u>, however <u>will</u> <u>plan</u> this year's event.

Correct: <u>Mr. Jones</u>, however, <u>will</u> <u>plan</u> this year's event.

In terms of structure, adverbial conjunctions are often nonessential elements. However, these conjunctions play an important role in writing style by giving clues to meaning and helping readers identify key points.

Practice 4.5

Rule 6: Parenthetical (PAR)

Instructions: Place commas where needed in the following sentences. For each main clause, underline the subject once and the verb twice.

Incorrect: Our contract however did not include delivery charges.

Corrected: <u>Our contract</u>, however, <u>did</u> not <u>include</u> delivery charges. .

1. Customer service I believe can best assist you with this issue.

2. T. J. therefore will work this weekend in my place.

3. Our invoice unfortunately was submitted incorrectly.

4. The new contract in my opinion meets specifications.

5. Brown Company of course recommended us to a vendor.

Note: See page 416 for the answer key.

WRITING TIP *A Note about Style*: Comma Parenthetical (PAR) shows you the correct way to punctuate a sentence when an adverbial conjunction occurs in the middle of a sentence, for example:

> Our sales representative, *therefore*, will assist you.

However, you can often make your sentence more reader friendly by moving the adverbial conjunction to the beginning of the sentence, for example:

> *Therefore,* our sales representative will assist you.

Adverbial conjunctions play an established role in writing. However, writers often interject introductory comments such as "I believe" or "I think," for example:

> *I think* the answer will become clear as we move forward.

These types of unnecessary expressions can generally be removed, for example:

> The answer will become clear as we move forward.

Can you see how theses changes make a sentence flow more effectively?

Rule 7: Direct Address (DA)

Use commas to set off the name or title of a person addressed directly.

Often the name of the person being addressed directly appears at the beginning of the sentence, but the name can also appear in the middle of the sentence or at the end of it, as shown below:

> *Donald*, <u>you</u> <u>can</u> <u>arrange</u> the meeting in Dallas or Fort Worth.

> <u>I</u> <u>gave</u> the invitation to everyone in the department, *Marge*.

> Your <u>instructions</u>, *Professor*, <u>were</u> clear and to the point.

In each of the above examples, notice that the name of the person being addressed is *not* the subject of the sentence.

The sentences below also contain a direct address, but the subject of each sentence is implied. As you read each sentence, ask yourself *who* is performing the action of the verb.

<u>Thank</u> you, *Astrid*, for speaking on my behalf.

<u>Feel</u> free to call my office at your convenience, *David*.

Traci, please <u>assist</u> me with the spring conference.

In the first sentence above, the implied subject is *I understood*; in the second and third, the implied subject is *you understood*:

I <u>thank</u> you, Astrid, for speaking on my behalf.

You <u>feel</u> free to call my office at your convenience, David.

Traci, *you* please <u>assist</u> me with the spring conference.

You will find that in sentences that contain a direct address, the subject is often implied.

After you complete the Practice below, work on Rule 8: Appositive.

Practice 4.6

Rule 7: Direct Address (DA)

Instructions: Place commas where needed in the following sentences. For each main clause, underline the subject once and the verb twice:

Incorrect: Johnny you should study that problem in more depth.

Corrected: Johnny, <u>you</u> <u>should study</u> that problem in more depth.

1. Give your report to the auditor by Friday Marcel.

2. Jason do you have tickets for the game?

3. Doctor I would like to know the results of my tests.

4. Would you like to attend the banquet Alice?

5. Thank you for inviting me George.

Note: See page 416 for the key to the above exercise.

Rule 8: Appositive (AP)

Use commas to set off the restatement of a noun or pronoun.

With an appositive, an equivalency exists between the noun and its descriptor. In the examples below, the appositives are show in italics:

> Carolyn, *my co-worker from Atlanta*, requested the date.

> Mr. Johns, *the building commissioner*, refused to give us a permit.

To check if the descriptor is an appositive, ask yourself questions that would indicate if an equivalency exists, such as the following:

> *Who is Carolyn?* My co-worker from Atlanta.

> *Who is my co-worker from Atlanta?* Carolyn.

> *Who is Mr. Johns?* The building commissioner.

> *Who is the building commissioner?* Mr. Johns.

For an appositive that occurs in the middle of a sentence, using only one comma not only creates a mistake but also changes the meaning of the sentence. Notice how the following sentences differ in meaning:

> **Incorrect:**   Josef, my former boss gave me the information.

> **Correct:**   Josef, my former boss, gave me the information.

In the first sentence above, the subject shifts to "boss" because of Rule 1 which states, "Do not separate a subject and verb with only one comma." In other words, leaving out the comma after "Josef" changes the meaning of the sentence: without the comma, grammar dictates that "boss" would become the subject rather than "Josef."

This rule applies to appositives that are not restrictive, but some appositives are restrictive. A restrictive appositive is not set off with commas because the appositive is essential for clear meaning.

For example, let's say your brother Charles is joining you for dinner. Here is how you would write the sentence as a *nonrestricted appositive*:

> **Appositive:**   My brother, Charles, will join us for dinner.

If you had only one brother, you could take "Charles" out of the sentence, and the reader would still know who you were talking about. However, what if you had five brothers? If you took "Charles" out of the sentence, would the reader know which brother would join you for dinner?

With commas setting off "Charles," the above sentence translates to: *My brother will join us for dinner.* Thus, for a *restricted appositive*, omit the commas:

Restricted Appositive: My brother Charles will join us for dinner.

Do not set off a *restricted appositive* with commas, as illustrated by the sentence above. However, focus on identifying nonrestrictive appositives until you clearly understand this principle: nonrestrictive appositives are far more common, and they are set off with commas.

Complete the Practice below before going on to Rule 9: Addresses and Dates.

Practice 4.7

Rule 8: Appositive (AP)

Instructions: Place commas where needed in the following sentences. For extra practice, underline the subject once and the verb twice in each main clause, for example:

Incorrect: Elaine my cousin taught business education subjects.

Corrected: <u>Elaine</u>, my cousin, <u>taught</u> business education subjects.

1. Jacob Seinfeld our associate director decided to hire Williams.
2. My lab partner Carol Glasco applied for a job here.
3. Jim Martinez the registrar approved your request.
4. The department chair Dr. George Schmidt did not receive your transcript.
5. The director asked Clair my sister to join us for dinner.

Note: See page 416 for the answer key to the above exercise.

Rule 9: Addresses and Dates (AD)

Use commas to set off the parts of addresses and dates.

The term *set off* means that commas are placed on both sides of the part of the address or date to show separation. For example, notice how commas surround *Massachusetts* and *California* as well as *August 15*:

Boston, Massachusetts, <u>is</u> the best city to host the conference.

<u>Sally has worked</u> in Long Beach, California, for the past five years.

On Wednesday, August 15, my <u>friends celebrated</u> the Ferragosta.

Does it surprise you to learn that a comma is required *after* the state name when a city and state are written together? If so, you are not alone; the following mistake is common:

Incorrect: Dallas, <u>Texas is</u> a great city to start a new business.

Correct: <u>Dallas</u>, Texas, <u>is</u> a great city to start a new business.

The same is true for dates; the second comma in the set is often left off incorrectly, as follows:

Incorrect: Jerome listed August 15, 2005 as his start date.

Correct: Jerome listed August 15, 2005, as his start date.

Another type of error occurs when a writer puts a comma between the month and the day, for example:

Incorrect: September, 4, 2006 was the date on the application.

Correct: September 4, 2006, was the date on the application.

Never, never, never put a comma between the month and the day as in the above incorrect example.

After completing the Practice that follows, work on Rule 10: Words Omitted.

Practice 4.8

Rule 9: Addresses and Dates (AD)

Instructions: Place commas where needed in the following sentences. For extra practice, underline the subject once and the verb twice in each main clause, for example:

Incorrect: The conference is planned for August 19 2009 in Denver Colorado.

Corrected: The <u>conference</u> <u>is</u> <u>planned</u> for August 19, 2009, in Denver, Colorado.

1. Send your application by Friday December 15 to my assistant.
2. San Antonio Texas has a River Walk and Conference Center.
3. Would you prefer to meet in Myrtle Minnesota or Des Moines Iowa?
4. Springfield Massachusetts continues to be my selection.
5. We arrived in Chicago Illinois on May 22 2009 to prepare for the event.

Note: See page 417 for the key to the above exercise.

Rule 10: Word Omitted (WO)

Use a comma in place of a word that has been omitted when its omission affects the flow of the sentence.

This type of comma occurs infrequently. Most of the time, the word that has been omitted is either *that* or *and*.

The problem is *that* the current situation is quite grim.

The problem is, the current situation is quite grim.

Mr. Adams presented the long *and* boring report to the board.

Mr. Adams presented the long, boring report to the board.

After the Practice below, work on Rule 11: Direct Quotation.

Practice 4.9

Rule 10: Word Omitted (WO)

Instructions: Place commas where needed in the following sentences. Underline the subject once and the verb twice for each main clause:

Incorrect: My suggestion is you should contain the situation now.

Corrected: My <u>suggestion</u> <u>is</u>, you should contain the situation now. (WO)

Corrected: My <u>suggestion</u> <u>is</u> *that* you should contain the situation now.

1. The president shared two intriguing confidential reports.

2. The photo shoot is on Tuesday at 5 p.m. on Wednesday at 6 p.m.

3. The problem is some of the results are not yet known.

4. Leave the materials with Alicia at the Westin with Marcia at the Hilton.

5. Silvia presented a short exciting PowerPoint on Italy.

Note: See page 417 for the key to the above exercise.

Rule 11: Direct Quotation (DQ)

Use commas to set off a direct quotation within a sentence.

A direct quotation is a person's exact words. In comparison, an indirect quotation does not give a speaker's exact words and would *not* be set off with commas.

Direct Quotation: Gabrielle said, "I have a 9 o'clock appointment," and then left abruptly.

Indirect Quotation: Gabrielle said that she had a 9 o'clock appointment and then left abruptly.

Direct Quotation: Dr. Gorman asked, "Is the environment experiencing global warming at a faster rate than previously predicted?"

Indirect Quotation:	Dr. Gorman asked whether the environment is experiencing global warming at a faster rate than previously predicted.

An exception to this rule relates to short quotations: a short quotation built into the flow of a sentence does not need to be set off with commas.

Short Quotations:	Marian shouted "Help!" as she slid on the ice.
	My boss told me "Do not sweat the small stuff" before he let me go.
	The advice "Give the project your best this time" sounded patronizing rather than encouraging.

With direct quotations, whether set off with commas or blending with the flow of the sentence, capitalize the first word of the quotation. Since using punctuation with quotation marks can be confusing, apply the following closed punctuation guidelines.

Punctuation placement with quotation marks:

- Place commas and periods on the *inside* of quotation marks.
- Place semicolons and colons on the *outside* of quotation marks.
- Place exclamation marks and question marks based on meaning: these marks can go on the *inside* or *outside* of quotation marks.

Regardless of where the punctuation mark is placed, never double punctuate at the end of a sentence.

You learn about each of the above points in detail when you work on Chapter 16, Quotation Marks, Apostrophes, and Hyphens.

Work on the following Practice before moving to your last comma rule, Rule 12: Contrasting Expression or Afterthought.

Practice 4.10

Rule 11: Direct Quotation (DQ)

Instructions: Place commas where needed in the following sentences. For each main clause, underline the subject once and the verb twice.

Incorrect: Jeffery insisted go back to the beginning before you decide to give up!

Corrected: <u>Jeffery</u> <u>insisted</u>, "Go back to the beginning before you decide to give up!"

1. Patrick shouted get back! before we had a chance to see the falling debris.

2. According to Tyler all children can learn if they find an interest in what is taught.

3. My father warned me when you choose an insurance company, find one with good customer service.

4. Sharon encouraged me by yelling go for the gold as I was starting the race.

5. Lenny said to me good luck on your exam before I left this morning.

Note: See page 417 for the key to the above exercise.

Rule 12: Contrasting Expression or Afterthought (CEA)

Use a comma to separate a contrasting expression or afterthought from the main clause.

A contrasting expression or afterthought adds an interesting twist to writing style. The expression at the end of the sentence certainly gets the reader's attention, for example:

> Go ahead and put the property on the market, if you can.

> I asked for the information so that I could help Bill make the sale, not take it from him.

My cousin Buddy, not my brother Chuck, drove me to the airport.

In fact, omitting the CEA comma is not a serious error; however, using the CEA comma makes your comments stand out and gives your writing a flow that is somewhat conversational.

After you complete the Practice below, complete the worksheets at the end of this chapter so that you get the practice that you need.

Practice 4.11

Rule 12: Contrasting Expression or Afterthought (CEA)

Instructions: Place commas where needed in the following sentences. For extra practice, underline the subject once and the verb twice in each main clause, for example:

Incorrect: Elaine attended Southern State University not Northern State.

Corrected: Elaine attended Southern State University, not Northern State.

1. You will find the manuscript in John's office not in Bob's.

2. Marcus secured the contract but only after negotiating for hours.

3. Chair the budget committee if you prefer.

4. Lester rather than Dan received the award.

5. Work to achieve your dreams not to run away from your fears.

Note: See page 418 for the key to the above exercise.

Recap

Have you stopped placing commas based on pauses?

Complete the worksheets at the end of this chapter. For best results, follow the directions exactly as prescribed. Though analyzing comma use in this way may seem challenging at first, you will improve your skills. For additional practice, go to the Web site, www.commasrule.com.

Basic Comma Rules

Rule 1: The Sentence Core Rules

Do not separate a subject and verb with only one comma.

Rule 2: Conjunction (CONJ)

Put a comma before a coordinating conjunction, such as *and* or *but*, when it connects two independent clauses.

Rule 3: Series (SER)

Put a comma between items in a series.

Rule 4: Introductory (INTRO)

Put a comma after a *word*, *phrase*, or *dependent clause* that introduces an independent clause.

Rule 5: Nonrestrictive (NR)

Use commas to set off nonessential words and phrases.

Rule 6: Parenthetical (PAR)

Use commas to set off a word or expression that interrupts the flow of a sentence.

Rule 7: Direct Address (DA)

Use commas to set off the name or title of a person addressed directly.

Rule 8: Appositive (AP)

Use commas to set off the restatement of a noun or pronoun.

Rule 9: Addresses and Dates (AD)

Use commas to set off the parts of addresses and dates.

Rule 10: Word Omitted (WO)

Use a comma to indicate a word is omitted when its omission affects the flow of the sentence.

Rule 11: Direct Quotation (DQ)

Use commas to set off direct quotations within a sentence.

Rule 12: Contrasting Expression or Afterthought (CEA)

Use a comma to separate a contrasting expression or afterthought.

Writing Workshop

Activity A. Writing Practice

Instructions: Write a short paper entitled, "What is Learning?"

John Dewey once said, "We become what we learn." Do you agree? How can you tell when you have learned something? How does it feel when you fail . . . or succeed? When you are motivated, do you work harder to learn?

If you can, discuss these questions with a peer before you start writing.

Activity B. Journal

Mistakes are an integral part of the learning process. Journal about a mistake that you recently made, and then discuss how you responded.

Could you have reacted differently? Do you ever try to be a perfectionist? Please explain.

Skills Workshop

As you complete the worksheets on the following pages, indicate the reason for each comma that you use. This additional step of analysis ensures that you will make conscious and educated decisions, bringing your skills to a higher level of expertise.

Analyzing comma use in this way may seem challenging in the beginning. However, this approach ensures that you will learn commas once and for all, a benefit throughout your writing career.

Note: See pages 418 - 421 for the keys to the worksheets that follow.

Worksheet 1: Practice for the following comma rules:

- **Conjunction (CONJ)**
- **Series (SER)**
- **Direct Address (DA)**

Instructions: Place commas where needed in the following sentences. For each main clause, underline the subject once and the verb twice. Also, indicate the comma rule for each comma that you use, for example:

Incorrect: You assisted me with the project and I appreciated it.

Corrected: You assisted me with the project, and I appreciated it. (CONJ)

1. I completed my report and Alice sent it to Wanda.
2. Wanda received the report but she did not yet file it with the department.
3. Thank you for letting me know about your concern Marsha.
4. Wanda will appreciate your telling her about the missing information for John Wilson Bill Jones and Mark Kramer.
5. Give Wanda the information today and you will save her some time.
6. The report often needs to be adjusted and Wanda kindly helps us with it.
7. Marsha you are wonderful to assist us with the extra work in our department.
8. Call Marcus Mary and Phil about the schedules and inventory.
9. You can ask for additional time but you may not receive it.
10. The training room needs new chairs tables and flip charts.
11. Go to the mail room to get the catalog for ordering supplies Mallory.
12. The accounting department issues guidelines for expenses and someone in that department can assist you with your expense account.

Worksheet 2: Practice for the following comma rules:

- **Introductory (INTRO)**
- **Appositive (AP)**
- **Direct Address (DA)**

Instructions: Place commas where needed in the following sentences. For each main clause, underline the subject once and the verb twice. Also, indicate the comma rule for each comma that you use, for example:

Incorrect: If you are able to assist me I would be relieved.

Corrected: If you are able to assist me, I would be relieved. (INTRO)

1. While I waited for a bus I completed the report.

2. However the report may need some major revisions.

3. Give me your honest opinion Mike.

4. Mr. Sisco our new office manager will use the report to make important decisions.

5. If I had known how important the report would be I would not have agreed to do it.

6. However I felt pressured to agree to do it because everyone has too much work.

7. You can ask Susan our sales representative for a second opinion.

8. When I started this job I had no idea about the long work hours.

9. However I would have taken it anyway because of its wonderful opportunities.

10. After you work here for a while you will appreciate your fellow workers.

Worksheet 3: Practice for the following comma rules:

- **Conjunction (CONJ)**
- **Addresses and Dates (AD)**
- **Nonrestrictive (NR)**
- **Parenthetical (PAR)**

Instructions: Place commas where needed in the following sentences. For each main clause, underline the subject once and the verb twice. Also, indicate the comma rule for each comma that you use, for example:

Incorrect: You are wonderful to help me and I will return the favor.

Corrected: You are wonderful to help me, and I will return the favor. (CONJ)

1. Mr. Gates started a computer company and Miller invested in it.

2. Miller however did not realize the potential at that time.

3. The company which is quite successful has satellites around the world.

4. He revealed that March 27 2010 will be the official kick-off date.

5. Arrive on time to the interview and you will make a good impression.

6. We have as a result chosen another vendor.

7. The time management seminar was excellent and its cost was reasonable.

8. Your paper unfortunately did not meet the standards.

9. Our management team assessed the damages and they recommended changes.

10. On September 4 2011 we will arrive in Denver Colorado for a meeting.

Worksheet 4: Practice for the following comma rules:

- **Introductory (INTRO)**
- **Series (SER)**
- **Words Omitted (WO)**
- **Contrasting Expression or Afterthought (CEA)**

Instructions: Place commas where needed in the following sentences. For each main clause, underline the subject once and the verb twice. Also, indicate the comma rule for each comma that you use, for example:

Incorrect: You are invited to the kick-off event and can bring a friend if you wish.

Corrected: You are invited to the kick-off event and can bring a friend, if you wish. (CEA)

1. If you choose to attend the event let us know by the end of the day.

2. Bring a guest to the luncheon if you prefer.

3. If you need extra tickets ask Elizabeth.

4. After the awards they will serve a meal of fish potatoes and broccoli.

5. Resume the program at the north branch not at the south branch.

6. Although the offer still stands our deadline quickly approaches.

7. Before they rescind their offer give them an answer.

8. After you review the contract let us know what you think.

9. The contract can be changed but only on our terms.

10. Your feedback should include items to add delete or change.

11. The fact is your input will assist us in many ways.

12. Begin the year with a detailed comprehensive plan.

Instructions: Now that you have had some practice, write a sentence demonstrating each of these rules:

Conjunction (CONJ):

_____

Series (SER):

_____

Direct Address (DA):

_____

Introductory (INTRO):

_____

Appositive (AP):

_____

Direct Address (DA):

_____

Editing Workshop

Instructions:

Insert commas where needed in the following e-mail message, and delete any commas that do not belong.

Dear Mrs. Adams:

We have an opening for an intern in our accounting department. Therefore please post the attached job order in your placement department.

Anyone interested in applying for the position, can contact Mary Jones our human resource recruiter. Mary, is expecting to hear from your students and she will interview, any students who apply. She is planning to conduct interviews, on Wednesday June 5 and Thursday June 13.

You have always been so helpful Mrs. Adams in encouraging students with great skills to apply for positions, at our company. As a result we contact you first when we have, an opening.

All the best,

Georgia Smith
All Pro Temporaries

Note: See page 421 for the key to this exercise.

5

Semicolon Rules

Most people find commas a necessity, sprinkling them throughout their writing even when unsure about how to use them correctly. It does not work that way with semicolons, however. Some people—maybe most people—develop an aversion to using semicolons, hoping to avoid them for life!

The truth is, you *can* avoid using semicolons. However, if you do not use semicolons, you are sometimes likely to put a comma where a semicolon belongs, creating a serious grammatical error. While semicolons are not similar to commas, they are similar to periods: semicolons, like periods, create major breaks in structure, for example:

- A semicolon is a full stop that is not terminal.

- A period is a full stop that is terminal.

A period brings the sentence to an end, but a semicolon does not. Most of the time, the following rule of thumb for using semicolons works:

Use a semicolon in place of a period.

In other words, if you cannot use a period, you probably should not use a semicolon either.

Since you never need to use a semicolon, why use one? Because, though you may not yet realize it, punctuation speaks to your reader in subtle, yet powerful ways.

Here are two things to consider about the semicolon:

1. The semicolon whispers to your reader that two sentences share a key idea.

2. The semicolon alerts readers to slight shades of meaning, helping readers see connections and draw relationships.

In addition, once you use your first semicolon correctly, you are likely to feel so excited about it, you will want to use the semicolon more often just for the thrill of it!

OK, so *thrill* might be a bit of a stretch; however, the more serious you become about writing, the more you will enjoy using the less common punctuation marks, such as semicolons, dashes, and ellipses (which you learn how to use in Chapter 14). These marks give you choices and options; but more importantly, they give your voice a fingerprint and add momentum to your message.

Here are the three basic semicolon rules:

1. **Semicolon No Conjunction**: use a semicolon to separate two independent clauses that are joined without a conjunction.

2. **Semicolon Bridge**: use a semicolon before and a comma after an adverbial conjunction that acts as a bridge between two independent clauses.

3. **Semicolon Because of Comma**: when a clause needs major and minor separations, use semicolons for major breaks and commas for minor breaks.

Before working on each of the semicolon rules, write two sentences, each of which contains a semicolon. Then check back after you work through these semicolon rules to see if you used each semicolon correctly.

1. _____

_____

2. _____

_____

REVIEW POINT While you are familiar with the role conjunctions play with comma use, you are not yet familiar with the role that they play with semicolon use.

- **Coordinating conjunctions** connect equal grammatical parts: and, but, or, for, nor, so, yet

- **Subordinating conjunctions** introduce dependent clauses and phrases: after, while, because, although, before, though, if, as, as soon as, and so on.

- **Adverbial conjunctions** introduce or interrupt independent clauses: however, therefore, for example, consequently, as a result, though, thus, fortunately, and so on.

Be cautious when a conjunction appears in the middle of a sentence as it may signal the use of a semicolon (see Rule 2: Semicolon Bridge and Rule 3: Semicolon Because of Commas).

Rule 1: Semicolon No Conjunction (NC)

Use a semicolon to separate two independent clauses that are joined without a conjunction.

This semicolon rule closely relates to the comma conjunction (CONJ) rule, which states "place a comma before a coordinating conjunction when it connects two independent clauses." When a conjunction is not present, separate the two independent clauses with a period or a semicolon, for example:

Comma Conjunction:	Al <u>went</u> to the store, *but* <u>he</u> <u>forgot</u> to buy bread. (CONJ)
Semicolon No Conjunction:	Al <u>went</u> to the store; <u>he</u> <u>forgot</u> to buy bread. (NC)
Period:	Al <u>went</u> to the store. <u>He</u> <u>forgot</u> to buy bread.

Notice how each sentence has a slightly different effect based on how it is punctuated. Do you see how choppy the writing sounds in the example above which uses a period, thereby breaking up the sentences?

In general, avoid writing short, choppy sentences. One way to achieve that goal is to use a semicolon instead of a period. The semicolon no conjunction (NC) rule is best applied when two sentences are closely related, especially when one or both sentences are short.

The examples and practice exercises in this book are designed to help you gain a better understanding of structure. Understanding structure provides a foundation that will help you improve your editing skills as well as your writing style.

Before moving to the next semicolon rule, do the exercise below so that you gain practice applying what you have just learned.

Practice 5.1

Rule 1: Semicolon No Conjunction (NC)

Instructions: Place semicolons where needed in the following sentences. For each main clause, underline the subject once and the verb twice, for example:

Incorrect: Addison arrived at 8 o'clock, she forgot the agenda.

Corrected: <u>Addison</u> <u>arrived</u> at 8 o'clock; <u>she</u> <u>forgot</u> the agenda.

1. Keri will not approve our expense account she needs more documentation.

2. Ask Bryan for the report he said that he completed it yesterday.

3. Arrive on time to tomorrow's meeting bring both of your reports.

4. A laptop was left in the conference room Johnny claimed it as his.

5. Recognize your mistakes offer apologies as needed.

Note: See page 422 for the key to the above exercise.

Rule 2: Semicolon Bridge (BR)

Use a semicolon before and a comma after an adverbial conjunction that acts as a bridge between two independent clauses.

This semicolon rule corresponds to the comma parenthetical (PAR) rule. With a comma parenthetical, an adverbial conjunction (shown in italics) interrupts one independent clause, for example:

Comma PAR: Bob, *however*, <u>will</u> <u>determine</u> the fees.

Instead, the semicolon bridge rule involves two complete sentences with an adverbial conjunction providing a bridge or transition between the two:

Semicolon BR: Bob <u>will</u> <u>determine</u> the fees; *however*, <u>he</u> <u>is</u> open to suggestions.

For those who avoided semicolons prior to working on this chapter, here is how you might have punctuated the above sentence:

Incorrect: Bob <u>will</u> <u>determine</u> the fees, *however*, <u>he</u> <u>is</u> open to suggestions.

In the above example, by placing a comma where a semicolon (or period) would belong, your result is a run-on sentence. This kind of error is common yet serious.

Whenever you see an adverbial conjunction in the middle of a sentence, read through the sentence at least twice to ensure that your punctuation is correct.

Here are more examples of the semicolon bridge rule (with the adverbial conjunctions shown in italics):

<u>Lidia</u> <u>wrote</u> the grant; *therefore*, <u>she</u> <u>should</u> <u>be</u> on the committee.

The <u>grant</u> <u>was</u> <u>accepted</u>; *as a result*, <u>we</u> <u>will</u> <u>receive</u> funding.

<u>You</u> <u>should</u> <u>call</u> their office; *however*, (<u>you</u>) <u>do</u> not <u>leave</u> a message.

Now that you have reviewed this rule, can you see how you may have sometimes used a comma when you should have used a semicolon?

Practice 5.2

Rule 2: Semicolon Bridge (BR)

Instructions: Place commas and semicolons where needed in the following sentences. For each main clause, underline the subject once and the verb twice, for example:

Incorrect: Feranda left, however, she forgot her briefcase.

Corrected: Feranda left; however, she forgot her briefcase.

1. Carol suggested the topic fortunately Carlos agreed.
2. The project management team offered assistance however their time was limited.
3. Ken compiled the data therefore Mary crunched it.
4. The numbers turned out well as a result our new budget was accepted.
5. Roger ran in the marathon unfortunately he was unable to finish.

Note: See page 422 for the key to the above exercise.

Rule 3: Semicolon Because of Comma (BC)

When a clause needs major and minor separations, use semicolons for major breaks and commas for minor breaks.

This semicolon rule differs from the other two rules because it does not involve a "full stop"; in other words, this rule does not follow the "semicolon in place of period" rule of thumb that you learned earlier.

In addition, the semicolon because of comma (BC) rule occurs less frequently than the other types of semicolons; that is because most sentences do not call for both major and minor breaks. Even though you will not use this semicolon rule as often as the others, this rule is nonetheless necessary at times.

Apply this rule when listing a series of city and state names, for example:

Semicolon BC: Joni will travel to Dallas, Texas; Buffalo, New York; and Boston, Massachusetts.

Since the state names need commas around them, reading the above sentence without semicolons would be confusing:

Incorrect: Joni will travel to Dallas, Texas, Buffalo, New York, and Boston, Massachusetts.

Also apply this rule when listing a series of names and titles:

Semicolon BC: The committee members are Jeremy Smith, director of finance; Marjorie Lou Kirk, assistant vice president; Carson Michaels, accountant; and Malory Willowbrook, broker.

A more complicated example would include major and minor clauses within a sentence:

Semicolon BC: Millicent asked for a raise; and since she was a new employee, I deferred to Jackson's opinion.

Semicolon BC: Dr. Jones suggested the procedure; but I was unable to help, so he asked Dr. Bender.

Practice 5.3

Rule 3: Semicolon Because of Commas (BC)

Instructions: Place commas and semicolons where needed in the following sentences. In each main clause, underline the subject once and the verb twice.

Incorrect: Gladys has lived in Boise, Idaho, Biloxi, Mississippi, and Tallahassee, Florida.

Corrected: Gladys has lived in Boise, Idaho; Biloxi, Mississippi; and Tallahassee, Florida.

1. Please include Rupert Adams CEO Madeline Story COO and Mark Coleman executive president.

2. By next week I will have traveled to St. Louis Missouri Chicago Illinois and Burlington Iowa.

3. Mike applied for jobs in Honolulu Hawaii Sacramento California and Santa Fe New Mexico.

4. Your application was received yesterday but when I reviewed it information was missing.

5. You can resubmit your application today and since my office will review it you can call me tomorrow for the results.

Note: See page 422 for the key to the above exercise.

Writing Style: Punctuation and Flow

Using punctuation *correctly* is one element of writing. Another element is applying punctuation *effectively*: punctuation packages your words, developing a rhythm that affects the style and tone of your writing.

Writing generally does not flow well when it consists of short, choppy sentences. However, at times short, choppy sentences create a desired dramatic effect, as in the following:

> Conan arrived late today. He resigned.

When you want to reduce the choppy effect that short sentences can create, semicolons can often add flow to your writing, but not always. Consider the following example:

> Jay priced the condo lower; he needs to relocate.

In the previous example, connecting the independent clauses with a semicolon does not necessarily reduce the choppy effect of the writing. The reader needs a transitional word to build a bridge between the "cause and the effect."

Here are some ways to solve the problem through the use of conjunctions:

> Jay priced the condo lower *since* he needs to relocate.

> Jay priced the condo lower *because* he needs to relocate.

> Jay priced the condo lower; *unfortunately*, he needs to relocate.

In each example above, the conjunction smoothed out the flow of the writing. By giving the reader a transitional word, the reader can more readily draw a connection between the meaning of the two clauses.

Recap

Punctuation is one more tool to help you connect with your reader and get your message across. Work with punctuation until you understand how it helps you to express your voice: experiment with punctuation and conjunctions until you gain a sense of how to use them effectively.

Semicolon Rules

Rule 1: Semicolon No Conjunction (NC)

Use a semicolon to separate two independent clauses that are joined without a conjunction.

Rule 2: Semicolon Bridge (BR)

Use a semicolon before and a comma after an adverbial conjunction that bridges two independent clauses.

Rule 3: Semicolon Because of Comma (BC)

When a clause needs major and minor separations, use semicolons for major breaks and commas for minor breaks.

Writing Workshop

Activity A. Writing Practice

Instructions: Read and analyze an article that discusses a goal that you want to achieve.

1. What is the overall purpose of the article or its thesis?

2. What audience does the article target?

3. Is the tone emotional or persuasive? Please explain.

4. Identify two or three key points that the article makes. Write a paragraph to summarize each key point.

5. What did you learn from the article that you will apply?

For a more formal start to your essay, give the author's first and last name, the title of the article, and then the purpose of the article, as shown below:

> In John Smith's article entitled "Write for Results,"
> Smith argues (or asserts or reveals) that writing is the
> most critical skill for career success today.

Activity B. Journal

Instructions: Describe the color green. What does *green* remind you of? Explore the feelings that the color green evokes, for example:

"The color green reminds me of summer and trees as well as money and my favorite shirt. When I think of green, I feel fresh and full of energy. . . ."

Write a minimum of one page.

Skills Workshop

Complete the worksheets on the following pages so that you get the practice that you need to apply the semicolon rules with confidence.

Note: See pages 423 - 425 for the keys to the following worksheets.

Worksheet 1. Semicolon No Conjunction (NC) and Comma Conjunction (CONJ)

Instructions: Place commas and semicolons where needed in the following sentences. For each main clause, underline the subject once and the verb twice. In addition, identify the reason for each mark of punctuation, for example:

Incorrect: Mark invited me to the Green Tree reception I accepted his offer.

Corrected: <u>Mark</u> <u>invited</u> me to the Green Tree reception; <u>I</u> <u>accepted</u> his offer. NC

1. The Green Tree reception was elegant it was a black tie event.

2. I arrived early to the event and everyone seemed very friendly.

3. The group expressed concern about the environment they all wanted to see immediate and substantial change.

4. The keynote speaker shared new data about climate change everyone listened attentively to the entire speech.

5. Mark suggested that we join the group so he inquired about the requirements for membership.

6. Membership required participation at various levels both of us were already overextended.

7. The group's mission appealed to me and I was excited about getting involved.

8. Mark thought it over for a while yet he was still not ready to commit.

9. The environmental movement grows every year but more help is urgently needed.

10. Mark finally agreed to join the group my excitement tipped him in the right direction.

11. Their first meeting is next week and we both plan to go to it.

12. I will volunteer for the same project that Mark works on working together is fun.

Worksheet 2. Semicolon Bridge (BR) and Comma Parenthetical (PAR)

Instructions: Place commas and semicolons where needed in the following sentences. For each main clause, underline the subject once and the verb twice. In addition, identify the reason for each mark of punctuation, for example:

Incorrect: Technology advances every day in fact most people have trouble keeping up with it.

Corrected: Technology advances every day; in fact, most people have trouble keeping up with it. BR

1. Keeping up with technology can however enhance career.

2. Different generations have different sorts of issues with technology for example younger people have an easier time learning new technology.

3. Today's young people used computers throughout their schooling consequently they find technology a natural part of their world.

4. Older generations however didn't have access to technology in school.

5. They needed to learn how to use computers and software on the job as a result many considered themselves "technologically illiterate."

6. It is never too late though to learn how to use a computer.

7. Taking classes at a local college can sometimes be inconvenient however you can research training opportunities online.

8. Online classes make learning convenient for example you can learn while you are in your own home office.

9. Most companies offer in-house training fortunately their employees stay at the cutting edge of technology.

10. Getting a job at a major corporation therefore helps ensure that you will keep your skills up-to-date.

11. Take advantage of all opportunities to build your skills for example keep an eye on your college and company newsletters.

12. Computer classes and other sorts of career classes are offered however only the most motivated enroll in them.

Editing Workshop

Instructions: Edit the following paragraph by making corrections for punctuation use.

Dear Ms. Allison:

Thank you, for your résumé and cover letter, your qualifications are excellent, however, we have no full-time positions available at the present time.

We will; however, have openings later in the year and I will certainly hold your résumé until that time, in the meantime I can offer you a position as a part-time floater.

A floater in case you are wondering shifts from task to task quickly, and must adapt to different environments. This position, might be perfect for you as new college graduate, you will be able to sample many types of projects. If you would like to discuss this option further; please call me.

I hope Ms. Allison that you will consider being a floater, we are sure to have full-time positions open within the next six months.

Best regards,

Margaret Parson

Note: See page 425 for the key to the above exercise.

PART 3: GRAMMAR FOR WRITING

Chapter 6: Verbs

Chapter 7: Pronouns

Chapter 8: Modifiers

Grammar defines the structure of a language. As you have learned, the sentence core plays a critical role in grammar and writing. Now in Part 3, you work on using elements of the sentence core correctly: verbs and pronouns.

The formal grammar of a language does not change much, even over long periods of time. However, every formal language has several informal, micro varieties.

For example, languages such as Spanish, French, and Italian have many different varieties. The Spanish that is spoken in Spain differs from the Spanish that is spoken in Mexico or South America. The French that is spoken in Paris differs from the French that is spoken in the south of France. In Italy, every region has its own *dialetto*, and each dialect is considered a valid, though informal, variety of Italian.

The same is true of English—many different "brands" of English are spoken. People from various English-speaking countries speak different varieties of English, and even people from the same country speak different varieties of English.

You can break down language use even further by saying that people speak different dialects within the same city or even within the same household. In fact, most people who speak English are fluent in more than one variety.

Varieties of a language vary in the following categories:

1. Grammar

2. Word Usage

3. Pronunciation

Do you speak differently when you are at school from when you are at home or with friends? Right now, you may not be fully aware of how you **switch codes**, which means change language patterns. However, if you focus on how you speak, you may find yourself making subtle shifts or using certain words in one situation that you would never use in another.

The chapters in this part explore how the grammar of Standard English, which is also called Edited English, differs from other varieties of English. To set the stage for language use, let's look at using language in context.

English and Its Varieties

In school, you are used to working with **Standard English** or **Edited English**. Your textbooks are written in Edited English, which corresponds closely to the way Standard English is spoken.

Standard English is the language that is spoken formally and used by most of the media. Just turn on the 6 o'clock news, and you will hear the newscaster speaking formal Standard English; however, listen to an interview with the man on the street, and you are likely to hear **local language**, a **micro-language** of Standard English.

A local language is an informal language pattern. In fact, each of us speaks one form of local language or another—no one speaks or writes formal English perfectly: *it ain't even possible!*

Here is what you need to know:

- **Edited English** or **Standard English** is known as formal English, and it facilitates communication in multi-cultural environments.

- **Local language** is known as informal language, and it is the language of choice with family and friends.

How do you know the difference between Standard English and local language? Rather than focusing on an official definition, think about what you already know.

- What does it sound like when someone is speaking "proper"?
- What does it sound like when someone is speaking "country"?

This way of describing formal and informal language patterns may make you giggle. However, each language pattern has its benefits, and the more you understand about using language in context, the more confident you will be in every situation.

Your goal now is to tune in to the difference between these two types of English. Since local language develops naturally, there is no need to work on it. However, most people need to work on their formal English, so that is what you will be doing when you work on verbs, pronouns, and modifiers in the following chapters.

Language Use and Context

To some degree, everyone is **bi-dialectal**, which means being proficient in different varieties of the same language.

By working on formal English—and keeping it separate from your local language—your bi-dialectal abilities will become even more defined than they are now.

In other words, your goal is to switch codes based on the context or environment, shifting from one language system to another with awareness and confidence. For instance, if you were on a job interview, using formal English would be the most effective choice, if that particular job called for it. However, when you are with your friends or family, local language is the natural choice.

Global Communication and Formal English

Global communication is multi-cultural communication: people from different backgrounds and different countries come together speaking the "same language." Knowing the difference between formal and informal language patterns becomes important with global communication.

People from non-English-speaking countries who study formal English also have their own brand of local English. For example, some people from India speak a local language called "Hinglish," which is a combination of Hindu and English. A combination of Spanish and English is called "Spanglish."

Local varieties, or dialects, in the United States include Appalachian, Boston English, Black Vernacular English, Cajun, Chicano, and Hawaiian Pidgin, among many others. In fact, every major city has its own form of local language. In Chicago and Boston, people use the term "yous guys"; in the South, people use "y'all"; in and around Ohio, people use "you'ins"; and in Texas, you will hear the term "all y'all." The formal equivalent for all of these terms is "you."

Just think how confusing communication would be in global settings if everyone spoke their own local English rather than formal English. More time would be spent trying to understand the meaning of the words than getting the job done.

The global environment that exists in most public arenas has brought a new urgency for proficiency in using Edited English. However, do not let formal English interfere with how you speak when you are in casual settings: Local language plays a key role in your relationships with friends and family. If you start to speak formally in places where formal language does not fit, your relationships may suffer.

Workshop Activity

Instructions: With a partner, discuss the differences in language that you hear all around you every day.

1. Make a list of words and phrases from local language and then translate them into Edited English.

2. Make a list of terms that you use in text messages, and translate them into Edited English. Is text messaging more similar to local language or Edited English? Please explain.

Note: As you complete the exercises in this chapter, use your local language as a springboard to improving your formal English skills, building a wall between the two language systems.

6

Verbs

Verbs are sources of power and energy, bringing ideas to life. Though vital, verbs can seem complicated. Fortunately, by learning only a few basic principles, you can use verbs effectively and confidently.

Here is what you will work on in this chapter:

- Regular and Irregular Verbs in Past Time

- Present Tense Third Person Singular: the *–S* Form

- Consistency of Verb Tense

- Active Voice

- Parallel Structure

- Subjunctive Mood

This chapter starts by reviewing verb parts, such as past tense forms and past participle forms, which cause writers unique problems.

After you do the basic work with verbs, you are introduced to topics that improve the quality and flow of your writing: the active voice and parallel structure. (These two topics are so important that an entire chapter is devoted to each: Chapter 9, Active Voice, and Chapter 10, Parallel Structure.)

Finally, this chapter covers the subjunctive mood. The subjunctive mood makes writing and speech sound more sophisticated for those times when you are in formal settings.

To refresh your memory, here is a list of action verbs.

Action Verbs:

Use strong verbs to add power to your writing.

accelerate	energize	lead	promote
acknowledge	enhance	learn	propose
admit	express	judge	recognize
argue	extend	justify	reconcile
analyze	focus	maintain	refute
assert	generate	modify	reinforce
charge	ignite	mold	reject
claim	illustrate	motivate	restore
challenge	implement	negotiate	revise
compile	imply	observe	simplify
concede	increase	organize	solve
consult	influence	orient	state
convert	initiate	originate	stimulate
create	inspire	perform	suggest
design	install	persuade	summarize
devote	interpret	predict	support
emphasize	invent	preserve	use
encourage	launch	produce	unify

For more information about verb tenses as well as additional exercises, visit the Web site www.commasrule.com.

Now let's get to work using verbs in past time.

Verbs in Past Time

Let's start by going over some basic information about verbs in past time. Some of this information was covered in Chapter 2, so here is a review:

1. All verbs have a base form: "to" plus a base form of a verb is called an *infinitive*; for example: *to see, to do, to be, to walk*.

2. All verbs have a *past tense* form and a *past participle* form:

   • A past tense form does <u>not</u> take a *helper verb* (also called an *auxiliary verb*).

   • A past participle form must be used with a helper verb.

Base	**Past Tense**	**Past Participle**
walk	walked	*have* walked
do	did	*have* done

3. Common helper verbs are *to have* and *to be*, as follows:

   Have: has, have, had

   Be: is, are, was, were

Based on the way past tense is formed, verbs are broken down into two broad categories: *regular verbs* and *irregular verbs*. Let's work with regular verbs first and then work with irregular verbs.

Practice 6.1

Instructions: Before you go any further in this chapter, find out which irregular verbs are troublesome for you.

1. With a partner, fill in the Irregular Verb Inventory on pages 139 to 140.

2. Which verbs do you and your partner need to work on?

3. Select a topic that you and your partner are both interested in, and together write a paragraph in past time.

Regular Verbs in Past Time

The vast majority of verbs are regular, which means that the past tense and past participle forms are both created by adding –ed to the base form, for example:

Base	**Past Tense**	**Past Participle**
walk	walked	*have* walked
file	filed	*has* filed
comment	commented	*had* commented
argue	argued	*have* argued

Here are some examples of how errors are made with past tense verbs in Edited English:

Incorrect: We *walk* to the store yesterday after class.

Correct: We *walked* to the store yesterday after class.

Incorrect: The committee *argue* all afternoon.

Correct: The committee *argued* all afternoon.

Incorrect: After we *had serve* the meal, we gave awards.

Correct: After we *had served* the meal, we gave awards.

If you leave off the –ed ending with past time regular verbs in your writing, in all likelihood you also leave off the –ed ending in your speech.

Notice your speech patterns: do you speak differently with your friends from the way that you speak in more formal environments, such as a classroom? If so, practice pronouncing the –ed ending so that you become as fluent with "school talk" as you are with local language. Repetitive practice is a key to language learning.

Here are more examples using verbs that have an –ed ending in Edited English:

Incorrect: The assistant *help* me with my application.

Correct: The assistant *helped* me with my application.

Incorrect: Mark had *refer* to the incident when we spoke last week.

Correct: Mark had *referred* to the incident when we spoke last week.

Work on the following exercise to gain practice using verbs in past time.

Practice 6.2

Regular Verbs in Past Time

Instructions: Correct the following sentences by using the Edited English past tense form of the verb.

Incorrect: My friend assist me with the class project.

Corrected: My friend *assisted* me with the class project.

1. The coach misplace the roster before the game began.
2. My counselor suggest that I submit my résumé.
3. Bart receive the award for most valuable player.
4. Last week no one on our team want the schedule to change.
5. When Jonika suggest that we meet after school, everyone was pleased.

Note: See page 426 for the key to the above exercise.

Irregular Verbs in Past Time

Irregular verbs are used differently in local language in two important ways from how they are used in Edited English.

First, in local language, an irregular past tense form is sometimes used with a helper, as in the examples that follow.

Local Language:	Edited English:
Lida *has wrote* the paper.	Lida *has written* the paper.
Bob *has spoke* to the director.	Bob *has spoken* to the director.
Alisha *has saw* that movie.	Alisha *has seen* that movie.

Second, in local language, an irregular past participle is sometimes used without a helper, as follows:

Local Language:	Edited English:
Lucas *seen* the paper.	Lucas *has seen* the paper.
Marc *spoken* to the director.	Marc *has spoken* to the director.
Alisha *done* good work.	Alisha *has done* good work.

As you can see, irregular verbs create different problems for writers than regular verbs do. To use irregular verbs correctly in Edited English:

1. Know the correct Edited English past tense of each irregular verb.

2. When using the past tense form, do <u>not</u> use a helper or auxiliary verb.

3. When using the past participle, use a helper.

Before doing Practice 6.3, Irregular Verbs in Past Time, let's take a look at one verb that seems to be especially troublesome. (Make sure that you select your choice *before* you read the explanation below.)

Which of the following sounds correct to you?

Choice 1: Jason loaned me his car.

Choice 2: Jason lent me his car.

The verb *lend* is irregular; its past tense form and past participle form are the same: *lent*. However, the word *loan* is a noun. As a noun, *loan* has neither action nor past tense forms. The correct choice above is Choice 2.

Using the noun *loan* as a verb is common, but it is local language nonetheless; for formal situations, use *lend*.

Practice 6.3

Irregular Verbs in Past Time

Instructions: Correct the following sentences by using the Edited English past tense form of the verb.

Incorrect: George has went to the meeting.

Corrected: George has *gone* to the meeting.

1. We already seen that movie last week.
2. The professor said that you had wrote a good paper.
3. I brang my lunch today, so you don't need to loan me money.
4. Bob loaned me $5 so that I could go to the game.
5. The assistant has took all the papers to the office.

Note: See page 426 for the key to the above exercise.

The –S Form: Third Person Singular

In Edited English, all third person singular verbs in simple present tense end in an *s*.

By referring to these verbs as the *–s* form, you remain aware of their unique "spelling." Here are some examples:

Incorrect: Bob **don't** give the information to anyone.

Correct: Bob **does not** (doesn't) give the information to anyone.

Incorrect: Martha **have** the right attitude about her job.

Correct: Martha **has** the right attitude about her job.

Incorrect: My teacher **say** that the paper is due on Friday.

Correct: My teacher **says** that the paper is due on Friday.

Work on the exercise below to get practice using the *–s* form.

Practice 6.4

The *–S* Form

Instructions: Correct the following sentences by using the *–s* form.

Incorrect: When Lenny have a question, he ask for advice.

Corrected: When Lenny *has* a question, he *asks* for advice.

1. The coach say that we need to practice for one more hour.
2. Our team finish in first place every year.
3. Taylor have chosen the players for both teams.
4. The coach have enough good players already.
5. If the group listen carefully, they will learn the information.

Note: See page 426 for the key to the above exercise.

Verb Tense and Consistency

When you are writing, do not shift verb tense unnecessarily. In other words, stay in present tense *or* past tense unless the meaning of the sentence demands that you change tenses.

Incorrect: Arthur says that the game started on time.

Correct: Arthur said that the game started on time.

Incorrect: After we went to the store, then we go to the movies.

Correct: After we went to the store, then we went to the movies.

Do the following exercise to get practice using verb tense consistently.

Practice 6.5

Verb Tense and Consistency

Instructions: Correct the following sentences so that the tense remains consistent.

Incorrect: My friend tells me that she had lunch already.

Corrected: My friend *told* me that she *had* lunch already.

1.   The note is not clear and needed to be changed.

2.   My boss says that I arrived late to work every day this week

3.   The new computers arrive today, so then I had to install them.

4.   Yesterday my counselor tells me I needed to take an extra elective.

5.   Last week my teacher tells me that I had to redo the paper.

Note: See page 426 for the key to the above exercise.

Active Voice

The active voice keeps writing clear and engaging. To understand active voice, let's start with a passive sentence:

Passive: The ball was thrown by Billy.

First, identify the main verb, which is *sent*. Next, identify the *real subject*. The real subject is the person or thing performing the action of the verb. In a passive sentence, the real subject is different from the grammatical subject, which precedes the verb in a statement.

In the passive example above, *who threw the ball? Billy did.*

Active: Billy threw the ball.

Here are the steps to change a sentence from passive to active voice:

1. Identify the main verb of the sentence.

2. Identify the real subject by asking, *who performed the action of the verb?*

3. Place the real subject at the beginning of the sentence.

4. Follow the real subject with the verb, making adjustments for agreement.

5. Complete the sentence with the rest of the information.

Let's use the above steps to translate the following sentence from passive voice to active voice:

> The team captain was replaced by the coach.

1. What is the main verb?   replaced

2. Who was doing the replacing?   the coach

3. Begin the sentence with the real subject: The coach . . .

4. Follow the real subject with the verb: The coach replaced . . .

5. Complete the sentence: The coach replaced the team captain.

Here is the structure for the **passive voice**:

What was done by whom.

Here is the structure for the **active voice**:

Who did what.

Do you see the difference between the passive voice and the active voice? Do you see that the active voice makes writing more direct, clear, and concise?

Practice 6.6

Active Voice

Instructions: Change the following sentences from passive to active voice.

Passive Voice: The meeting had been planned by Suzie.

Active Voice: Suzie had planned the meeting.

1. The assignment was given by my math instructor.

2. The car was purchased for me by my Uncle John.

3. The new soccer jersey was chosen by the entire team.

4. An annual art exhibit will be planned by the Art Council.

5. Your invoice should be paid by the beginning of the month.

Note: See page 427 for the key to the above exercise.

Parallel Structure

Parallel structure means putting similar sentence elements, such as words and phrases, in the same grammatical form. Parallel structure adds balance, which helps writing flow well.

Parallel structure often involves infinitives and gerunds. As you will recall, an infinitive consists of "to" plus the base form of the verb, as in *to see*, *to go*, or *to keep*. A gerund is the "ing" form of the verb, as in *seeing*, *going*, or *keeping*.

Even though the words *go*, *see*, and *keep* are verbs, they function as nouns when they are in their infinitive or gerund form. When you list items in a sentence, be consistent: use gerunds *or* infinitives.

Inconsistent structure:	My favorite activities are *to jog*, *swimming*, and *going to the park and golfing*.
Parallel structure:	My favorite activities are *jogging*, *swimming*, and *golfing*.

Likewise, when you create a list, apply parallel structure to the way you list your items. Here is an inconsistent list:

Goals for tomorrow:

1. Buy new tennis outfit.

2. Making an appointment with tennis coach.

3. Time for doing homework must be planned in.

To make this list parallel, start each item with a gerund or an infinitive:

Gerunds:

1. Buying new outfit.

2. Making an appointment with tennis coach.

3. Planning time for homework.

Infinitives:

1. (To) Buy new tennis outfit.

2. (To) Make an appointment with tennis coach.

3. (To) Plan time for homework.

Notice that using an infinitive without the word *to* is the same as using an active verb. You will go over this topic and other elements of parallel structure in Chapter 10, Parallel Structure.

Besides gerunds and infinitives, also make sure your sentences do not shift from active voice to passive voice, as shown in the examples that follow.

Unnecessary Shift: Bob received his brother's old car because a new car was bought by his brother.

Parallel Structure: Bob received his brother's old car because his brother bought a new car.

Work on the following sentences to practice applying parallel structure.

Practice 6.7

Parallel Structure

Instructions: Edit the following sentences for parallel structure.

Incorrect: Our assignment included reading, to write a paper, and it was necessary to give a presentation as well.

Corrected: Our assignment included *reading*, *writing*, and *giving* a presentation.

1. My professor asked me to submit a new paper and handing it in on Friday was required.

2. My friends and I plan to visit a cathedral and seeing the ancient ruins in Rome.

3. Everyone focused on showing good team spirit and to win the game.

4. Your attitude will go a long way toward achieving success and get what you want in life.

5. I received the new soccer jerseys, and now they must be passed out.

Note: See page 427 for the key to the above exercise.

Subjunctive Mood

In addition to tense, verbs also express mood, which represents the writer's attitude toward a subject.

Here are the possible moods that verbs can convey:

- Indicative: straight-forward, matter of fact
- Imperative: exclamatory
- Subjunctive: possibility, contrary to fact

The indicative mood is the most common mood; and most writing, including this text, is written in the indicative mood. Less common is the imperative mood, but the imperative mood is easy to recognize. For example, sentences ending in an exclamation mark express emotion and are considered imperative: *Stop! Don't go there!*

The most challenging mood to use correctly is the subjunctive mood. The subjunctive mood expresses improbability, and an improbability often comes in the form of a *wish* or *a possibility*. The subjunctive mood is also used with certain requests, demands, recommendations, and set phrases.

- For the **past subjunctive**, *to be* is always expressed as *were*. For example: If I *were* you . . . I wish I *were* . . . and so on.

- For the **present subjunctive**, the verb is expressed in the **infinitive** form. For example: It is critical that John *attend* the program.

When the subjunctive mood is used, language sounds sophisticated and formal. Therefore, by developing expertise in using the subjunctive mood, you have the option of using it when you are in formal settings.

Past Subjunctive

Statements following "wish" and "if" are written in the past subjunctive. In a past subjunctive statement, the verb *to be* is always represented as *were.*

Local Language:	Edited English:
I *wish* I *was* the captain.	I *wish* I *were* the captain.
Barb *wishes* she *was* captain.	Barb *wishes* she *were* captain.
Bob *wishes* it *was* true.	Bob *wishes* it *were* true.

When a sentence begins with the word *if*, often the statement that follows is a *condition* rather than a statement of fact. Express such conditional statements in the subjunctive mood.

Incorrect:	If he *was* certain, we would buy the product.
	If she *was* here, she would understand.
	If I *was* you, I would go to the game.

Correct:	If he *were* certain, we would buy the product.
	If she *were* here, she would understand.
	If I *were* you, I would go to the game.

Practice using the subjunctive mood until you feel comfortable using it so that you have the option of using it in formal situations.

Present Subjunctive

The present subjunctive occurs in *that clauses* expressing wishes, commands, requests, or recommendations. The present subjunctive is expressed by the infinitive form of the verb, regardless of the person or number of the subject.

The coach said that it is imperative (that) you be on time.

It is essential (that) your brother assist you with the project.

Malcolm suggested (that) the team be invited to the opening.

The counselor requested (that) Mark submit his paperwork.

The word *that* is essential when the words *said* or *reported* precede it, thereby showing that a direct quote does not follow. However, the word *that* is implied even when removed.

Practice 6.8

Subjunctive Mood

Instructions: In the following subjunctive sentences, circle the correct form of the verb. (The correct answer is shown in bold below.)

Example: The instructions require that the package (is, **be**) sent via UPS.

1. The president insisted that Melba (attends, attend) the reception.
2. Jacob wishes that he (was, were) on this year's team.
3. If Dan (was, were) your team captain, would you support him?
4. My mother said that it is imperative that my sister (complete, completes) her college education.
5. If I (was, were) you, I would run for office.

Note: See page 427 for the key to the above exercise.

Recap

Verbs can be complicated, but a few basic principles can solve most writing questions.

➢ Do not use a helper verb with past tense forms, but do use a helper with past participle forms.

➢ End all third person singular verbs in an *s* (the *–s* form).

➢ Within a sentence, do not shift verb tense unnecessarily.

➢ Use the active voice to produce writing that is clear and concise.

➢ Apply parallel structure to produce writing that flows well.

➢ Use the subjunctive mood to express possibility, but not fact.

➢ For the past subjunctive, use *were* for the verb *to be*; for the present subjunctive, represent verbs in their infinitive form.

➢ Practice until you feel confident: repetition is the key to achieving success with any type of skill development.

Writing Workshop

Activity A. Writing Practice

Compose a brief description of yourself using the prompts below. Each response should be at least five sentences, but you can write as much as you would like beyond the minimum. This activity is an opportunity to apply your newly refreshed knowledge of verb tense.

"I Was, I Am, I Will Be, I Wish I Were"

1.) At one time in my life, I was . . .

2.) At this time in my life, I am . . .

3.) In five years I will be . . .

4.) I wish I were . . .

Activity B. Journal

Choose one special or memorable experience from your life, and write about it.

What incident pops into your mind? Why is it significant? How old were you? What did you learn from it?

Writing about significant incidents in your life is an excellent form of self-reflection . . . and an excellent way to start your memoir.

Skills Workshop

Irregular Verb Inventory

Instructions: Fill in the past tense and past participle forms below. Use a helper verb, such as to be (is, are, was, were) or to have (*has*, *have*, or *had*) with each past participle. (*Note*: See page 144 for the key to the Irregular Verb Inventory.)

Base Form	Past Tense	Past Participle
arise	arose	*have* arisen
become	became	*has* become
break	broke	*was* broken
bring	_____	_____
buy	_____	_____
choose	_____	_____
do	_____	_____
drink	_____	_____
drive	_____	_____
eat	_____	_____
fly	_____	_____
forget	_____	_____
freeze	_____	_____
get	_____	_____
forget	_____	_____
go	_____	_____
know	_____	_____
lend	_____	_____
prove	_____	_____
say	_____	_____
see	_____	_____
set	_____	_____
sink	_____	_____
sit	_____	_____
show	_____	_____
speak	_____	_____
stand	_____	_____
take	_____	_____
throw	_____	_____
write	_____	_____

Note: See pages 428 - 429 for the keys to the exercises below.

Worksheet 1: Verbs in Past Time

Instructions: In the following paragraph, change verbs from local language to Edited English.

When I had gave my manager notice that I was resigning, she ask me for a formal letter of resignation. However, I had never wrote that kind of letter, so I didn't know how to get started. One of my friends says that she would help me, so I felt relieve. Last Saturday, it seem that we work all day on that letter until we finally come up with a professional version. By the time that I had finish the letter, I have decided not to quit my job. I sure hope that my change of mind goes over well with my manager!

Worksheet 2: Third Person Singular, Present Tense: the -S Form

Instructions: Correct the following sentences by using the –s form.

Incorrect: My assistant have the papers you need.

Corrected: My assistant *has* the papers you need.

1. Melissa don't have the correct information.

2. Her friend Jeanne have given her misleading advice.

3. When she ask me, I always tell her the truth.

4. The economy have not done well this year.

5. Willis don't know anyone to ask to join our team.

6. If you are looking for a job, Jerrod know the right people to contact.

7. The professor pass out reports at the beginning of every class.

8. My paper have not yet been completed.

9. The library close at noon but reopen at 1 p.m.

10. Though my manager don't belong to that organization, she should.

Worksheet 3: Subjunctive Mood: Present and Past

Instructions: In the following paragraph, make corrections in the subjunctive mood where necessary.

The athletic department announced the swim team will have its first meeting on Friday. If I was you, I would go. The captain said that if you want to be considered for the team, it is imperative that you are on time. In fact, I wish that I was as talented in sports as you are. If I was, I would try out for more than one sport.

Worksheet 4: Verb Tense, Agreement, and Consistency

Instructions: Choose the correct form of the verb.

1. Bob should not have (went, gone) to the luncheon on Friday.
2. Our receptionist (don't, doesn't) give that information to anyone.
3. The new president had (spoke, spoken) at the annual event.
4. Randle (loaned, lent) me the material for the team project.
5. You should have (wrote, written, writen) a draft first.
6. The phone must have (rang, rung) 20 times while we were there.
7. I should have (brang, brung, brought) another copy of my paper.
8. Who has (drunk, drank) the last glass of milk?
9. We were (froze, frozen) before the game even began.
10. You should have easily (saw, seen) the error in the report.
11. Everyone in the room was (took, taken) by surprise.
12. It felt as if we had (swam, swum) with sharks.
13. My heart (sunk, sank) when she gave the news.
14. The budget is (froze, frozen) until next quarter.
15. Bob was displeased that he (is, was) not able to complete the project.

Standard Verb Tenses

SIMPLE TENSE		DESCRIPTION
Past	spoke	an action that ended in the past
Present	speak	an action that exists or is repeated
Future	will speak	an action that will happen in the future

PROGRESSIVE TENSE

Past	was speaking	an action that was happening in the past
Present	am/is/are speaking	an action that is happening now
Future	will be speaking	an action that will happen in the future

PERFECT TENSE

Past (Distant Past)	*had* spoken	an action that ended before another action in the past
Present (Recent Past)	*has/have* spoken	an action that started in the past and was recently completed or is still ongoing
Future	will have spoken	an action that will end before another future action or time

PERFECT PROGRESSIVE TENSE

Past	had been speaking	an action that happened in the past over time before another past action or time
Present	has/have been speaking	an action occurring over time that started in the past and continues into the present
Future	will have been speaking	an action in the future occurring over time before another future action or time

IRREGULAR VERBS

Base Form	Past Tense	Past Participle
arise	arose	arisen
become	became	become
break	broke	broken
bring	brought	brought
buy	bought	bought
choose	chose	chosen
dive	dived, dove	dived
do	did	done
draw	drew	drawn
drink	drank	drunk
drive	drove	driven
eat	ate	eaten
fall	fell	fallen
fly	flew	flown
forget	forgot	forgotten
freeze	froze	frozen
get	got	got, gotten
give	gave	given
go	went	gone
grow	grew	grown
know	knew	known
lend	lent	lent
prove	proved	proved, proven
ride	rode	ridden
say	said	said
see	saw	seen
set	set	set
sink	sank	sank
sit	sat	sat
show	showed	showed, shown
speak	spoke	spoken
stand	stood	stood
swim	swam	swum
take	took	taken
throw	threw	thrown
wear	wore	worn
write	wrote	written

7

Pronouns

Most people are not aware of the mistakes that they make with pronouns, so keep an open mind as you go through this chapter. You see, you may be making common mistakes with pronouns but not be aware of it. For example, is it "between you and *I*" or "between you and *me*"? Should you give the report to "John and *myself*" or to "John and *me*"?

In case you need a refresher, a **pronoun** is a word that is used in place of a noun or another pronoun; for example, *I, you, he, she, it, we,* and *they* as well as *who, that, which, someone,* among others.

One of the biggest mistakes that people make with pronouns is using a formal-sounding pronoun such as *I* in place of a less-formal sounding pronoun such as *me*. That kind of mistake is called a **hyper-correction**.

Hyper-correction is common. Unsure speakers pick up incorrect pronoun use almost the way they would pick up a virus, changing their speech so that it "sounds right." If you want to use pronouns correctly, base your decisions on how they *function* in a sentence and not how others use them; then you will have sound and principle on your side.

Pronouns are classified by **case**: the four cases of personal pronouns are **subjective**, **objective**, **possessive**, and **reflexive**. In this chapter, you first review how pronouns function based on case. Then you review pronoun viewpoint and how to use pronouns consistently within sentences and paragraphs. Finally, you work with other types of pronouns, such as **relative**, **indefinite**, and **demonstrative pronouns**.

Learning a few basic principles about pronouns will give you control and confidence in the say that you use them, so let's get started.

Review the following chart for a quick refresher of personal pronouns.

Personal Pronouns: Four Cases

	Subjective	Objective	Possessive	Reflexive
Singular				
1st Person	I	me	my, mine	myself
2nd Person	you	you	your, yours	yourself
3rd Person	he	him	his	himself
	she	her	hers	herself
	it	it	its	itself
Plural				
1st Person	we	us	our, ours	ourselves
2nd Person	you	you	your, yours	yourselves
3rd Person	they	them	their, theirs	themselves

Here is a summary of the role that each case plays in a sentence:

- **Subjective** case pronouns function as **subjects** of verbs, and thus a subjective case pronoun is used as the subject of a sentence.

- **Objective** case pronouns function as **objects**, usually of verbs or prepositions.

- **Possessive** case pronouns **show possession** of nouns or other pronouns.

- **Reflexive** case pronouns reflect back to subjective case pronouns; reflexive case pronouns are also known as **intensive case pronouns**.

Subjects vs. Objects

Your first step in gaining control of pronouns lies in using subjective case and objective case pronouns correctly.

At the core of pronoun use, here is the question you need to answer:

Does the pronoun function as a subject or as an object?

Here is why it is easy to use subjective case and objective case pronouns incorrectly:

1. Subjective case pronouns sound more formal than objective case pronouns. An unsure speaker will use *I* or *he* as an object, when *me* or *him* would be correct.

2. When a pronoun is part of a pair, incorrect pronoun use can sound correct.

Here are some examples:

Incorrect:	Bill asked Mike and *I* to assist him.
Correct:	Bill asked Mike and *me* to assist him.
Incorrect:	George and *me* went to the game last Friday.
Correct:	George and *I* went to the game last Friday.

In place of a subjective case pronoun or an objective case pronoun, some writers incorrectly substitute a reflexive case pronoun.

Incorrect:	George and *myself* went to the game last Friday.
Incorrect:	Bill asked Mike and *myself* to assist him.
Correct:	Sue and *yourself* can work on the project.

Instead, use reflexive case pronouns only when they refer to a subjective case pronoun or a noun that is already part of the sentence.

Here are some examples using reflexive case pronouns correctly:

I will do the work *myself*.

You can complete the project *yourself*, if you have the time.

Susan referred to *herself* as the person in charge of hiring.

The *dog* bit *itself* in the foot, mistaking his foot for a bone!

To use subjective case and objective case pronouns correctly, first identify whether the pronoun functions as a *subject* or as an *object*. If the pronoun stands alone, it is easier to test by sound. If the pronoun is part of a pair, use the following substitutions:

1. Use *I* if you could substitute *we*:

    Sam and I went to the game: *We* went to the game.

2. Use *me* if you could substitute *us*:

    Sally asked *Juan and me* for help: Sally asked *us* for help.

3. Use *he* or *she* if you could substitute *they*:

    Martin and he finished the project: *they* finished the project.

4. Use *him* or *her* if you could substitute *them*:

    Melissa encouraged *LaTika and her* to go: Melissa encouraged *them*.

Another way would be to simplify your sentence by taking out the "other person" and then testing for sound. Using examples from above, here is how you would test your pronoun based on sound:

Incorrect:	Sam and *me* went to the game.
Simplify:	~~Sam and~~ *me* went to the game.
Correct:	Sam and *I* went to the game.
Incorrect:	Sally asked Juan and *I* for help.
Simplify:	Sally asked ~~Juan and~~ *I* for help.
Correct:	Sally asked Juan and *me* for help.

Incorrect:	Martin and *him* finished the project.
Simplify:	~~Martin and~~ *him* finished the project.
Correct:	Martin and *he* finished the project.

Incorrect:	Bill asked Mike and *myself* to assist him.
Simplify:	Bill asked ~~Mike and~~ *myself* to assist him.
Correct:	Bill asked Mike and *me* to assist him.

WRITING TIP

Rule of Thumb Substitution: If you can substitute *we* for a pair, use *I*. If you can substitute *us,* use *me.*

Practice 7.1

Subjects and Objects

Instructions: Correct the following sentences for pronoun usage.

Incorrect:	When you call the office, ask for myself or Alice.
Corrected:	When you call the office, ask for *me* or Alice.

1. If you can't reach anyone else, feel free to call myself.
2. The director told Catie and I to try the scene again.
3. Fred and her collected for the local food drive.
4. His manager and him have two more reports to complete.
5. That decision was made by Jim and I.

Note: See page 429 for the key to the above exercise.

Pronouns Following *Between* and *Than*

Using pronouns after *between* and *than* can be confusing. The local language versions are so common that they sound "more correct" than the correct usage. Let's start with *between*.

Which of the following sounds correct to you? (Select your choice *before* you read the explanation that follows.)

> **Choice 1:**   Between you and *I*, we have too much work.
>
> **Choice 2:**   Between you and *me*, we have too much work.

Remember the saying, "What is the object of the preposition?" The word *between* is a preposition, and an object would follow it. When *between* is followed by a pronoun, the correct choice would be an objective case pronoun such as *me* or *him* or *her* or *them*. Therefore, the correct choice is "between you and *me*."

Now let's work with the conjunction *than*. Which of the following sounds correct to you?

> **Choice 1:**   Paco is taller than *me*.
>
> **Choice 2:**   Paco is taller than *I*.

Since the word *than* is a conjunction, a subject *and* a verb would follow it. Oftentimes the verb is implied, which makes an objective case pronoun sound correct even when it is not correct. If you selected the second choice above, you would be correct. The statement actually reads, "Paco is taller than I (am)."

Here is what you need to know:

- Use the objective case after the preposition *between*.

> **Incorrect:**   You can split the project between *Bob* and *I*.
>
> **Correct:**   You can split the project between *Bob* and *me*.
> You can split the project between *us*.

Incorrect: That issue should remain between *yourself* and *I*.

Correct: That issue should remain between *you* and *me*.

- Use the subjective case after the conjunction *than* when a subject and implied verb follow it. To be correct without sounding too formal, include the implied verb in your speech and writing.

Incorrect: Mitchell has more time than *me*.

Correct: Mitchell has more time than *I (have)*.

Incorrect: Erin runs faster than *me*.

Correct: Erin faster than *I (run)*.

Once again, using pronouns correctly involves knowing the principle and avoiding the habit of hyper-correcting!

Practice 7.2

Pronouns Following *Between* and *Than*

Instructions: Correct the following sentences for pronoun usage.

Incorrect: The discussion was between John and I.

Corrected: The discussion was between John and *me*.

1. Between you and I, who has more time?

2. Beatrice sings better than me.

3. The decision is between Bob and yourself.

4. The Blue Jays are more competitive than us.

5. You can split the work between Margaret and I so that it gets done on time.

Note: See page 429 for the key to the above exercise.

Pronoun and Antecedent Agreement

An **antecedent** is a word to which a pronoun refers. In the following example, *teachers* is the antecedent of *they* and *their*.

> All *teachers* said that *they* would submit *their* monthly progress reports on time.

Pronouns must agree in number and gender with their antecedents. Many antecedents are not gender specific, such as *person* or *doctor* or *teacher* or *lawyer*. For a singular antecedent that is gender neutral, use combinations of pronouns to refer it, such as *he/she* or *him/her*. For example, the antecedent "doctor" is gender neutral.

> When a *doctor* performs *his* or *her* duties, *he* or *she* must remain attentive to *his* or *her* patients.

Lack of agreement between pronouns and their antecedents usually occurs within sentences that contain an antecedent that is singular. Here are some examples:

Incorrect: When a *person* writes, *they* need to stay focused.

Correct: When a *person* writes, *he* or *she* needs to stay focused.

Incorrect: Every *attendee* should make *their* own reservations.

Correct: Every *attendee* should make *his* or *her* own reservation.

An easier way to correct the above sentences would be to make the antecedent and its corresponding pronouns plural:

Correct: When *people* write, *they* need to stay focused.

Correct: All *attendees* should make *their* own reservations.

To get some practice correcting pronoun-antecedent agreement, complete the following exercise.

Practice 7.3

Pronoun and Antecedent Agreement

Instructions: Correct the following sentences for pronoun-antecedent agreement.

Incorrect: When an employee calls in sick, they should give a reason.

Corrected: When *employees* call in sick, *they* should give a reason.

1. When a teller does not relate well to their customers, they need more training.
2. A server is going beyond her job description when they prepare carry-out orders for customers.
3. A pilot has a challenging job because they work long hours under difficult conditions.
4. When a student does not turn in their work, they should expect penalties.
5. A writer needs to submit their work in a timely manner.

Note: See page 430 for the key to the above exercise.

Point of View and Consistency

Besides making sure that your pronouns agree with their antecedents, also make sure that you remain consistent with your point of view. Any of the following viewpoints are acceptable, depending on the piece that you are writing:

	Singular	**Plural**
First or person:	I	We
Second person:	You	You
Third person:	He, She, It	They

Each point of view has a different effect. If you are writing about your own experience, use the *I* point of view. If you are communicating directly with your reader, use the *you* point of view.

I Viewpoint: When *I* started this project, *I* implied . . .

You Viewpoint: (*You*) Take your time as you read the examples so that *you* can . . .

In business, writers often use the *we* point of view to stress that they represent their company, as in the following:

We Viewpoint: *We* at First Trust Bank value your business.

When you summarize a research article, use the third person point of view stating the author's name, for example:

Barnes argues that Internet sites distract learners, ultimately creating more stress than genuine enjoyment.

Once you select a point of view, use that point of view consistently throughout the piece that you are writing. In other words, do not shift point of view within sentences and paragraphs.

Here are the various points of view:

When *I* speak, *I* must pay attention to *my* audience.

When *you* speak, *you* must pay attention to *your* audience.

When a *person* speaks, *he* or *she* must pay attention to *his* or *her* audience.

When *we* speak, *we* must pay attention to *our* audience.

When *people* speak, *they* must pay attention to *their* audience.

Though the use of *one* as a pronoun is not common in the United States, other English-speaking countries commonly use the *one* point of view, for example:

When *one* speaks, *one* must pay attention to *one's* audience.

Here are some examples of shifting point of view:

Incorrect: *I* like to swim because it's good for *you*.

Correct: *I* like to swim because it's good for *me*.

Incorrect: *An employee* should follow the rules because *you* never know when *your* manager is observing *you*.

Correct: *An employee* should follow the rules because *he* or *she* never knows when *his* or *her* manager is observing *him* or *her*.

Even though the above sentence is correct, notice how tedious it is to present it in third person singular. A better choice would be to make the antecedent plural or to use the *you* viewpoint:

Correct: *Employees* should follow the rules because *they* never know when *their* manager is observing *them*.

Correct: *You* should follow the rules because *you* never know when *your* manager is observing *you*.

How you adapt your topic to your audience helps determine the point of view you select. Once you select a point of view, the key is using it consistently. Edit individual sentences for consistency, and also edit paragraphs for consistency. At times, even entire documents must maintain consistency.

Another issue with pronouns relates to unclear pronoun and antecedent agreement. Restate the antecedent when using a pronoun would lead to an unclear meaning, for example:

Incorrect: Sam and Mike went to the meeting together so that *he* could present the information himself.

Correct: Sam and Mike went to the meeting together so that Mike could present the information himself.

Practice 7.4

Point of View and Consistency

Instructions: Change the following local language sentences to Edited English.

Incorrect: I appreciate having time off because it relieves your stress.

Corrected: I appreciate having time off because it relieves *my* stress.

1. I enjoy jogging because exercise keeps you fit.
2. You should follow the guidelines until we finish the project.
3. As long as you stay motivated, I won't mind finishing the project.
4. A person should strive to get the best education possible so you can have a satisfying career.
5. Sue and Mary worked on the project together, and she will present it at the next conference.

Note: See page 430 for the key to the above exercise.

Relative Pronouns: *Who, Whom,* and *That*

When writers do not know how to use *whom* correctly, they often misuse the pronouns *who* and *that*. Let's take a look at how to use each pronoun correctly.

1. Use *who* as the subject of a clause or a sentence.

   > Who gave you the report?
   > Who said that the program starts now?

2. Use *whom* as an object of a preposition, a verb, an infinitive, or other verb phrase.

   > To whom are you referring?
   > You are referring to whom?

3. Use *that* when referring to things, not people.

> The yellow car is the one that is broken.
> ***Not:*** Mary is the person *that* spoke first.

4. Use *who* as a subject complement of a linking verb such as *is*, *are*, *was*, or *were*.

> *Who* do you want to be when you grow up?
> You want to be *who* when you grow up?

When you are having difficulty choosing among the relative pronouns *who*, *whom*, and *that*, choose *who*.

When in doubt, use *who*.

Here is why:

1. *Whom* is falling out of use: only a small fraction of the population use *whom* correctly.

2. People who use *whom* correctly reserve its use for highly formal situations.

3. Using *whom* incorrectly sounds strange.

To improve your speech as well as your writing, instead focus on pronouncing your words clearly.

Local Language:	*Whoja* go to the ballgame with?
Informal English:	*Who* did you go to the ballgame with?
Formal English:	With *whom* did you go to the ballgame?

Work on the exercise that follows to gain additional practice using *who*, *whom*, and *that*.

Practice 7.5

Relative Pronouns: *Who, Whom,* and *That*

Instructions: Circle the correct pronoun in the following sentences.

Examples: (**Who,** Whom) presented the information to Alice's team?

Michael is the person (**who,** that) operates the machinery.

1. (Who, Whom) completed the monthly report?
2. (Who, Whom) are you going to the meeting with?
3. Is Jim the person (who, whom) spoke with you?
4. The doctor (that, who, whom) saw you yesterday is not available.
5. Every person (who, that) arrives late will be turned away.

Note: See page 430 for the key to the above exercise.

Relative Pronouns: *That* and *Which*

Though *that* and *which* are somewhat interchangeable, here is how to decide between the two.

- Use *that* with *restrictive* information, which is information that should not be removed if the meaning is to remain clear.

- Use *which* with *nonrestrictive* information, which is information that can be set off with commas and removed.

Here are some examples with a brief explanation following each:

Example 1: Our house that we bought last summer needs a new roof.

Example 1 gives the impression that "we" own more than one home—it is the house that we bought last summer that needs a new roof.

Example 2: Our house, which we bought last summer, needs a new roof.

Example 2 indicates that "we" have only one house and that "we" bought the house last summer.

Example 3: The report that came out in August reveals our position.

Example 3 indicates that more than one report came out, and the report of interest is the one that came out in August.

Example 4: The report, which came out in August, reveals our position.

Example 4 indicates that there was only one report, and that one report came out in August.

Now let's work on demonstrative pronouns.

Demonstrative Pronouns

Demonstrative pronouns modify nouns by "pointing to" them. Similar to possessive pronouns, demonstrative pronouns can be used in place of nouns. The four demonstrative pronouns are *this*, *that*, *these*, and *those*.

- *This* and *these* indicate something is nearby.
- *That* and *those* indicate something is away from the speaker.

Here are the kinds of errors that speakers and writers make when they use demonstrative pronouns:

1. Using *the* instead of *this*.
2. Using *that there* instead of *that*.
3. Using *them* instead of *these* or *those* (depending on the meaning).

Here are some examples:

Local Language:	Edited English:
That there Web site is good.	*That* Web site is good.
The paper is good.	*This* paper is good.
Them reports need updating.	*Those* reports need updating.
	These reports need updating.

Using demonstrative pronouns in local language relates as much to speaking as it does to writing.

Practice 7.6

Demonstrative Pronouns

Instructions: In the following sentences, correct the demonstrative pronouns; for example:

Incorrect: I gave them reports to Sylvia.

Corrected: I gave *those* reports to Sylvia.

1.   The manuals are on that there table in the corner.

2.   Anderson asked for them pamphlets, not the ones you are sending.

3.   Are them your clients you are referring to?

4.   That there is a good reason to give them the project.

5.   Jacob asked that we solve them problems before it's too late.

Note: See page 431 for the key to the above exercise.

Indefinite Pronouns

Indefinite pronouns are words that replace nouns without specifying the noun they are replacing. To use an indefinite pronoun correctly, first determine whether it is singular or plural.

Singular Indefinite Pronouns:

another	everybody	each	neither	somebody
anyone	everything	either	nobody	something
anybody	much	every	one	
everyone	nothing	no one	someone	

- Singular indefinite pronouns always take a singular verb:

  Every situation *calls* for a different response.

  Neither of the girls *works* here.

  Someone is ready for a promotion.

Plural Indefinite Pronouns:

  both, few, many, others, several

- Plural indefinite pronouns always take a plural verb:

  Many (of the participants) *were* unprepared.

  Several (invoices) *arrive* daily.

Indefinite Pronouns, Singular or Plural:

  all, none, any, some, more, most

- Indefinite pronouns that can be singular or plural are generally followed by a prepositional phrase that contains a noun. If the noun that the indefinite pronoun refers to is singular, then the pronoun is singular. If the noun is plural, then the pronoun is plural.

Here are examples of indefinite pronouns; make special note of the noun in the prepositional phrase that follows each:

> *None* of the cake *was* eaten.
>
> *None* of the cookies *were* gone.

> *All* of the paint *has* spilled.
>
> *All* of the brushes *are* spoiled.

Work on the Practice below; also make a list of the indefinite pronouns that are troublesome for you, and practice using them until you build your skill.

Practice 7.7

Indefinite Pronouns

Instructions: Correct the following sentences for pronoun-antecedent agreement.

Incorrect: Throw away any of the pens that doesn't work.

Corrected: Throw away any of the pens that *don't* work.

1. Either one of the programs work perfectly.

2. Everyone who finished the project are free to go.

3. None of the employees sends e-mail on Saturday.

4. Some of the assignments needs to be distributed before noon today.

5. Everything run much better when we are all on time.

Note: See page 431 for the key to the above exercise.

Recap

To make a correct choice with pronouns, focus on the way that the pronoun functions in the sentence: is the pronoun being used as a subject or as an object?

➤ Subjective case pronouns function as subjects of verbs.

➤ Objective case pronouns function as objects of verbs, objects of prepositions, and objects of infinitives.

➤ Reflexive case pronouns refer back to a subjective case pronoun or noun; for example: *I* will do the work *myself.*

➤ The pronoun *who* functions as a subject; *whom*, as an object.

➤ *Who* refers to people; *that* refers to objects.

➤ When in doubt, choose *who*.

➤ Pronouns must agree in number and gender with their antecedents and in number with any items of possession.

➤ The key to using pronouns and antecedents consistently is to use plural antecedents.

Writing Workshop

Activity A. Writing Practice

Instructions: Select a topic that you would like to write about. Write two paragraphs: one from your viewpoint (first person singular) and another from the third person viewpoint (singular or plural), for example:

First Person:	"I enjoy vacations, and I take one in June."
Third Person:	"A vacation helps people relax and enjoy life."

When you are finished, compare your paragraphs with a partner.

Activity B. Journal

Instructions: In Chapter 2, you identified a goal that you wanted to achieve and wrote about it. Have you made progress toward your goal? What are some steps to get you closer to achieving your goal?

Skills Workshop

Worksheet 1: Pronoun Case

Instructions: In the following sentences, circle the pronoun (shown in bold below) that correctly completes the sentence based on Edited English usage. (*Note:* See pages 431- 433 for the keys to worksheets in this chapter.)

Incorrect: John and (I, me) worked on the project together.

Corrected: John and (**I**, me) worked on the project together.

1. John and (I, me) completed the project yesterday.

2. Barbara was more competent than (he, him).   (Implied verb?)

3. Why were the materials delivered to (she, her) and Bob?

4. Between you and (I, me), we have enough expertise.

5. My manager required Bob and (I, me, myself) to attend the seminar.

6. You can ask George or (I, myself, me) for the updated report.

7. They are more competent to do the job than (we, us).

8. Dave said to divide the case among you, Alice, and (myself, me).

9. She asked who would do the report, my secretary or (me, myself, I).

10. Margaret is taller than (I, me).   (Implied verb?)

11. Bill likes Sue better than (I, me). (Implied verb?)

12. The professor told my associate and (I, me, myself) to complete our report.

13. The information was sent to (she and I, her and me, her and I).

14. Bill and (me, I) watched the game before (he, him) and (I, me) left.

15. Upon recommendation, he gave the project to Jim and (I, me, myself).

16. Bob has more time than (me, I).

17. The project will be split between John and (I, me, myself).

18. She asked Phyllis and (me, myself) to attend the board meeting.

19. The problem should remain between Bob and (you, yourself).

20. I am going to make (me, myself) an excellent dinner.

Worksheet 2: Pronoun and Antecedent Agreement

Instructions: Change the sentences below from local language to Edited English.

I

Example:　When ~~you~~ feel a lot of stress, it's easy for me to get side-tracked.

1. When a patient asks for more medicine, you must tell them to check with their doctor.
2. I like to eat lunch before the afternoon because it is better for your health.
3. When one works hard at a task, he/she usually gets good results.
4. I usually work late on Thursdays because you can get a lot done at the end of the week.
5. Bob said that their department is exceptionally productive when you least expect it.
6. If you listen carefully, we can hear inconsistencies in their response.
7. When one graduates from college, your first worry usually is finding a job.
8. For many graduates, however, his or her first worry is credit card debt.
9. Many banks offer credit cards to college students knowing that you are least likely to pay off all of your debt.
10. In this way, creditors can make quite a bit of money off the interest it charges one.
11. College students are hurt in many ways by his or her credit card debt.
12. College students should consider the post-graduation monthly cost of their student loans before you accept a credit card offer.

Editing Workshop

Instructions: In the following paragraphs, make corrections in pronoun usage.

By sending a thank-you note after your interview, one has another opportunity to make a good impression. By taking the time to send a note to the person that interviewed you, you will be letting them know that your sincerely interested in the position.

You will also be letting him know that you are a candidate whom is different from other candidates. By mentioning something that yourself and they discussed during the interview, you will show that one was paying attention.

The format of the note is also important, and they should be written with care. Use the business card that the interviewer gave yourself to address the note so that you get important details correct.

Note: See page 433 for the key to the above exercise.

8

Modifiers

A **modifier** is a word or group of words that describes another word or even a complete sentence. Common modifiers are adjectives and adverbs as well as infinitive phrases and gerund phrases.

Though a modifier is not a core element of a sentence, a modifier can be an important element. Writers sometimes use modifiers excessively, thinking that the modifier will intensify their meaning; instead, a modifier can have the opposite effect and detract from meaning.

While modifiers add richness and depth when used necessarily and correctly, modifiers are just as often overused or misused. For example, certain categories of modifiers known as **hedges** and **emphatics** create the opposite of their desired effect. In other words, when you say that you are going to a "really, really important meeting," you would sound more effective by saying that you are going to "an important meeting." To keep your writing clear and concise, use modifiers sparingly and correctly.

Other issues with modifiers relate to hyper-correcting, such as using *more* or *less* along with the suffix *–er*, as in *more prettier* or *more better*. Another form of hyper-correcting is using double negatives, as in "B. J. *didn't* make *no* sense at yesterday's meeting."

To use a modifier correctly, place the modifier close to the word or words that it modifies. At times, misusing a modifier can be amusing. For example, when someone says, "Bill gave the assignment to our staff that no one wanted," should *the staff* feel offended?

Modifiers have as much to do with speaking as they do with writing. In this chapter, you once again work with local language patterns, translating them into Edited English. Let's start by working on the basics and then work through the other types of issues that occur with modifiers.

Modifiers: The Basics

The most basic point about modifiers relates to whether the modifier describes a noun or a verb:

- Adjectives modify nouns and pronouns.

- Adverbs (which often end in *ly*) modify verbs, adjectives, and other adverbs.

In the following examples, *good* is an adjective modifying the noun *paper* and *well* is an adverb modifying the verb *did*.

> Everyone in economics turned in a *good* paper.

> Everyone in economics did *well*.

Here are some common errors that writers make with adjectives and adverbs:

- Modifying action verbs with adjectives.

  Incorrect: Bill drives *good*.

  Correct: Bill drives *well*.

- Modifying state of being verbs with adverbs.

  Incorrect: I felt *badly* about the situation.

  Correct: I felt *bad* about the situation.

- Using *more*, *most*, *less*, or *least* and adding a suffix such as *–er* or *–est* to form a comparative or superlative modifier.

  Incorrect: We were *more busier* yesterday than today.

  Correct: We were *busier* yesterday than today.

- Misplacing a modifier; that is, placing a modifier away from the word or words it modifies.

Incorrect:	The *book* was placed on the shelf *with the bent cover*.
Correct:	The *book with the bent cover* was placed on the shelf.

- Dangling a modifier; that is, placing a modifier in a sentence without clearly stating in the sentence the word that it modifies.

Incorrect:	*Walking into my office*, the coffee spilled on the carpet.
	Who was walking into the office? *I was.*
Correct:	*Walking into my office*, *I* spilled coffee on the carpet.

Because gerund phrases and infinitive phrases need a subject, the first noun that follows the phrase is considered the subject of the phrase. In the above incorrect example, the sentence literally reads that "the coffee is walking into the office."

To correct a dangling modifier, either turn the phrase into a clause (*as I walked into my office*) or put the subject of the phrase immediately after it (*Walking into my office, I . . .*).

Modifiers and Verbs

The two broad categories of verbs are **action verbs** and **state of being verbs**, which are also called *linking verbs*.

Common linking verbs are forms of *to be* (is, are, was, were), *appear, become, seem*, and at times *smell, taste, feel, sound, look, act*, and *grow*.

- **Action verbs** are modified by **adverbs**:

  The computer <u>runs</u> *well.*

  The presenter <u>spoke</u> *loudly.*

  (You) <u>Drive</u> *safely.*

- **Linking verbs** express **state of being**. The words following a linking verb modify the subject rather than the verb. Thus, a **modifying word** following a linking verb would be an **adjective** (subject complement):

> I <u>feel</u> *bad* about the situation.

> The proposal <u>sounds</u> *good.*

> The situation <u>is</u> *bad.*

One of the most common mistakes that speakers make is to say "I feel badly" when they are referring to their own state of being. Instead say "I feel bad."

Practice 8.1

Modifiers and Verbs

Instructions: Correct the following sentences:

Incorrect: When you speak too loud, you may get an unwelcome response.

Corrected: When you speak *too loudly*, you may get an unwelcome response.

1. Drive slow so that you do not get in an accident.

2. George feels badly about the situation.

3. The trainer spoke too loud, and our group was offended.

4. The music sounds well to all of us.

5. The entire group felt badly about the change in management.

Note: See page 433 for the key to the above exercise.

Comparative and Superlative Modifiers

When using adjectives or adverbs to compare, use *more, less, most,* or *least* or a suffix such as *–er* or *–est* to show the degree of comparison (but do not use both). Follow these rules:

1. When you compare *two items*, use the **comparative** form of the modifier. The comparative is formed by adding the suffix *–er* or by adding *more* or *less*.

2. When comparing *three or more* items, use the **superlative** form of the modifier. The superlative is formed by adding the suffix *–est* or by adding *most* or *least*.

Speakers as well as writers need to be aware of this principle, for example:

Incorrect: Brad is the *most tallest* player on the team.

Correct: Brad is the *tallest* player on the team.

Incorrect: I am *more hungrier* now than I was an hour ago.

Correct: I am *hungrier* now than I was an hour ago.

Practice 8.2

Comparative and Superlative Modifiers

Instructions: Correct the modifiers in the following sentences.

Incorrect: I felt more hungrier after I ate lunch than before.

Corrected: I felt *hungrier* (or *more hungry*) after I ate lunch than before I ate.

1. Use your editing skills to make this letter more better than it was before.

2. Toni made the most silliest comment at the board meeting on Tuesday.

3. I was the most hungriest person in the room but the last to be served.

4. Of all the people at this college, I live the most farthest from campus.

5. Our committee is more further along on this project than I could have imagined.

Note: See page 434 for the key to the above exercise.

Implied Words in Comparisons

At times statements include incomparable items because implied words are left off. This kind of error often occurs when making comparisons using the conjunction *than*, for example:

Incorrect:	Our products are better than our *competitor*.
Correct:	Our products are better than our *competitor's products (are)*.
Correct:	Our products are better than our *competitor's (products)*.
Incorrect:	This production line runs faster than *anyone else*.
Correct:	This production line runs faster than *any other (production line runs)*
Correct:	This production line runs faster than *anyone else's production line (runs)*.

Notice how incomparable items are made comparable by placing a subject and verb (which is often implied) after the conjunction *than*.

Work on the exercise that follows to gain practice with this principle.

Practice 8.3

Implied Words in Comparisons

Instructions: In the following sentences, make corrections in adjectives and adverbs, for example:

Incorrect: Macy's introduced their line of clothing faster than us.

Corrected: Macy's introduced their line of clothing faster than *we introduced ours.*

1. Roger's office is nicer than our manager.
2. My office has more windows than you.
3. Reggie learned to use the software sooner than me.
4. The executives ordered their lunches before us.
5. However, our desserts were much tastier than them.

Note: See page 434 for the key to the above exercise.

Modifiers and Their Placement

Placing modifiers close to the word or words they modify keeps meaning clear. In fact, placing modifiers separate from the words they modify can create a grammatical error as well as an ambiguous meaning.

When you place modifiers correctly, your writing has better flow and clearer meaning. Here are some examples of misplaced modifiers:

Incorrect: The report was assigned to the Albuquerque office *on policy errors.*

Correct: The report *on policy errors* was assigned to the Albuquerque office.

Incorrect: The applicant was the best candidate *arriving late to the interview.*

Correct: The applicant *arriving late to the interview* was the best candidate.

Incorrect:	Our merger created chaos for us *with the other company.*
Correct:	Our merger *with the other company* created chaos for us.

Incorrect:	The truck pulled into the dock area *with huge dents.*
Correct:	The truck *with huge dents* pulled into the dock area.

Some modifiers, such as gerund and infinitive phrases, take as their subject the nearest noun or pronoun. When an "incorrect" subject is placed next to the phrase, the result can be amusing.

Here are some examples of dangling modifiers:

Incorrect:	Arriving late, the presentation ran over the time limit.
Correct:	Arriving late, the *presenter* ran over her time limit.

Incorrect:	Following my manager's instructions, the papers were filed incorrectly.
Correct:	Following my manager's instructions, *I* still filed the papers incorrectly.
Or:	Although *I followed* my manager's instructions, the papers were filed incorrectly.

Incorrect:	Entering the conference room, Bob's notebook fell to the ground.
Correct:	Entering the conference room, *Bob* dropped his notebook.
Or:	As *Bob entered* the conference room, he dropped his notebook.

Incorrect:	To achieve a higher grade, Sue's paper needed to be revised.
Correct:	To achieve a higher grade, Sue needed to revise her paper.

Misplaced modifiers are easy to overlook because, as the speaker or writer, you understand what you are trying to say. As you edit, be on the lookout for these faulty constructions.

Practice 8.4

Modifiers and Their Placement

Instructions: Place modifiers close to the words they modify.

Incorrect: George will give a presentation at this week's meeting *on how to select the right cell-phone package*.

Corrected: George will give a presentation *on how to select the best cell-phone package* at this week's meeting.

1. The report is due in September on policy change.
2. Major issues must be addressed at the fall meeting relating to dress policy.
3. Filling out the forms, a mistake was made by the applicant.
4. The letter was sent out yesterday giving details about the incident.
5. Answering the phone, my feet slipped right out from under me.

Note: See page 434 for the key to the above exercise.

More on Correct Placement

Whereas adjectives are generally placed before or after the word they modify, most adverbs can be placed in various positions depending on the meaning the writer wishes to convey.

However, place adverbs such as *only, nearly, almost, ever, scarcely, merely, too,* and *also* directly before or after the word they modify. When these adverbs are placed a distance from the word or words that they modify, meaning can get distorted.

Consider how the position of *only* changes the meaning of the following sentence:

Only I intend to assist you.   . . . no one else will.
I intend *only* to assist you.   . . . and do nothing else.
I intend to assist *only* you.   . . . and no one else.

Be on the lookout when you see any of these adverbs so that you ensure that they are placed directly before or after the word they modify.

Practice 8.5

More on Correct Placement

Instructions: Adjust the following sentences for adverb placement.

Incorrect: Bob only was trying to help you.

Corrected: Bob was *only* trying to help you.

1. I only received three copies of the report.

2. Louis almost bought all of the new software in the catalog.

3. During the meeting, we nearly finished all of the doughnuts and coffee cake.

4. Congratulations, Jerry, you nearly have ten years on the job!

5. We will only need to purchase one computer for the research team.

Note: See pages 434 - 435 for the key to the above exercise.

Double Negatives

To negate a statement, use only one negative. If you use a **double negative**—more than one negative in a sentence—your statement actually becomes positive.

The word *not* is commonly used word for negating; less common words used to negate are *nothing, never, hardly, barely,* and *scarcely.*

Incorrect:	I *can't hardly* get my work finished.
Correct:	I *can hardly* get my work finished.
Or:	I *can't* get my work finished.

Incorrect:	The crew *wasn't barely* finished before the rain started.
Correct:	The crew *was barely* finished before the rain started.
Or:	The crew *had just* finished when it started to rain.

The negative form of the word *regard* is *regardless*. However, some speakers add the prefix *ir* to the already negative form *regardless*, resulting in a word that has a built-in double negative: *ir-regard-less*.

Practice 8.6

Double Negatives

Instructions: Correct the double negatives or incorrect forms in the following sentences.

Incorrect:	Jim couldn't hardly believe what the contractor said.
Corrected:	Jim *could hardly* believe what the contractor said.
Or:	Jim *couldn't* believe what the contractor said.

1. The receptionist wouldn't give us no information over the phone.

2. Martha didn't have no intention of helping us with the proposal.

3. Sylvestri couldn't barely wait to tell us his answer.

4. The contractors will not start construction irregardless of what we offer them.

5. The accountants won't give us nothing for the charity deduction.

Note: See page 435 for the key to the above exercise.

Hedges and Emphatics

A hedge qualifies a statement; an emphatic "supposedly" places emphasis on the word it describes. However, a message is clearer without hedges and emphatics. As Robert Browning said, *less is more*.

Weak: The meeting is *very* important, so you *certainly* must attend.

Revised: The meeting is important, so you must attend.

Here are some common hedges *to avoid*:

> kind of, sort of, rarely, hardly, at times, tend, sometimes, maybe, may be, perhaps, rather, in my opinion, more or less, possibly, probably, seemingly, for all intents and purposes, to a certain extent, supposedly, usually, often, almost always, and so on.

Example:

For all intents and purposes, listening is an important part of communicating. Listening *may* help you connect with your audience by understanding *some of* their needs. By becoming a better listener, *to certain extent* you become a better communicator, *at least in my opinion*.

Here are some common emphatics; *use emphatics sparingly*, or they will detract from the meaning:

> very, most, many, often, literally, virtually, usually, certainly, inevitably, as you can plainly see, as everyone is aware, as you know, always, each and every time, totally, it is quite clear that, as you may already know, undoubtedly, first and foremost, and so on.

Example:

As everyone knows, listening is a *really* important part of communicating. Listening *certainly* helps you connect with your audience by understanding *most, if not all, of* their needs. By becoming a better listener, you *literally* become a better communicator, *as you may already know*.

Without hedges and emphatics, here is the short paragraph:

> Listening is an important part of communicating. Listening helps you connect with your audience by understanding their needs. By becoming a better listener, you become a better communicator.

The next time that you use an emphatic or a hedge, assess if your point is clearer without it.

Fillers and Tag-ons

Fillers and tag-ons are empty and add no value to your message. Two words that are often inserted as fillers in speech and writing are "just" and "like."

Incorrect: She *like just* said that we could *like* go to the meeting.

Correct: She said that we could go to the meeting.

Incorrect: I *just like* went to the meeting before *like* I knew it was cancelled.

Correct: I went to the meeting before I knew it was cancelled.

In addition to fillers, pay attention to *tag-ons*. In general, sentences should not end in prepositions; at times, speakers and writers place a preposition unnecessarily at the end of the sentence as a tag-on. Tag-ons are grammatically incorrect. The word "at" is a common tag-on.

Incorrect: Where do you work *at*?

Correct: Where do you work?

Incorrect: Where did you go to school *at*?

Correct: Where did you go to school?

Have you ever used words such as *like, just,* or *totally* at times when those words were not needed?

Quantifiers

Quantifiers modify nouns; they tell us *how many* or *how much*. Some quantifiers are used with count nouns (for example, *trees*) and others with non-count nouns (for example, *dancing*).

- Use the following quantifiers with count nouns:

  many, a few, few, several, a couple of, none of the

- Use the following quantifiers work with non-count nouns:

  not much, a little, little, a bit of, a good deal of, a great deal of

- Use these quantifiers with count and non-count nouns:

  all of the, some, most of the, enough, a lot of, plenty of, a lack of

In formal academic writing, use *many* and *much* rather than phrases such as *a lot of, lots of,* and *plenty of.*

Weak: *A lot* of the problems remain unresolved.

Revised: *Many* of the problems remain unresolved.

Complete the exercises at the end of this chapter before moving on to the next part, Part 4: Editing for Clarity.

Recap

Use modifiers correctly and, for the most part, sparingly.

➢ Adjectives modify nouns and pronouns.

➢ Adverbs often end in –ly, and they modify verbs, adjectives, and other adverbs.

➢ When comparing *two* items, form the comparative by adding the suffix –er or by adding *more* or *less.*

➢ When comparing *three or more* items, form the superlative by adding the suffix –est or by adding *most* or *least.*

➢ Place modifiers close to the word or words that they modify.

➢ Do not use double negatives and avoid using *ir-regard-less.*

➢ Avoid using hedges, emphatics, fillers, and tag-ons.

ADVERBS AND ADJECTIVES

Adverbs modify verbs, adjectives, and other adverbs as well as infinitives, gerunds, and participles. Adverbs answer questions such as:

Why? How? When? Where? To what degree?

Adjectives modify nouns, including gerunds, and pronouns. Adjectives answer questions such as:

Whose? Which? How much? How many? What kind of?

Use adjectives after linking verbs such as *be* (am, is, are, was, were) and *feel* when the verb expresses the condition or state of being of the subject.

> **Examples:**   The report is *good*.
> Sue feels *bad* about the changes.

USE ADJECTIVES AND ADVERBS TO COMPARE

Adjectives and adverbs indicate degrees of comparison through three forms:

- The **positive form** makes no comparison; the positive form is the simple form of the modifier: *red*, *slow*, *seriously*.
- The **comparative form** compares two things, indicating an increase or decrease over the positive form: *redder*, *slower*, *more seriously*.
- The **superlative form** indicates the greatest or least degree among three or more objects: the *reddest*, the *slowest*, the *most serious*.

IRREGULAR MODIFIERS

Positive	Comparative	Superlative
bad	worse	worst
good, well	better	best
far	farther, further	farthest, furthest
little	less, lesser, littler	least, littlest
many, some, much	more	most

Writing Workshop

Activity A. Writing Practice

Instructions: To gain more practice using modifiers, complete Part 1 and Part 2 below. For Part 1, work with a partner or in a small group. For Part 2, exchange your paragraph with a partner, and compare your use of modifiers.

Part 1.

In a small group, think of as many descriptive words as you can to describe the room that you are in now. When you have a substantial list, work together to write a paragraph describing the room. When you are finished, take turns with other groups to read each description out loud.

Part 2.

Step 1. Describe your favorite room or place. List the tangible elements first: tangible things are those that you can see, touch, and even smell. Next, explore the intangible aspects of the room: what kinds of activities and feelings are attached to the room and why? How does the room make you feel?

Step 2. Reread your paragraph describing your favorite room or place. How much sensory detail did you include? Make a quick list of the descriptive words and phrases that you used. Would someone else be able to visualize this place if you took away those descriptive phrases?

Experiment revising parts of your description by replacing abstract terms such as *cute dog* with concrete, specific words that help the reader get a visual picture, such as the *100-pound black Labrador wearing a red scarf and wagging his tail wildly* . . .

Activity B. Journal

Instructions: How do you use local language on a daily basis? Identify some of your local language patterns and their Edited English equivalents.

Are you more aware of how you use language than you were a month or two ago? Give examples of changes that you have made in your speech or writing.

Skills Workshop

Worksheet 1: Adverbs and Adjectives—the Basics
Instructions: Correct the sentences below for their use of adjectives and adverbs. (*Note*: See pages 435 - 437 for the keys to the exercises below.)

Incorrect: If you feel badly about the situation, change it.

Corrected: If you feel *bad* about the situation, change it.

1.   You did good on your latest report.

2.   Her new computer crashes more frequently than you.

3.   Riki felt badly about firing Sue.

4.   You will be able to go more faster if you take the train than if you walk.

5.   Our bookstore finds the most latest technology available.

6.   Your team works more diligently than anyone.

7.   I can't hardly wait until summer break.

8.   The lesser of your worries is how many vacation days you have left.

9.   The middle managers have requested more better working conditions.

10. Why didn't the client have no way of getting to the open house?

11. Leaving the corporate world was one of the most hard decisions I've ever had to make.

12. The client seemed more happier after we waived the initial fees.

Worksheet 2: Place Modifiers Correctly
Instructions: Revise the following sentences so that modifiers are placed correctly.

Incorrect: Taylor asked to use the conference room for the meeting *next to his office*.

Corrected: Taylor asked to use the conference room *next to his office* for the meeting.

1. All of our managers attended the conference in Tulsa on international trade.

2. Give the information to Doris about the revised plan.

3. The account was lost to our competitor for new car loans.

4. Mr. Jordan is the man talking to Joe with the briefcase in his hand.

5. You will find the new forms in the supply closet for joint accounts.

6. The driver left 20 minutes ago in the black sedan.

7. The group would like to have lunch served at noon meeting in Room 202.

8. You can pick up the proposal from the development office for new business today.

9. The official title for the new position is development director in our New Jersey office.

10. File the papers early in the day for incorporation to meet the deadline.

Worksheet 3: Dangling Modifiers

Instructions: Correct the following sentences by placing modifiers next to their subject or by turning phrases into clauses.

Incorrect: *Getting return business on the new account,* increased revenues came to *Spencer.*

Corrected: *Getting return business on the new account, Spencer* increased his revenues.

1. Following the account closely, a mistake was still made by the new sales representative.

2. Applying a service fee, the account was overdrawn by the bank.

3. To achieve the best results, a plan was developed by our team.

4. Leaving in frustration, the meeting was cancelled by our team leader.

5. To open an account, first the forms must be filled out.

Editing Workshop

Instructions: In the paragraph below, correct errors in the use of comparative and superlative adverbs, as well as other common errors.

One of the most greatest lessons you can ever learn is to never say nothing negative about people you work with. It can like really cause you problems if the person like ever finds out what you said about them. Even if you feel badly about what you said, you can't never take your words back. Until you learn this lesson good, you are not likely to never change. Be kindly to people, and you will reap the most best results.

Note: See page 437 for the key to the above exercise.

PART 4: EDITING FOR CLARITY

In the first three parts of this book, you learned principles about correct writing, which are elements of proofreading. Now you work with principles of editing. Editing improves the quality and style of writing, making it more readable and engaging.

Your writing style results from the decisions that you make about how to present your ideas. When you present your ideas in a clear, concise way, your writing style aids readers in understanding your message.

Though you had an introduction to active voice in Chapter 6, Verbs, you work with active voice again in Chapter 9. Passive voice creeps into people's writing as they progress through the academic system. In other words, you will not find many eighth graders writing in the passive voice, but you will find a lot of college students writing passively. By graduate school, many writers use the passive voice without question.

Once writers start using the passive voice, they struggle to keep it. Because the passive voice becomes more prominent with more education, some writers think that passive voice makes them sound smarter: only smart people can produce complicated writing, right? However, in today's fast-paced world, clear and concise writing is superior to complicated writing. As Albert Einstein once said, "Everything should be made as simple as possible, but not simpler."

In this part, you also cover parallel structure and conciseness. Parallel structure is about keeping similar grammatical elements in the same form, giving writing rhythm and flow. Being concise involves cutting the clutter, such as background thinking and empty ideas as well as redundant words and phrases.

As you go through Part 4, Editing for Clarity, always keep in mind to apply the principles that you are learning as you edit, not as you compose. As you compose, you are clarifying your thinking (and probably putting a lot of clutter in your draft). Now you are learning how to cut the clutter and become a ruthless editor, a skill that will serve you well throughout your entire career.

As you edit, keep in mind that *less is more*.

9

Active Voice

If you find yourself struggling to understand what you are reading, your first thought may be that your reading skills need a tune-up. In fact, the more likely answer is that the writing is full of the passive voice and other complex constructions.

Passive voice complicates meaning because the passive verb does not create action, which is its prescribed job in a sentence.

- With **active voice**, the verb *performs* action.

- With **passive voice**, the verb *describes* action.

Active voice assists in making writing clear and concise precisely because the various sentence parts play their designated roles. In other words, the verb performs action, and a real subject drives that action. With the passive voice, the real subject is more of a back-seat driver, if it is in the sentence at all. If this analogy does not mean anything to you right now, revisit it after you finish this chapter.

Though active voice is generally the voice of choice, passive voice has a legitimate and necessary place in all types of writing when used purposely. In fact, in scientific writing, the passive voice is used to place focus on a method or procedure rather than the person who is carrying it out.

Since real subjects play a deciding role in the active voice, let's start by reviewing the difference between grammatical subjects and real subjects.

Grammatical Subjects vs. Real Subjects

Real subjects drive the action of verbs; however, as you have already learned, the *grammatical subject* of a sentence is not always its *real subject*.

- The grammatical subject precedes the verb.
- The real subject drives the action of the verb.

When the real subject precedes the verb, the real subject and grammatical subject are one and the same, for example:

> Jane's manager gave her a laptop.

However, in the following sentence, the real subject (manager) is not the grammatical subject (Jane).

> Jane was given a laptop by her manager.

Since the real subject appears in the sentence, the above example is considered a **full passive**. In comparison, the following sentence has a grammatical subject, but not a real subject.

> A laptop was given to Jane.

Who gave Jane the laptop? Based on the above sentence, we do not know. When a passive sentence does not contain a real subject, it is called a **truncated passive.**

Even though you covered active voice in Chapter 6, Verbs, let's go over active voice from the beginning. Active voice is that important.

Active Voice

The active voice is the most clear, direct, and concise way to phrase a sentence because each part of the sentences fills its prescribed role. Let's start with a passive sentence and then revise it to active voice:

> **Passive:**   The papers were sent to Sue by Bob.

To change the above passive sentence to active voice, first identify the main verb, which is *sent*. Next, identify the real subject by asking who performed the action: *Who sent the papers? Bob did.* Finally, change the order in the sentence so that the real subject (Bob) is also the grammatical subject.

Active: Bob sent the papers to Sue.

Follow these steps to revise a passive sentence to active voice:

1. Identify the main verb of the sentence.

2. Identify the real subject by asking, *who performed the action of the verb?*

3. Place the real subject at the beginning of the sentence, making it the grammatical subject.

4. Follow the real subject with the verb, adjusting it for agreement, and then complete the sentence.

Let's revise another passive sentence:

Passive: The merger was rejected by their new CEO.

1. Identify the main verb: rejected

2. Identify "who" was doing the rejecting: their new CEO

3. Begin the sentence with the real subject: Their new CEO

4. Follow the real subject with the verb: Their new CEO rejected

5. Complete the sentence: Their new CEO rejected the merger.

Here is the structure for the **active voice:**

Who did what.

Here is the structure for the **passive voice**:

What was done by whom.

When the real subject is present in a passive sentence, the real subject is in the object position. Can you see that by changing from the passive voice to the active voice that your writing becomes more direct, clear, and concise? Work on the following exercise to practice the active voice.

Practice 9.1

Active Voice

Instructions: Edit the following sentences by changing passive voice to active voice.

1. Sean was asked by his manager to lead the diversity team.
2. Phelps was given another chance by his coach to swim in the relay.
3. The holiday event was hosted by our department last year.
4. A new policy on reimbursement for travel expenses was implemented by our president.
5. The program was cancelled by the mayor due to lack of interest.

Note: See page 437 for the key to the above exercise.

Passive Voice, the Tactful Voice

Since the real subject does not need to be present in a passive sentence, here are some times when passive voice is preferred over active voice.

- Whenever you do not want to focus on a specific person because it would be more tactful not to "point a finger," use passive voice, for example:

   Passive: A mistake was made on the August invoices.

Who made the mistake? An active sentence needs an actor or agent performing the action of its verb; however, a passive sentence does not need an actor or agent because its verb does not create action.

- Whenever you do not know *who* performed an action, use passive voice, for example:

Passive: The bank was robbed at gunpoint.

You will find that you use the truncated passive naturally in these situations. For these situations, the passive voice is natural and necessary. While truncated passives play a vital role in writing, full passives that are unnecessary interfere with the quality and the flow of writing.

Another element that complicates writing is nominals, which are often used in conjunction with the passive voice. After working on the Practice below, you will work on getting rid of unnecessary nominals.

Practice 9.2

Passive Voice, the Tactful Voice

Instructions: Edit the following sentences by changing passive voice to active voice. Then determine which sentences would sound more tactful written in the passive voice.

Passive: Your check should have been mailed last week to avoid a penalty.

Active: You should have mailed your check last week to avoid a penalty.

Active or passive?   Passive is more tactful.

1. An error in invoicing was made on your account (by Meyers).
2. If you wanted to avoid an overdraft, your check should have been deposited before 4 p.m.
3. Your receipt should have been enclosed with your return item.
4. Your order was sent to the wrong address and apologies are being made.
5. Your invoice needed to be paid before the first of the month to avoid penalties.

Note: See page 437 for the key to the above exercise.

Nominals

Nominals are verbs that change forms to function as nouns. The actual term for transforming a verb into a noun is *nominalization*.

You have already worked with two forms of nominals: gerunds and infinitives.

- To form a gerund, add *ing* to the base form of a verb: *go* in its gerund form is *going*.

- To form an infinitive, add *to* to the base form of a verb, as in *to go*.

As they are nominalized, some verbs change forms completely, following no specific pattern. For example, the verb *analyze* turns into the noun *analysis* . . . the verb *fail* turns into the noun *failure* . . . and the verb *maintain* turns into the noun *maintenance*.

Many verbs, however, commonly turn into nouns by adding the suffix *–ment* or *–tion*; for example, *define* turns into *definition*, and *commit* turns into *commitment*.

Verb	Nominal
accomplish	accomplishment
connect	connection
decide	decision
dedicate	dedication
develop	development
encourage	encouragement
evaluate	evaluation
facilitate	facilitation
institute	institutionalization
separate	separation
verify	verification

Obviously, nouns have no action and, for the most part, words originating as nouns cannot be used as verbs. When people turn nouns into verbs, the construction often sounds awkward, as in "Let's *lunch* together" or "Do you *lotto*?" One word, however, has taken a unique place in English, and that word is *Google*. Google is a proper noun that also functions as a verb. Can you think of any other proper noun that can also function as a verb?

Nominalization changes a verb's "DNA," so to speak, by stripping it of its action: nouns have no action. When writers use nominalizations unnecessarily, their writing becomes more complicated. However, just as passive voice at times adds value, nominalization can also add value when used effectively.

Here is an example of the verb *appreciate* and its nominalized form *appreciation*.

Nominalized: I want to express my **appreciation** for your help.

Active: I **appreciate** your help.

In the nominalized version above, the weak verb *want* replaces the strong verb *appreciate*. As well as stripping *appreciate* of its action, the nominalized version is more wordy. However, at times nominalizations work well, as in the following:

I value your *appreciation*.

Without the nominalization, the same sentiment would be expressed awkwardly, as follows:

When you appreciate my work, I value it.

Here is another example using the verb *commit* and its nominalized form *commitment*:

Nominalized: A **commitment** of resources for the disaster in Haiti was made by our CEO.

Active: Our CEO **committed** resources for the disaster in Haiti.

Once again, the more complicated writing is, the less effective it is. When using nominals, make sure that you use them purposefully, just as you would use the passive voice purposely.

When writers refuse to give up the passive voice, they may mistakenly believe that they sound sophisticated. Unfortunately, some writers fall into the same trap with nominalizations. Unnecessarily long four-syllable words do not improve the flow of writing. Follow Leonard Da Vinci's advice when he said:

Simplicity is the ultimate sophistication.

As an effective writer, make complex messages as *simple* as you can: use nominals *only* when they improve the efficiency of your writing, and use passive voice *only* when it improves the tone of your writing.

Here is one more example that shows how the passive voice and nominalizations are quite naturally used together:

Nominalized: **Encouragement** was given to me by my coach and teammates.

Passive: I **was encouraged** by my coach and teammates.

Active: My coach and teammates **encouraged** me.

The first sentence uses the nominalized form of the verb *encourage,* which is *encouragement*. In the second sentence, the nominal is removed, but the sentence is still passive. In the third sentence, *encourage* is an active verb in its past tense form.

Understanding these principles is much easier than actually applying them to your own writing. To achieve active writing, you need to edit diligently. The more committed you are, the more changes you will make in your writing.

Get some extra practice by doing the following exercise.

Practice 9.3

Nominals

Instructions: Rewrite the following sentences by changing nominals into active verbs.

Passive: The distribution of the product was made by Mary Lou.

Active: Mary Lou distributed the product.

1. The implementation of the dress policy was made official by management in August.
2. A suggestion was made by Jane that all new hires start on the first day of the month.
3. Information about that stock was given to us by our broker.
4. A discussion of the new account occurred at our last team meeting.
5. An announcement about the merger was made by our president before the deal was final.

Note: See pages 437 - 438 for the key to the above exercise.

Style, Tone, and Meaning

One of the biggest arguments against letting go of the passive voice is that changing a sentence from passive voice to active voice changes its meaning. However, shifting from one voice to another does not necessarily change the meaning, but it does change the tone.

When all actors are present in a sentence, changing from passive voice to active voice is an exercise in *translation*. Active voice is direct and clear. Passive voice is indirect and abstract to the point that the person performing the action is not necessarily in the sentence, for example:

Passive: The problem will be solved.

However, *who* is solving the problem?

Passive: A solution will be developed.

However, *who* is developing a solution?

For the above sentences to be active, each would need a real subject performing the action. Also, in each of the above passive sentences, no one is taking responsibility for the actions that purportedly will take place.

When sentences are long and complicated, the tone of the writing is much different from sentences that are clear and to the point. With passive voice, writers do not connect with their own words in the way that they must with active voice, for example:

Passive: A discussion of the issue ensued at length before an acceptable compromise could be established.

Once again, who discussed the issue? By adding "people" to the mix, the sentence becomes much more reader friendly.

Active: We discussed the issue at length before we reached a compromise.

Though passive voice sounds more formal, today's culture no longer supports that kind of distant formality. Changing your style of writing is difficult: breaking out of an academic or a corporate mold takes courage, commitment, and vigilance.

When you write in the active voice, your readers appreciate your clear, direct writing style that saves them time and energy.

Style and Process

Even though you now have good editing tools in your writing toolkit, you still may be trying to get your words down "right" as you compose.

Remember, the first and final draft approach does not work: when you try to write "the perfect sentence" as you compose, you are sabotaging your writing. As you write, you need freedom to put ideas on the page in whatever way they take shape in your mind. If you interfere with that process, writing is much more challenging for you than it needs to be.

The next chapter covers parallel structure, another topic that ranks high along with the active voice in making your writing effective.

Recap

Changing from passive voice to active voice improves the quality and readability of writing.

> ➤ Active voice is clear, concise, and direct.

> ➤ Passive voice is complicated and abstract but perfect for those situations that call for tact.

> ➤ Nominalization removes the action from verbs and complicates writing.

> ➤ Turn nominals back into active verbs.

If you have been able to identify passive sentences in your own writing and to revise them, savor your sense of accomplishment. Stay vigilant in your quest to write actively: active voice makes writing powerful because active voice brings writing to life.

Writing Workshop

Lessons Learned

Activity A. Writing Practice

Instructions: Take out a paper that you wrote a while back. Can you find any passive sentences that you could revise to the active voice?

Find a newspaper or a magazine article that interests you, and assess whether the writer uses the active voice or the passive voice.

Are you beginning to see the difference voice makes?

Activity B. Journal

Instructions: What is an important lesson that you have learned? Find a photo of yourself when you were ten or more years younger than you are now.

What advice would you give to that younger and more naïve version of yourself?

Skills Workshop

Worksheet 1: Active Voice

Instructions: Edit the following sentences by changing passive voice to active voice. (*Note*: See pages 438 - 439 for the keys to the following exercises.)

Passive: A call should have been made on Monday if you wished to avoid a penalty.

Active: You should have called on Monday if you wished to avoid a penalty.

1. Your order must have been canceled by one of the sales representatives.

2. To reinstate the order, a new order form must be submitted by you.

3. If the form is received by us today, your order can be filled today.

4. Your check should have been sent by Monday.

5. The loyalty of its customers is valued by every company.

6. A copy of your book was sent to me by your publisher.

7. Your book was enjoyed by our staff.

8. A request was made by our staff to have a workshop presented by you.

9. The event would be attended by most of our staff.

10. A book signing could be arranged by our human resource department.

11. If you agreed, a contract could be drawn up by our attorney.

12. In addition to providing a motivating event for our staff, good public relations would be built by you and your publisher.

Worksheet 2: Active Voice and Nominals

Instructions: Edit the following sentences by changing passive voice to active voice; also change nominals into active verbs as needed.

1. The package was returned unopened by the customer.

2. A full refund was issued by customer service.

3. Bill was given a recommendation for the job by his coach.

4. Encouragement was given to Bill from everyone on his team.

5. His acceptance of the job was a surprise to no one.

6. A short surgical procedure will be performed by Dr. Wyatt.

7. Dr. Wyatt will receive assistance from a surgical nurse.

8. The novel on wizardry was written by an author from London.

9. A rejection of the novel was made by several publishing companies.

10. Regret was expressed by many publishers because the book was not given more thoughtful attention.

11. After a year, the novel was turned into a film script by its author.

12. Acclamation for the book was widespread among people who had read the book.

Editing Workshop

Instructions: For the most part, editing passive sentences to the active voice is a matter of translation. Keep that in mind as you revise the following letter.

Dear Helen,

Every five years, an update is made on all active accounts by our data processing unit. The procedure is simple. The data on file is sent out to clients such as yourself so that changes can be made with a minimum of inconvenience.

Please find enclosed your data form. As your information is reviewed, any necessary changes should be made and initialed. Once all information has been updated, your signature is needed on the line provided.

Finally, please find enclosed a postage paid, self-addressed envelope so that the updated and signed form can be returned directly to our data processing unit. Let me convey my appreciation for your prompt attention to this account revision.

Sincerely yours,

Mitchell Szewczyk
Account Executive

Note: See page 439 for the key to this exercise.

10

Parallel Structure

When writing sounds choppy and disjointed, check to see if it lacks parallel structure. Parallel structure means that similar sentence elements are expressed in the same grammatical form; that is, noun for noun, verb for verb, phrase for phrase, and clause for clause.

Parallel structure gives writing balance, rhythm, and flow. As a result, parallel structure enhances understanding, which readers appreciate. In sentences, shifts in structure often occur with the following:

- Gerunds and infinitives

- Active and Passive Voice

- Verb Tense

Also check for parallel structure when using bullet points or creating lists. This chapter covers each of these topics and more.

Throughout the centuries, speakers and writers have used parallelism in a variety of ways to draw attention to their point. On a broad level, consider the parallel features of Martin Luther King's speech, *I Have a Dream*. King's repetition not only built up listeners' expectations but also added an indelible rhythm to his speech. When you listen to an especially effective speech, consider if the speaker uses parallel repetition to draw you in.

On a macro level, parallel structure involves using repetitive phrases or sentences to draw in readers and build their expectations. On a micro level, parallel structure involves putting similar sentence elements in the same grammatical form. On all levels, parallel structure creates rhythm and flow.

Let's get to work on the smaller elements of parallel structure that affect your writing on a daily basis.

Nouns

Writers have various ways of shifting structure when using nouns, thereby losing parallel structure.

Inconsistent:	You need *rest, relaxation,* and *weather that is warm.*
Parallel:	You need *rest, relaxation,* and *warm weather.*
Inconsistent:	During summers, I worked as *a secretary, assistant cashier,* and *did tutoring.*
Parallel:	During summers, I worked as *a secretary, an assistant cashier,* and *a tutor.*

Another common way to lose parallel structure is to shift from infinitives to gerunds. Infinitives and gerunds are nominals, so they function as nouns, not as verbs.

- An infinitive is the base form of the verb plus *to,* as in *to see, to go,* and *to keep.*

- A gerund is the base form of the verb plus *ing,* as in *seeing, going,* and *keeping.*

For parallel structure, the key to using gerunds and infinitives is using one or the other, but not both.

Inconsistent:	My favorite activities are *to jog, swimming,* and *to go to the park and golfing.*
Parallel:	My favorite activities are *jogging, swimming,* and *golfing.*

Next, you will work with parallel structure using adjectives.

Adjectives

With lists of adjectives, writers sometimes drift from an adjective to a phrase or a clause.

Inconsistent:	Marguerite is *nice, pretty*, and *has a lot of talent.*
Parallel:	Marguerite is *nice, pretty*, and *talented.*
Inconsistent:	The program is *short, intense*, and *many people like it.*
Parallel:	The program is *short, intense*, and *popular.*

When you see yourself shifting from an adjective to a phrase, revise your sentence so that it is parallel.

Phrases

Parallel agreement with phrases can be tricky, especially with prepositional phrases. For example, the preposition may not fit all of the phrases that follow it, necessitating the addition of a preposition that would fit:

Inconsistent:	I am disappointed *about the situation* and *the people* who caused it.
Parallel:	I am disappointed *about the situation* and *with the people* who caused it.

You may find a prepositional phrase followed by another type of structure:

Inconsistent:	Our company applauds them *for their dedication* and *because they are passionate about their cause.*
Parallel:	Our company applauds them *for their dedication to* and *for their passion about* their cause.

Once again, edit these kinds of inconsistencies out of your writing.

Clauses

When a sentence shifts from active voice to passive voice, or vice versa, the sentence lacks parallel structure, for example:

Inconsistent:	Bob received his brother's old car because a new car was bought by his brother. (active-passive)
Parallel:	Bob received his brother's old car because his brother bought a new car. (active-active)
Inconsistent:	We ran out of money in our budget, so that project was dropped. (active-passive)
Parallel:	We ran out of money in our budget, so we dropped that project. (active-active)

The following sentences will give you practice applying parallel structure.

Practice 10.1

Clauses

Instructions: Edit the following sentences for parallel structure.

Inconsistent: I am going to Florida and will be joined by my family.

Parallel: I am going to Florida, and my family will join me.

1. My manager asked me to attend the annual meeting, and arriving early on Friday was his suggestion.
2. My family will join me in Florida, and reservations will be made for them by my assistant.
3. Though I gave input, my schedule was planned by my manager.
4. If my schedule can be adjusted, I will take time off for some fun with my family.
5. The extra time was approved by my boss, so now I must change my travel arrangements.

Note: See page 439 - 440 for the key to the above exercise.

Tenses

Do not shift verb tense unnecessarily. In other words, stay in present tense or past tense unless the meaning of the sentence requires that you change tense.

Inconsistent: Tim *tells* me last week that the competition *was* over.

Parallel: Tim *told* me last week that the competition *was* over.

Inconsistent: Management *says* that our team won.

Parallel: Management *said* that our team won.

To get practice using verb tense consistently, do the following exercise.

Practice 10.2

Tenses

Instructions: The following sentences shift tense unnecessarily. Change the verbs so that tenses are consistent.

1. The message is not clear and needed to be changed.
2. My boss says that their account was closed for some time now.
3. The new computers arrive today, so then I had to install them.
4. Yesterday my co-worker tells me that I was supposed to attend the budget meeting.
5. First Mary says that she wants the position then she says that she didn't.

Note: See page 440 for the key to the above exercise.

Lists

Pay special attention when listing items within a sentence or displaying items using bullet points or numbering.

When displaying lists, you can use various forms as long as you are consistent. For example, you can display items using active voice, nouns, gerund phrases, or infinitive phrases.

When writing a list of instructions, by far the most effective style to choose is the active voice. Active voice communicates to the reader what must be done in the most simple, direct way.

Below is an inconsistent list which is then displayed in the various styles: active voice, nouns, gerund phrases, and infinitive phrases.

Incorrect:

1. Paper on environmental risks

2. Selecting a location for meeting

3. Topics for meeting agenda

Corrected:

Active Voice:

1. Write paper on environmental risks

2. Select a location for meeting

3. Identify topics for meeting agenda

Nouns:

1. Paper on environmental risks

2. Location for meeting

3. Topics for meeting agenda

Gerund phrases:

1. Writing paper on environmental risks

2. Selecting a location for meeting

3. Identifying topics for meeting agenda

Infinitive phrases:

1. To write a paper on environmental risks

2. To select a location for meeting

3. To identify topics for meeting agenda

Here is a list of instructions that lacks parallel structure:

Instructions for Tallying the Call Volume

1. A tally should be taken of the call volume.
2. You need to complete the tally by 9 a.m. for the previous day's calls.
3. The call volume is recorded in the black binder labeled "Call Volume."
4. Then you should report the number to the sales manager.
5. When you are finished, the binder must be returned.

Here is the same list in the active voice:

Call Volume Tally

1. Tally the previous day's sales calls by 9 a.m.
2. Record the number in the black binder labeled "Call Volume."
3. Report the number to the sales manager.
4. Return the binder.

In the exercise below, put the listed items in parallel structure.

Practice 10.3

Parallel lists

Instructions: Make the following list parallel by using active verbs.

- Creation of High Performance Teams
- Development of Effective Communication Skills
- Effective Job Performance Coaching
- Conflict Resolution
- Recruitment and Retention of Managers
- Valuing Personality Differences in the Workplace
- Climate Assessment in Change Efforts

Note: See page 440 for the key to the above exercise.

Correlative Conjunctions

Here are common pairs of conjunctions—notice that the second word in the pair is a coordinating conjunction:

> either . . . or
> neither . . . nor
> both . . . and
> not . . . but
> not only . . . but also
> whether . . . or

When using correlative conjunctions, follow the second part of the correlative with the same structure as the first part.

Inconsistent:	We will *not only* upgrade your account *but also* are providing monthly reports.
Parallel:	We *not only* will upgrade your account *but also* will provide monthly reports.
Parallel:	We will *not only* upgrade your account *but also* provide monthly reports.

Complete the following exercise for additional practice.

Practice 10.4

Correlative Conjunctions

Instructions: Edit the following sentences for parallel structure.

1. My boss not only asked me to complete the report but also presenting it at the meeting was required.
2. Milly applied both for the job and got it.
3. Our team neither focused on winning the game nor to show good team spirit.
4. The solution makes not only sense but also saves time.
5. Neither my new car has a warranty nor does it run well.

Note: See pages 440 - 441 for the key to the above exercise.

Recap

Parallel structure comes in all shapes and forms. Developing a keen eye for similar sentence elements takes time and commitment. As you focus attention on parallel structure, you will see connections that you did not previously see.

➤ Put similar sentence elements in the same grammatical form: noun for noun, verb for verb, phrase for phrase, and clause for clause.

➤ Start bulleted lists with gerunds, infinitives, or active voice.

➤ Use active verbs in the *you viewpoint* when writing instructions.

➤ Pay special attention to parallel structure when using correlative conjunctions.

Writing Workshop

Activity A: Writing Practice

Use your newly refreshed understanding of parallel structure to give instructions on how to accomplish a task. Start by selecting a task that takes several steps to complete, such as cooking a recipe, completing a chore, or following directions to a specific location. Then break the task down into steps, and list each step in the active voice.

In other words, write your list of instructions so that anyone could pick up your list and accomplish your chosen task. (See an example on page 209.)

Activity B: Journal

Instructions: Short of telepathy, one person cannot transfer feelings and thoughts to another person in pure form. In other words, something is always lost in translation when words leave one person's lips and enter another's ears.

1. Describe an experience in which you misinterpreted someone's words or actions.

2. What did you learn from the experience?

Skills Workshop

Instructions: Edit the following sentences, correcting for parallel structure.

1. Getting too many phone calls distracts me and are causing me to make mistakes.

2. Mathew's job duties are writing quarterly reports and to edit the company newsletter.

3. The director gave her employees two options: attending the meeting or to complete the report.

4. The applicants are similar in that both have good qualifications and their experience is extensive.

5. The director suggested that our committee focus on novel solutions, outside advice should be sought, and remaining open to our options.

6. Please suggest research studies that are informative, will be interesting, and provoke our thinking.

7. Weekly meetings help your staff to stay current with department goals, innovative solutions can be developed, and they keep everyone updated.

8. John either will complete the report on time or he will not.

9. We discussed the project over lunch and an agreement was made to go forward with it

10. To improve how I manage my time, my supervisor advised me to structure my time, staying focused on one task at a time, and similar projects should be consolidated.

Note: See page 441 for the key to this exercise.

Editing Workshop

Instructions: Work on the following bulleted list, using active voice to make the items parallel.

At the Leadership Institute, you will achieve the following:

• An understanding of state-of-the-art leadership qualities

• The development of strategies to improve productivity

• Best practices for training programs are identified and applied

• Creation of a personal network for problem solving

• Gain insight into the processes that create effective teams

• Acquisition of tools for managing training programs

Note: See pages 441 - 442 for the suggested revision.

11

Conciseness

When you write, do you ever have magical moments? You know the ones—when you can simply sit down and write what you mean without effort. Most of the time, writing does not work that way. Even seasoned writers struggle with their words until their thoughts become clear. The real magical moments are the insights, the clarity, the next step revealed.

Adapt your expectations so they are in line with the reality of the writing process, and writing will not disappoint you. Writing develops your thinking: compose freely until you understand your point. Then edit your writing so that you say what you mean in the most simple and most concise way.

To get rid of the clutter in your writing, you may need to change some ways of thinking, giving up some security blankets. This chapter shows you the kinds of information to edit out of your writing, and here is the principle to follow:

Less is more.

If you find yourself in a quagmire of words, remember the following:

1. Simple words and short messages convey information more effectively than complex words and long messages.

2. Using big, four-syllable words is *not* a sign of intelligence.

In other words, along with empty information, let go of artificial and abstract language. As Mark Twain once said, "The more you explain it, the more I don't understand it."

Wordiness also relates to the writing process; let's review that issue before learning how to cut redundant words and phrases.

Compose to Learn—Edit to Clarify

Creating a concise message is a function of editing, not composing.

Wordiness plays an essential role in the composing process because writers learn their message as their ideas unfold on the page. Trying to figure things out in your head *before* you start writing leads to procrastination and insecurity: start writing, and you begin to solve the problem at hand.

Use mind maps to capture your ideas, use page maps to organize them and create a visual map, and last but not least:

Compose fearlessly—edit ruthlessly.

As a wise writer once said, "This would have been shorter if I had more time." Cutting excess comes after you have clear insight into your purpose.

Put Purpose First

When you are composing, you eventually reach an insight, which often arrives as you write the last sentence or two as you convey a key point. Those are the moments of insight when you say to yourself, "Wow, that's what I was trying to say—now I can stop writing."

Those light-bulb experiences are the best moments of writing, making the struggle worthwhile. Once you know your key point, follow these steps:

1. Highlight your key point,

2. Copy it and cut it, and then,

3. Paste your key point to the beginning of your message.

At that point, delete any other information that the reader does not need: you may find yourself cutting quite a bit of background information, or "deadwood" leading in to your key point.

Deadwood comes in various categories—let's start with the smaller details that merit cutting before identifying the bigger chunks of information to cut.

Eliminate Redundant Pairings

Some redundant pairings have been passed on for centuries, such as "various and sundry" and "first and foremost." Do you even know what *sundry* means? If you list something *first*, isn't it also *foremost*?

Though redundant pairings seem to fit together like bookends, you need only one of the words: when you use both, you are automatically and unconsciously . . . oops, is that a redundant pairing?

For the following pairings, which word would you cut? Cover the revised words as you go through the originals.

Original	Revised
and so on and so forth	and so on
any and all	any *or* all
basic and fundamental	basic
each and every	each *or* every
fair and equitable	fair
first and foremost	first
full and complete	complete
if and when	if *or* when
hopes and desires	hopes
hope and trust	trust
issues and concerns	issues
more and more	more
null and void	void
questions and problems	questions
true and accurate	accurate

Also cut unnecessary verb add ons:

Verb Add Ons	Revised
add up	add
add together	add
advance forward	advance
continue on	continue
combine together	combine
refer back	refer
repeat again	repeat
rise up	rise

Cut Redundant Modifiers

Some words simply do not need to be modified. For example, have you ever wondered about *free gifts*? If gifts are not free, are they still gifts? What about *terrible tragedies* and *advance reservations*? Aren't all tragedies terrible and all reservations made in advance?

Redundant modifiers come in all shapes and sizes. Once again, cover the revised words as you work through the originals.

Original	Revised
advance warning	warning
close proximity	close
cold temperature	cold
combine together	combine
completely demolished	demolished
completely eliminate	eliminate
completely finish	finish
difficult dilemma	dilemma
each individual	each
end result	result

exactly identical	identical
final outcome	outcome
foreign imports	imports
frozen ice	frozen, ice
future plans	plans
general public	public
honest truth	truth
new breakthrough	breakthrough
one hundred percent true	true
past memories	memories
personal beliefs	beliefs
sudden crisis	crisis
true facts	facts
tuna fish	tuna
unexpected surprise	surprise
12 noon/12 midnight	noon *or* midnight

Work on the following sentences to gain practice cutting unnecessary words.

Practice 11.1

Cut Redundant Modifiers

Instructions: Edit the following sentences to remove empty information, redundancy, and outdated expressions.

1. We hope and trust that you find our services helpful and worthwhile.

2. Our new breakthrough in design makes our laptop even more perfect than it was before.

3. The final outcome of this project depends on each individual employee doing his or her best.

4. Before you finish this step to go on to the next step in the process, please review and examine all the items in your shopping cart.

5. We want you to be absolutely certain that you have not ordered multiple items that are exactly alike.

Note: See page 442 for the key to the above exercise.

Cut Vague Nouns

If you use vague nouns as a lead in to your point, cut them. For example, nouns such as *area, factor, manner, situation, topic,* and even *purpose* are often fillers during the composing phase. Say what you mean and be specific.

Wordy:	My field of study is the area of sociology.
Revised:	I am studying sociology.
Wordy:	I have found myself in a situation in which I am forced to make a decision.
Revised:	I am forced to make a decision.
Wordy:	The topic that I have chosen to write about is gender differences.
Revised:	Gender differences answer common questions about miscommunication . . .
Wordy:	The purpose of my paper is to explore climate change.
Revised:	Climate change affects all living species . . .

Can you think of any vague nouns that you use?

Eliminate the Obvious

Isn't *round* a shape and *red* a color? Go through the list below, cutting the obvious.

audible to the ear	of an uncertain condition
brief in duration	period of time
bright in color	rate of speed
consensus of opinion	red in color
dull in appearance	re-elected for another term
extreme in degree	round in shape
filled to capacity	soft to the touch
heavy in weight	unusual in nature
honest in character	visible to the eye

In fact, when you find yourself using the following phrases, simply delete them and get right to your point:

all things considered	in a manner of speaking
as a matter of fact	in my opinion
as far as I am concerned	my purpose for writing is
for the most part	the point I am trying to make
for the purpose of	what I am trying to say is that
I wish to take this opportunity	what I want to make clear is

Besides stating the obvious, writers often used canned and outdated phrases.

Update Outdated Phrases

Be confident about your writing and stop using outdated phrases, even if someone you respect still uses them.

Once again, to turn this into a learning activity, cover the right column that shows current use as you work through the outdated column.

Outdated	Current
as per our discussion	as we discussed
as per your request	as you requested
at all times	always
at the present time	now, today
at your earliest convenience	give a specific date
attached please find	attached is
due to the fact that	because
during the time that	while
gave a report to the effect	reported
gave assistance to	helped
in the event that	if
in a situation in which	when
in almost every instance	usually
in the near future	soon
in receipt of	"Thank you for . . ."
in reference to	about
is of the opinion that	believes
I wish to thank you	don't wish *and* thank
may I suggest	don't ask permission
prior to	before
subsequent to	after
sufficient number of	enough
thank you in advance	thank you
thank you again	one thank you is sufficient
the manner in which	how
this day and age	today
with regard to	about *or* concerning

Practice 11.2

Remove Redundancy and Outdated Expressions

Instructions: Edit the following sentences.

Wordy: In the event that you hear from George, give him the news.

Revised: If you hear from George, give him the news.

1. Attached please find the papers that you requested.
2. You have our complete and absolute confidence, and we appreciate and value our business partnership.
3. As per our discussion, the new policy should be received and reviewed this week.
4. You can completely eliminate any questions or problems by sending your agenda early in advance of the meeting.
5. I would like to thank you in advance for your cooperation, support, and assistance.

Note: See page 442 for the key to the above exercise.

Avoid Legalese

Today even attorneys avoid using the following terms:

Legalese	Revised
as stated heretofore	as stated
aforementioned	as mentioned
concerning the matter of	concerning
enclosed herewith please find	enclosed is
enclosed herein	enclosed is
notwithstanding	without
pursuant to	regarding
the writer/the undersigned	use "I" or "me"
until such time as	until

People who write passively and use outdated verbiage do so at their own choice. Remember, "If you wouldn't say it that way, don't write it that way."

Use Simple Language

Some people think that using complicated words rather than simple ones make them sound smart. However, savvy writers choose simple words. As Leonardo da Vinci pointed out, "Simplicity is the ultimate sophistication."

Outdated	Revised
apprise	inform
ascertain	find out
cognizant of	aware of
contingent upon	dependent on
deem	think
endeavor	try
facilitate	help
implement	start, begin
initiate	begin
is desirous of	wants
methodology	method
prior to	before
render	make, give
render assistance	assist
referred to as	called
termination	end
transpire	happen
transmit	send
utilization	use

For example, instead of saying:

We <u>utilize</u> that vendor.

I am <u>cognizant of</u> the change.

We <u>endeavor</u> to be the best.

<u>Prior to</u> working at Macy's . . .

Say this:

We <u>use</u> that vendor.

I am <u>aware</u> of the change.

We <u>try</u> to be the best.

<u>Before</u> working at Macy's . . .

Complete the exercise below to practice this principle.

Practice 11.3

Use Simple Language

Instructions: Simplify the following sentences.

Weak: What transpired subsequent to their involvement?

Revised: What happened after they became involved?

1. We are utilizing that product, and the marketing department is cognizant of our choice.
2. Subsequent to the merger, we have endeavored to compromise as much as possible.
3. As per your request, an omission of that information is being made.
4. If the merger is contingent upon our utilization of their facilities, we should endeavor to change locations.
5. If you are cognizant of their objections, endeavor to make respective changes.

Note: See page 443 for the key to the above exercise.

Modify Sparingly

As you reviewed in Chapter 8, Modifiers, two specific kinds of unnecessary modifiers that creep into writing and are **hedges** and **emphatics**.

Example using hedges:

> *For the most part*, trust is best established from the beginning and, *in my opinion*, difficult to regain once breached. Assume that every communication *may* have the potential to build *some kind of* trust. And also realize that every communication *to a certain extent* has the potential to destroy trust.

Example using emphatics:

> *As you may already know*, trust is best established from the beginning and *really* difficult to regain once breached. *First and foremost*, assume that *each and every* communication has the potential to build trust. And also realize that every communication also has the potential to *totally* destroy trust.

Without the hedges and emphatics, here is the short paragraph:

> Trust is best established from the beginning and difficult to regain once breached. Always assume that every communication has the potential to build trust. Also realize that every communication has the potential to destroy trust.

Practice 11.4

Modify Sparingly

Instructions: Remove unnecessary modifiers from the sentences below.

1. In my opinion, you should feel really certain what the true facts are before you sign the contract.
2. Can you confirm that it is totally true that they might possibly back out of their agreement?
3. I would kind of like for you to speak to the person who really knows a lot about this topic, literally.

Note: See page 443 for the key to the above activity.

Edit Out Background Thinking

Background thinking is different from explaining an issue or giving evidence to support a point. Learn to identify the difference between your own background thinking and key information that makes a point.

As you compose your message, you may go down many different lines of thought to get to your main point. All or most of the details leading up to your main point could be background thinking.

As you read the following, identify information to cut.

> After we spoke, I continued to think about the situation in which we find ourselves. Not that long ago, the economy was strong and we were looking for different ways to invest our profits. Now, with the sudden change in the economy, we are faced with uncertainty—many of our clients will be tightening their belts and looking for ways to avoid buying our product. Here's my point: we can go right on using the same methods to sell our product, or we can look for new, innovative approaches—something we've never tried before. Let's open up a contest among our sales reps to see what they can come up with. What do you think?

Write your revision in the space provided below:

_____

_____

_____

_____

Note: See Endnote 1, page 232, for the key to the above example.

Leave Out Opinions and Beliefs

Though you may find that writing about your opinions helps you get to your key points, opinions are usually not relevant once you find your key point. If you find yourself rambling off the point, that is an indication to start cutting.

Be cautious when using phrases such as *I believe*, *I think*, and *I feel*. These types of phrases make you sound less sure of yourself; so unless you use these phrases as you give advice to a colleague, they are simply *I statements* that merit deletion.

Also, do not tell your reader *how* to interpret your message; these added comments may give the reader the impression that you are unsure of your message or that you lack confidence. Thus, remove phrases or sentences that tell your readers *how you think* they will react.

As you read the following example, identify the opinions and beliefs that you could cut.

> I'm not sure if you are going to like this idea, but I've been thinking about this for a few weeks now, tossing over the pros and cons. In fact, one of our guys in the field mentioned it to me, and I was surprised that he was thinking about it too. But if this is just another message suggesting something you are already thinking about or have decided won't work, sorry that I wasted your time.
>
> I am suggesting that we cut the sales meeting by one day this summer. Generally our productivity goes down by the last day, and we could save about 20 percent of our costs and probably accomplish just as much in the shorter time frame. Let me know what you think.

Write your revision in the space provided below:

_____

_____

_____

_____

Note: See Endnote 1, page 232, for the key to the above example.

Recap

Whenever you can, simplify your writing: *less is more*.

➤ Put purpose first, and you will have a clear idea of what to cut.

➤ Get rid of your background thinking and your opinions.

➤ Modify sparingly, paying special attention to hedges and emphatics.

➤ Be direct and say what you mean.

➤ Remember, compose freely—cut when you edit and revise.

Writing Workshop

Activity A. Writing Practice

Instructions: Select two or three pieces of your writing. Identify information that you could cut. Analyze the information by seeing if it fits in any of the following categories:

- Redundant pairings (including redundant subjects and redundant verbs)
- Vague nouns
- Hedges and emphatics
- Background thinking and opinions
- *I think, I believe, I feel* statements

Remember, *less is more*.

Activity B. Journal

Instructions: Write a short self-assessment identifying your strengths.

What do you do well? What have you accomplished that makes you feel good about yourself? What situations have you turned around, making something good come from something challenging? What are your personal qualities that assist you in getting a job done effectively?

Identify how you feel when you focus on your strengths, and then identify how you feel when you focus on your weaknesses. Do words make a difference? Can you affect your self-confidence with self-talk?

Skills Workshop

Using Simple Language

Instructions: Simplify the following sentences.

Weak: We will ascertain the cause of the problem and a correction will be made immediately.

Revised: We will find out the cause the problem and correct it immediately.

1. The decision for the utilization of that product was made by our advertising department.

2. Subsequent to their involvement, we made little progress.

3. As per your suggestion, I have brought the issue of our competitor accepting our coupons to my immediate supervisor.

4. It would be so appreciated if you would fill me in on the new manager's background.

5. Pursuant to your request, my assistant is sending you several brochures and flyers.

6. In the event of a power outage, the generator will keep our file server running.

7. On behalf of everyone in the entire marketing department, we would like to welcome you to the company.

8. Was the committee cognizant of the Jones Company's history of defaulting on loans?

9. If the merger is contingent upon our utilization of their software, we should endeavor to make the change.

10. Always endeavor to do your best, especially when you are cognizant of the challenges.

11. We utilize the best materials in our new product line.

12. The termination of the project will absolutely occur in June.

Note: See pages 443 - 444 for the key to this exercise.

Editing Workshop

Instructions: Edit the following message, paying special attention to redundant and outdated working.

Also consider using bullets or numbering to make expectations or desired actions clear.

Jaclyn,

Per my voicemail I will need more information in order to troubleshoot the problem that needs to be addressed immediately. Any yes, you are contacting the right person—I should be able to help, and with the information that I am requesting, we can get the process started. As you said in your message earlier today, Carrie Thompson tried to make an International call from her cell phone, and it would not work—even though previously it did work. I realize this is a serious issue because she travels a lot and not having access to her phone can be frustrating. So once I have the following information, I'm confident that I can get her back up and running:

Where is Carrie currently located? (i.e. Is she out the country? If so, where?)

What kind of product does she have (in other words, what brand cell phone does she use?) Where is Carry trying to call? (If she's out of the country, is she trying to call here or another country?) Where was Carry calling from when her cell phone did work? Any help you can give would be greatly appreciated. Hope you are having a great day—talk to you soon.

Matteo

Note: See page 444 for the suggested revision to this exercise.

Endnotes

1. **Background Thinking Revised:**

   Since the market has changed, we need some fresh ideas. What do you think about opening up a contest among our sales reps to see what they can come up with?

2. **Reader's Perception's Revised:**

   How about cutting the sales meeting by one day this summer? Generally our productivity goes down by the last day, and we could save about 20 percent of our costs.

12

Formatting

Right now, you may be spending extraordinary efforts to craft your message while overlooking the obvious: the overall appearance of your document on the page.

Regardless of what you are writing, make it your objective to give your readers easy access to your ideas. When you use formatting effectively, formatting becomes a form of visual persuasion as well as an element of your writing style.

- **Formatting speaks to your reader** at first glance, and correct formatting gives your document credibility.

Lop-sided documents can give the impression that the writer either did not know how to format or simply did not care. When documents are framed beautifully with balanced margins, the difference becomes obvious with a glance. However, well-formatted documents do more than present a "pretty picture":

- **Formatting gives visual cues** to aid the reader in understanding the content.

Formatting tools include the use of headings, bullets and numbering, font, color, bold, underscore, and italics. However, at times the most important element may be none of these, but rather the unused portions of the page often referred to as **white space**. To present an effective finished product, all elements must work together harmoniously.

Formatting Basics:
Special Features and White Space

To achieve an instantaneous rapport between your reader and your document, break your message into manageable chunks. Position your text so that it is well-balanced on the page, and display key ideas prominently. Such visual cues allow your reader to scan the document and understand its meaning before actually reading it.

Here is an overview of elements that affect formatting:

- Displaying key ideas with bullet points or numbering.

- Organizing a topic by using headings and subheadings.

- Incorporating special features such as bold, underscore, and italics.

- Setting off explanations or descriptive information with parentheses.

- Selecting fonts for ease of reading.

- Following official guidelines for white space.

In addition to following official formatting guidelines, another way of adding white space is to break information into readable chunks. Just as a sentence is more readable under 25 words, a paragraph is easier to read when it does not appear too lengthy.

The following is a general "rule of thumb": for papers, consider 8 lines a maximum length for paragraphs; for letters, consider limiting paragraph length to 6 lines; for e-mail, keep your paragraphs to 4 lines or fewer.

In fact, with e-mail, getting right to the point is critical, so messages are often short. As a result, even individual sentences can effectively be set off as "paragraphs."

As you learn official guidelines for using formatting features and white space, you will see documents differently. In other words, you will build an expertise for knowing how to format a document so that it looks balanced and professional.

Bullet Points and Numbering

Have you ever written an e-mail message that included three or four questions; but when you received your response, only two questions were answered? Next time, consider numbering your questions, leaving a line of white space between each one.

Bullet points and numbering are strong visual cues. They not only make key points instantly visible for your reader but also organize and prioritize your key points.

- For items of equal importance, use bullet points.

- For items with different degrees of value, use numbers and list the most important items first.

For bullets or numbered items, you have a variety of different styles from which to choose. Stay consistent with the bullet or numbering style throughout your document, and shift from one style to another only if you have a special purpose for changing styles. For example, use a larger bullet for major points and a smaller bullet for minor points.

By numbering questions in an e-mail, you make it easier for your reader to give you a complete response. By making your key ideas instantly visible, you aid the reader in responding to your requests, which in turn aids you in getting your job done.

Display bullet points in parallel structure: noun for noun, verb for verb, phrase for phrase. For example, if you start with an active verb, start every item in the list with an active verb in the same tense.

Though you worked extensively with parallel structure in Chapter 10, Parallel Structure, use the following examples as a brief review. The following list is displayed as *nouns*.

Here are items to discuss at our next meeting:

- Employee Dress Policy

- Holiday Schedule

- Summer Hours

You can represent the same list more specifically starting with *verbs*:

At our next meeting, we need to do the following:

- Revise employee dress policy
- Review holiday schedule
- Implement summer hours

Adding *–ing* to the verbs turns them into *gerunds* (a noun form):

The following are topics for our next meeting:

- Revising employee dress policy
- Reviewing holiday schedule
- Implementing summer hours

You can also use complete sentences:

Here is what we expect to accomplish at our next meeting:

- We will revise the employee dress policy.
- We will clarify our holiday schedule.
- We will establish summer hours and a date to implement them.

If you present your information in complete sentences or short phrases, you can end your bulleted or numbered points with a period.

Experiment using bullets and numbering until you feel comfortable using them.

Sections and Headings

Headings are relevant for writing papers and long letters, adding white space and visual appeal. Break your text into manageable and cohesive chunks of information so that both you and your reader have an easier time navigating your document.

You can create centered and side headings during the composing or revising phase of writing.

- **Composing:** create a page map of your major ideas. (Page mapping was presented in Chapter 1.) Use key words from your page map as centered section headings and side headings. A page map may be the most effective means for starting any document that is longer than one page.

- **Revising:** as you revise your work, you further refine your thinking. Organize and prioritize your ideas as you pull out key terms for centered and side headings.

There are various patterns to follow for headings. Once you choose a pattern for your document, remain consistent with spacing, font, and display. For each level of heading, maintain parallel structure within that level. Clean up your document for consistency as you revise it.

Here is one pattern to follow:

- **Document titles and chapter openings**: Type the title of your report or chapter in all capital letters and use boldface type 2 inches from the top of the page (space down 6 lines from the default top margin in your computer template).

- **Centered headings (for sections or parts):** A section or part represents a major break in content. The centered section heading can be in 12-point all capital letters. (For caps and lowercase, capitalize the first letter of every main word but not the first letter of a preposition or an article with fewer than four letters, unless it is the first or last word.)

  ° Center section headings and follow them by a double space.

  ° Triple-space before a section heading; if you start a section on a new page, leave a 2-inch top margin.

- **Side Headings: A side heading**, also referred to as a **subheading**, starts at the left margin. Type the heading in bold, either all-caps or caps and lowercase. Start the text content a double space below the side heading.

- **Run-in headings:** A **run-in heading** is also known as a **paragraph heading.** Indent the run-in heading ½ inch from the left margin, and type it in bold cap and lowercase letters followed by a period. (A colon can be used instead of a period.) Space twice and begin your text.

- **Second pages.** Use a correct and consistent pattern to identify second pages. For papers and reports, the preferred method is placing the page number in the upper right-hand corner. Unless you start a new paragraph, make sure you carry over at least two lines of the last paragraph.

When you do a final screening of your document, make sure that your document is consistent and balanced. Also make sure that you represent headings within each level in parallel structure.

Formatting Features and Marks

Formatting features include **bold**, <u>underscore</u>, and *italics*; special marks include parentheses and quotation marks.

You probably understand not to use all caps to stress words or phrases, as all caps connote shouting. Instead, use bold, underscore, or italics to stress words, as explained below:

- **Bold**: Put words or key ideas in boldface type to make them stand out.

- **Underscore**: Stress key words by underscoring them.

- **Italics**: Stress words or give definitions in italics; display book titles or foreign terms in italics.

- **Quotation Marks**: Enclose direct quotes and technical terms presented for the first time in quotation marks.

- **Parentheses**: Put parentheses around information that gives a brief explanation or that does not directly relate to your topic. Also put parentheses around a paraphrase or an abbreviation.

- **Caps**: Follow traditional capitalization guidelines; do not use all capital letters (all caps) to make words stand out.

Within a document, be consistent in the way that you display these features and marks. Since the bold and underscore features provide a similar purpose, use one or the other, not both at once.

Sometimes, especially in e-messages, writers think they are making an idea stand out by using all caps. Instead, readers may infer that the writer is shouting at them. To stress a word or phrase in any document, including e-mail, use bold, underscore, or italics (but not all caps).

Many writers also think that putting a word between quotation marks makes the idea stand out (such as, *it's a really "good" idea*). Instead, when quotation marks are used for no valid reason, readers think that the writer is implying the *opposite* of what the word actually means. Be careful: Do not use quotation marks unless you are certain about how you are using them.

Use quotation marks to:

1. Enclose a direct quote of three or fewer lines within the body of a document.

2. Identify technical terms, business jargon, or coined expressions which may be unfamiliar.

3. Use words humorously or ironically (if you think your reader will miss the humor).

4. Show a slang expression, poor grammar, or an intentionally misspelled word.

Use italics to:

1. Refer to a word as a word; for example, the word *listen* has many shades of meaning.

2. Emphasize a word, phrase, or entire sentence.

3. Display foreign terms (such as *Merci, Grazie, Dobra, Domo Arigato*) and Latin abbreviations (such as *i.e.* and *e.g.*).

4. Display book titles. In the past, book titles were underscored. However, now that we have access to the variable spacing and special features of computers, using italics is the preferred method.

Use parentheses to:

1. Include a brief explanation within a sentence.

2. Insert a sentence that does not directly relate to the topic of your paragraph.

3. Supply abbreviations.

Using parentheses tells the reader that the information relates to the broader topic without going into detail of how or why. Thus, you can sometimes avoid writing a lengthy explanation by enclosing a few words in parentheses.

Font Size and Color

For most professional documents, select conservative fonts and keep them to traditional sizes. Common fonts are Times New Roman and Arial. Most business and academic documents are written in a 12-point font, which means there are 12 characters per inch. This traditional size is a carry-over from the typewriter, which only had two sizes (10 or 12 point). Now, with electronic processing, almost any font size is possible.

The traditional color for print and e-mail messages is black. However, for e-mail, some professionals use blue for the body of their message or their automatic sign-off. Colors other than blue or black may be considered unprofessional; in fact, some business executives are annoyed when untraditional colors or special features appear in an e-mail. These individuals may or may not be justified for feeling this way; however, entrants into the workforce should be aware of possible critics before sending out blazing red or purple messages (or animation) thinking they are being creative. To avoid criticism, use accents of color conservatively. Also consider the following:

- Limit font types to two per document so that your work does not appear cluttered.

- Use a larger-sized font for the title of your document (size 14) and major text headings (title, chapter, and section headings).

If you know that your reader has visual difficulty, increase font size. Most e-mail templates are set for a size 10 font; increase the font size to 12 or 14. You may use the bold feature to make the message especially clear.

White Space and Balance

The term **white space** refers the unused areas of your document, such as top and side margins and spacing between lines. Official guidelines dictate a range of minimum to maximum spacing to leave between parts. After you learn official guidelines for spacing, which are reviewed in the following pages, you will develop a trained eye for document placement.

White space gives your readers' eyes a place to rest and delineates the various parts of your document. White space also gives readers a place to make notes and comments. White space controls the way your document looks at a glance. Therefore, before you consider any document complete, ask yourself the following questions:

- Does this document look balanced, appealing, and professional?

- Is too much information crowded into too little space?

- Does the document look lop-sided or does it look as if it has a *picture frame* of white space?

Documents should look balanced, with top and bottom margins being roughly equal; side margins should be somewhat equivalent. The easiest mistake to make is to leave too little space at the top of a document, resulting in too much empty space at the bottom. A professional rule of thumb is to aim for a picture-framed effect.

Use the page preview feature on your computer to examine how your document looks before you print it. (Page preview can be found in the File menu on your toolbar.)

The following pages contain basic guidelines and examples of these commonly-used documents:

- Business Letter

- E-Mail

- Fax

For each document, notice the amount of white space to leave between parts.

Note: For vertical spacing (up and down), 6 lines take up 1 inch of space.

Basic Parts of a Letter

1. **Letterhead**. This part includes the name, address, phone number, fax number, and web address of a company or individual.

2. **Date Line**. The day, month, and year on which the letter is typed.

3. **Inside Address**. The name, title, and company name and address of the recipient. Use two-letter state abbreviations, but avoid using other types of abbreviations in addresses.

4. **Salutation**. The traditional greeting for letters starts with "dear," as in "Dear Mr. Jones" or "Dear Sue"; follow the salutation with a colon.

5. **Body**. The text of your message should be single spaced with 1 blank line between paragraphs; do not indent paragraphs.

6. **Complimentary Closing**. A common closing is "Sincerely."

7. **Writer's Signature Block**. The writer's name is typed along with a title, when used.

8. **Reference Initials**. If the typist is different from the writer, indicate the typist's initials.

9. **File Name Notation**. This code indicates where a document is stored. When used, file names often have three components: a name, a dot used as a separator, and an extension consisting of 1 to 3 characters.

10. **Enclosure Notation**. This notation alerts the recipient (and you) that something is enclosed with the letter.

11. **Delivery Notation**. This notation indicates that a letter was sent in a special way, such as UPS, FedEx, Express, and so on.

12. **Copy Notation**. A "cc" notation (courtesy copy) indicates to whom copies of the letter are being sent.

13. **Postscript**. A post script is an afterthought; represent the post script with or without periods and with or without a colon; however, use capital letters (PS, P.S., or PS:).

Reginald D. Piper [1]

4900 East Wilson
Chicago, IL 60608
312-555-5555 / rdp@email.com

July 11, 2009 [2]   *(Return 3 to 5 times, depending on length)*

Mr. Bob Allison [3]
Communication Network, Inc.
333 West Wacker Drive
Chicago, IL 60610   *(Return 2 times)*

Dear Mr. Allison: [4]   *(Return 2 times)*

In the first paragraph, connect with your reader. If you are writing a **direct message**, state your main point in the first paragraph. [5]

In the body of your letter include details, examples, and rationale. With an **indirect message** (also referred to as a *bad news* letter), state your main point toward the end of the body or the beginning of the conclusion, after you have given your rationale.

In the last paragraph define **action needed** or next steps. Also invite the reader to contact you by including your phone number and Web address.

Sincerely, [6]   *(Return 4 to 6 times, depending on length)*

Reginald D. Piper [7]
Instructional Designer   *(Return 2 times before notations)*

djy [8]
allison.711 [9]
Enclosure [10]
By UPS [11]
cc: Michael Jones [12]

PS Before you print your letter, use the print preview function to make sure that margins are balanced, creating a "picture frame" effect. [13]

Basic Parts of an E-Mail Message

With e-mail, software templates provide the heading; writers need only fill in the necessary information. For the body of an e-mail, make sure that you leave adequate vertical spacing, or white space, after the salutation, between paragraphs, and before your closing. Also take note of the following points:

- When you expect recipients to take action based on information in your message, list their names in the *To* section, not the *Cc* section.

Reserve Cc use for when you are copying a message to someone but not expecting the Cc recipient to take action. With messages that you are forwarding, feel free to add a note at the top of the message stating expected action from recipients.

- Use an accurate **subject line** and update it as your conversation evolves.

In other words, when you exchange several messages about the same topic, update the subject line to reflect new information.

- Use a **greeting,** even it is as simple as the recipient's name.

A greeting personalizes a message and helps you connect with your reader. When you write to several people, use a greeting such as "Hello, team," "Hi everyone," or "Good day." When you write to one person, use the person's name followed by a comma; if you wish, also use "Hi" or "Hello." If the e-mail is formal, use "Dear."

- Keep the message short.

Try to keep your messages to about one screen in length. If your message is long, consider phoning.

- Use a simple **closing**.

An e-mail is not as formal as a business letter, so you can use an informal closing such as "Best regards," "All the best," "Enjoy your day," or "Take care," among others.

- For professional messages, include a sign-off that lists your company name, address, phone number, and other relevant contact information.

Standard E-Mail Message

Notice the use of white space in the e-mail message below. White space is an element of visual persuasion because it aids the reader in understanding your message.

From: **Bob Allison**
To: **Reginald Piper**
Cc:
Subject: **Policy Manual Update**

Hi Reggie,   *(Return 2 times after the salutation)*

Thank you for helping us with our company policy manual. Please make sure that you stress the following:

1. Use correct grammar and punctuation in all e-mail.

2. Follow standard rules for capitalization.

3. Avoid using abbreviations.

Also, please include a section advising employees *not* to send messages if they have any doubts. When they feel unsure about their message, they should either save the message as a draft or make a phone call.

We look forward to seeing the first draft.

Best regards,   *(Return 2 times after the closing)*

Bob   *(Return 2 times)*

Bob Allison   *(Create your automatic sign-off)*
Communication Network, Inc.
333 West Wacker Drive
Chicago, IL 60610
Phone: 312-555-1212
Fax: 312-555-1234

Standard Fax Cover Sheet

When faxing information, create a cover sheet, as shown below. Send your fax cover sheet with your document to ensure that everyone on the receiving end clearly understands who sent the fax, who should receive the fax, and how many pages in total to expect.

FAX COVER SHEET

TO: Angelina Lopez   **FAX:**   800-555-9215

FROM: Jennifer Pitt   **PHONE:** 888-555-9242
                              FAX: 888-555-9243

* 3 Pages Follow *

Angie, attached is the real estate contract for the property in Long Grove. The closing is next Friday at 10 a.m. Please call me if you have questions.

I look forward to seeing you there.

Jenny

White Space Guidelines

Letters

- Start most letters 2 inches from the top the page (after the 6 blank lines that your computer automatically leaves, space down 6 lines from your computer page template).

- Use the default margins for most letters.

- For short letters, add more vertical space before the dateline, between the date and address, and between the complimentary close and the signature line.

- For long letters, leave less vertical space between parts and at the top and bottom.

- Do not justify right margins (readers find justified lines more difficult to follow).

Reports

- Start your first page 2 inches from the top of the page (down 6 lines from the default top margin).

- Type the title in 14-point all-caps or bold caps and lowercase; type the body in a 12-point font.

- Use 1-inch margins or the default margins.

- Type the second-page continuation heading 1 inch from the top of the page; for the heading, include the title, page number, and date, if applicable. After the heading, space down 3 lines before continuing the body of your report.

Memos

- Most companies (and software packages) provide a memo template.

- To start the body of the memo, space down 3 times (leaving 2 blank lines) after the heading.

- Leave 1 blank vertical line between paragraphs.

Follow established guidelines for research and academic papers. These rules vary slightly from source to source; for specifics, consult the reference source your instructor recommends.

Basic Letter Structure: Connect – Tell – Act

The business letter is an excellent vehicle to build business relationships. Your letters represent you and your company and may be the only image your client has of your company.

Although the purpose and content of letters vary, you can organize most letters successfully by applying the following basic structure:

- In the introduction, **connect** with the reader as one human being communicating with another. Connect your purpose to the reader's needs and interests; be friendly rather than stiff and abstract.

- In the body, **tell** your reader details, explanations, and facts. Summarize and highlight information supporting your purpose.

- In the closing, state the **action** or next steps that you will take or that you request the reader to take. Express good will; invite the reader to contact you for more information.

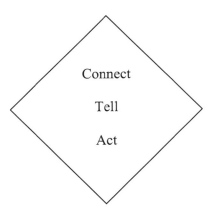

When you write a letter, you also need to determine whether you will communicate information using a **direct approach** or an **indirect approach**.

The Direct Message

Most letters take a direct approach to conveying information, putting the purpose and main point in the first paragraph. Once readers understand the purpose, the supporting information in the body confirms and expands their understanding of your message.

The bulk of the letter is in the body, which can consist of one paragraph (or as many paragraphs as it takes to convey your message). Give as many details as necessary, but do not stray from the principle *less is more*.

The closing in a direct message is usually short; the closing states the action or the next steps that you intend to take or that you request your reader to take. The closing also expresses good will and opens the door for additional communication.

To simplify the structure, think of the direct message as a diamond: the top represents a short introduction; the middle, the bulk of the information; and the bottom, a short closing (see illustration, page 248).

The Indirect Message

Some letters purposely take an indirect approach. When conveying unexpected or bad news, first explain the rationale before stating your main point or decision. This approach equips the reader to accept the "bad news" by understanding the logic behind it. The indirect approach is tactful and shows respect to the reader.

In the introduction, state the purpose in a general way. Then give enough explanation so that the rationale leading to the news makes sense to the reader (or as much sense as possible). State your main point or bad news toward the end of the body or possibly in the conclusion.

Direct Message	Indirect or Bad News Message
Connect with the reader	Connect with the reader
State purpose/get to the point	State general purpose
Give supporting details	Give supporting details
Close with desired actions or next steps	State main point or conclusion
	Close with cordial words (and next steps if they apply)

As in the direct message, the closing paragraph of an indirect message lets your reader know that he or she may contact you or someone else for additional information.

Recap

Here are some of the points stressed in this chapter:

➤ Ensure that you leave an appropriate amount of white space between each part of every document.

➤ Use special features such as bolding, underscoring, and italics to make key ideas stand out.

➤ Use bullets so that your key ideas are instantly visible.

➤ Use numbering to make it easier for your recipient to respond to a series of questions.

➤ Add side headings to give your documents visual appeal.

As you experiment using these tools to enhance the visual appeal of your documents, you will become more confident and use them with ease.

Writing Workshop

Activity A: Writing Activity

What Is Your Legacy? What do you want to be remembered for? Take a moment to reflect on your strengths and values. Are you doing what you want to do? Are you doing what you need to do so that you leave the mark you desire to leave?

Also reflect on your dreams. Are you pursuing your passions? If not, what changes do you need to make to bring your dreams and passions into your life? When you were a child, what did you dream of becoming?

Activity B: Journal

Start a joy journal. Take a few minutes every day to list the things that you appreciate and that bring you joy. Or rather than starting a separate journal, finish your daily journal by doing this activity.

Editing Workshop

Instructions: Edit the following message paying special attention to formatting. In fact, consider whether you can use bullets or numbering to enhance your revision.

Jesse,

April 12, June 7, and September 27 are the dates for the training sessions in Washington, D.C. Two flip charts, markers, and name tents are the only supplies that will be needed. A u-shape is how the room should be set up. Fifteen participants will be attending, so that's how many set-ups that will be needed. Muffins and coffee have been ordered for breakfast; sandwiches, chips, soft drinks, and cookies have been ordered for lunch. Invoices have been prepared and should be received by participants by next week. Should participants be contacted by me before the training?

Best regards,

Diana

Note: See pages 445 for the suggested revision to this exercise.

PART 5: MORE MECHANICS

Though you have already covered the critical elements of mechanics, many little details still linger. Since you are well on your way to becoming an incurable editor, now is the time to work on the final details to becoming an expert editor.

This part starts with similar words, such as *affect/effect* and *loan/lend*. Then you work with colons, ellipses, and dashes: these punctuation marks give you variety in the way you express yourself and give your writing flair.

Capitalization and number usage may give you headaches, but learning only a few simple rules will help clear up the confusion. Then there are quotation marks, apostrophes, and hyphens. Memorizing how to use these marks is unrealistic, so instead go over them with the goal of becoming familiar with them. You will know where to find the rules when you need to use them.

Grammar and mechanics are trivial compared to the critical thinking side of writing: your ability to use writing to solve problems is one key to creating a successful career. However, knowing the grammar and mechanics of writing will give you more confidence and credibility. Now go have some fun with the mechanics of writing!

13

Word Usage

Are you ready for some surprises? In all likelihood, this chapter will reveal several words that you have been using incorrectly without any clue they were "wrong." For example, did you know that *alright* is not a Standard English spelling? Or when was the last time you *loaned* someone something or drove *thru* the car wash?

Besides using common words incorrectly or spellings that "do not really exist," the English language has many common words that confuse writers. These are the words that sound alike but are spelled differently and have different meanings, such as *its* and *it's* or *affect* and *effect*. These kinds of words are called *similar words* or *homophones*.

In addition to similar words, this chapter also includes other words that can also be confusing for any variety of reasons. Like any skill, the only way to build your vocabulary is through practice and repetition. Use new words in context, and you are more likely to remember them. Also, practice new words until you reach a comfort zone using them.

Plan time into your daily or weekly routine to build your vocabulary, targeting ten new words at a time. (Start by using the five spelling lists at the end of this chapter.) Also, keep a running list of words that you are likely to misuse or misspell.

The format of this chapter is quite different from the previous chapters in that you start with a short pretest. Take the pretest on the following page to identify the words that give you problems.

Pretest

Instructions: In the sentences below, cross out any words that are used incorrectly, and write in the correct word above it or to the right of the sentence.

1. Will that decision effect you in a positive way?

2. The principle on my loan is due on the 1st of the month.

3. My advise is for you to get a job before you buy that new car.

4. Please ensure my manager that I will return in one-half hour.

5. Its been a challenging day, but things are getting better.

6. Their are a few issues that we need to discuss.

7. The agency gave are report a new title.

8. Pat lives further from work than I do.

9. You can have a meeting everyday, if you prefer.

10. Whose going to the ballgame?

11. I enjoy movies more then I enjoy plays.

12. Megan assured that the project would be successful

13. It's alright for you to contact the manager directly.

14. I didn't mean to infer that you were late on purpose.

15. Try and be on time for the next meeting.

Note: See page 445 for the answer key to this pretest.

Similar Words: Tricky Combos

This part contains some of the most common similar word combos. Write two or three sentences for each word that you are serious about mastering. With each new word that you learn, the next new word becomes a bit easier to learn, even if it does not feel that way at the moment.

adverse/averse: *Adverse* is an adjective meaning "unfavorable or bad"; *averse* is an adjective meaning "reluctant or unenthusiastic."

> I have an *adverse* reaction to dog racing.

> Jaclyn is *averse* to working on that project.

advice/advise: *Advice* is a noun and means "recommendation"; *advise* is a verb and means "to give advice or to make a recommendation."

> Please give me some *advice* about my paper.

> I *advise* you to trust the writing process.

affect/effect: Though each of these words can be a noun and a verb, they are primarily used as follows:

> *Affect* is a verb meaning "to influence."

> *Effect* is a noun meaning "result."

When you cannot figure out which word fits, substitute its definition:

> How will this *affect* (influence) you?

> The *effect* (result) is good.

As a noun, *affect* refers to emotions and is used primarily within the field of psychology; as a verb, *effect* means "to cause to happen" or "to bring about," for example:

> My sister was diagnosed with an *affective* (emotional) disorder.

> The new policy will *effect* (bring about) change within our organization.

When in doubt, use *affect* as a verb and *effect* as a noun.

alright/all right: *Alright* is not considered a Standard English spelling. Use *all right*. Here is a memory trick: something is either "all right" or "all wrong," for example:

Are you feeling *all right* about the changes?

among/between: *among* is a preposition meaning "together with or along with"; *between* is a preposition that means basically the same thing as *among*. Use *among* when three or more people or objects are discussed, but use *between* when only two people or objects are discussed.

Among the three of us, we have all the talent we need.

Between the two of us, you have more time than I do.

appraise/apprise: *Appraise* is a verb meaning "to assess or evaluate"; *apprise* is a verb meaning "to inform."

After the realtor *appraises* the house, she'll *apprise* you of your options.

are/hour/our: *Are* is a present tense form of the verb *to be*; *hour* is a noun that refers to 60 minutes of time; and *our* is the possessive pronoun for *we*.

What *are our* options? We have an *hour* to decide.

assure/ensure/insure: These three verbs are somewhat similar in sound and meaning, but they have distinct uses, for example:

assure: to give *someone* confidence

ensure: to make certain that some *thing* will happen

insure: to protect against loss

Here is the rule of thumb to follow: when you use *assure*, make sure that a "person" is the object, for example:

I *assure* **you** that we will meet the deadline.

When you use *ensure*, make sure that a "thing" is the object:

I *ensure* the **product** will arrive on time.

When you use *insure*, make sure that it refers to insurance.

You can *insure* against losses with our company.

breath/breathe: breath is a noun meaning a "lungful of air"; breathe is a verb meaning "to take in breaths."

I need a *breath* of fresh air.

When I *breathe* fresh air, I feel much better.

don't/doesn't: *Don't* and *doesn't* are both contractions of *do not*. *Doesn't* is the contraction of *does not*, which is the third person –s form of Edited English. However, speakers often mistakenly use *don't* for third person singular subjects in place of *doesn't*.

She *doesn't* have a care in the world.

Not: She *don't* have a care in the world.

Bob *doesn't* go to school here anymore

Not: Bob *don't* go to school here no more.

everyday/every day: Use *everyday* as a modifier meaning "ordinary" or "daily"; if you can insert the word *single* between *every* and *day*, you know that it is two words.

That is an *everyday* routine.

We do that procedure *every (single) day*.

farther/further: Though similar in meaning, *farther* refers to actual distance that can be measured; *further* indicates progress that is intangible and not measurable, such as "to a greater or lesser degree or extent."

Sue lives *farther* from work than you do.

Let's discuss this proposal *further*.

has/have: *Has* and *have* are both present tense forms of *to have*. Use *has* for third person singular (he *has*, she *has*, and it *has*) and *have* for all other persons: I *have*, you *have*, we *have* and they *have*. However, writers sometimes use *have* for third person singular in place of *has*.

A block of rooms *has* been reserved.
Not: A block (of rooms) *have* been reserved.

The car *has* a few dents on its fender.
Not: The car *have* a few dents on its fender.

infer/imply: These two verbs are opposite in meaning: *infer* means "to deduce, conclude, or assume"; *imply* means "to express or state indirectly."

From your statement, I *inferred* that Len was at the meeting; is that what you meant to *imply*?

its/it's: The word *its* is a possessive pronoun, whereas *it's* is a contraction of *it is* or *it has*, for example:

You can't judge a book by *its* cover.

It's been a great day.

Writing Tip One way to improve your use of these words is to stop using the contraction *it's*; every time you use *it's*, see if you can substitute "it is" or "it has."

loan/lend: Most people confuse these words without realizing it, even people in high level banking positions! Here is what you need to know:

Loan is a noun, not an action.

Lend is a verb; its past tense form is *lent*.

For example: The bank will give you a *loan*, but it will *lend* you money.

In other words, you cannot really "loan" someone your book, but you can *lend* it. Practice these words until the meaning becomes clear.

may be/maybe: *May be* is a verb form that suggests possibility; *maybe* is an adverb that means "perhaps."

This week *may be* the right time to submit our request.

Maybe you can get the information from Fred.

Not: I *maybe* able to help you.

principal/principle: At one point, you may have learned that the *principal* of your school was your "pal." That is true; however, *principal* has a broader meaning, which is "chief or main." So you may be surprised to learn that your loan consists of "*principal* and interest." *Principle* means "theory or rule of conduct."

What is the *principal* on your loan?

We all try to live by our *principles*.

In fact, I would rather pay my *principal* than my interest!

saw/seen: *Saw* is the past tense of the verb *to see*; *seen* is the past participle. The past tense form of a verb does not take a helper verb; however, the past participle form must have a helper. Contrary to Edited English usage, in local language speakers sometimes use a helper with *saw* but leave out the helper with *seen*.

We all *saw* Tasha enter the conference room.

Not: We all *seen* Tasha enter the conference room.

We had *seen* that movie twice already.

Not: We had *saw* that movie twice already.

sight/site/cite: *Sight* is a noun referring to vision or mental perception; *site* is also a noun that refers to a location, as in *Web site*; *cite* is a verb meaning "to quote" or "to name."

The pilot's *sight* was impaired due to the accident.

My Web *site* is under construction.

I was *cited* for driving without my license.

supposed to/used to: In speech the –ed ending of *supposed* and *used* is not always distinguished from the –t of *to*. Therefore, the –ed is often left off of these words erroneously. These words are regular verbs and as such require the –ed ending for their past tense and past participle forms.

You *are supposed* to attend that class. I *used* to go to that school.

Not: You are *suppose* to assist in the lab.

than/then: the word *than* is a conjunction used in comparisons; *then* is an adverb referring to time, as in "after that." To help remember, use *then* when it has to do with a "when."

I would rather get up early *than* sleep late.

After you complete the project, *then* I will have more time.

their/there/they're: *Their* is the possessive form of *they* and will always be followed by a noun; *there* is an adverb meaning "in or at that place" or a pronoun which functions as an anticipating subject; *they're* is the contracted form of *they are*.

Their apartment is next to mine.

There are a lot of people in the lobby. Go *there* if you choose.

They're standing next to the reception desk.

themselves/theirselves: *Themselves* is the reflexive form of *they*; *theirselves* is not a Standard English spelling.

The team members can help *themselves* to refreshments.

through/threw/thorough/thru: *Through* is a preposition meaning "by means of; from beginning to end, or because of"; *threw* is a verb and the past participle of *throw*; *thorough* is an adjective meaning "carried through to completion"; and take special note: *thru* is an incorrect spelling of *through* (use *thru* as a hyphenated form of *drive-thru*).

Walk *through* the room quietly.

Jenkins *threw* the paper at the judge.

We all did a *thorough* job on the report.

to/too: The preposition *to* is often used when the adverb *too* should be used. Remember, when you are describing something that relates to quantity, use the adverb *too*. *Too* also means *also*.

It's *too* late to go to the meeting.

The proposal has *too* much fluff and *too* little substance besides being *too* late to make a difference.

I will go to the conference *too* (also).

try to/"try and": The verb *try* is not followed by the word *and*. Instead, *try* is followed by an infinitive, such *to be*, *to see*, *to go*, and so on. Many people inadvertently say "*Try and* be on time" when they really mean to say "*Try to be* on time."

Try to get your work done early.

Try to be there before anyone else.

were/we're/where/wear: *Were* is one of the past-tense forms of the verb *to be* (as in *you were, we were, they were*). *We're* is a contraction for *we are*. The adverb *where* (pronounced the same as *wear*) is often confused with the past tense verb *were*. The verb *wear* means *to dress in*.

Where were you when the decision was made?

We're about to enter a new phase.

Wear that suit to the meeting.

who's/whose: The contraction *who's* stands for *who is* or *who has*. *Whose* is the possessive pronoun of *who*.

Who's chairing the meeting?

Whose book is that?

you/yous/y'all: *You* is a subjective pronoun, and *you* is singular or plural. In some areas, such as Chicago, the word *yous* is used as a local language plural form of *you*, as in "yous guys." While this is considered colloquial in the United States, *yous* is an acceptable pronoun in Ireland.

You all should go to the game this Friday.

In southern and southwestern portions of the U.S., the equivalent to *yous* is *y'all*, with *all y'all* being used with larger groups. An additional form is *you'uns* or *you'ins*.

These variations add life and color to the language when speaking; however, edit them to standard usage in your writing so that people from all parts of the globe can understand the meaning of your message.

you're/your: *You're* is a contraction for *you are*. *Your* is a possessive pronoun for *you*.

You're the one I want on my team.

Your personality makes the difference.

The similar words listed in this part are only a handful of similar words that you will come across. If you have a question about a word that is not listed here, go to the Internet and do a search. Several professional sites are likely to offer a complete explanation of the word in question.

Spelling Tips

One of the reasons spelling is difficult is that only about 40 percent of English words are spelled according to phonetics, which is how they sound. In other words, about 60 percent of English words are written with silent letters or other non-phonetic qualities, thereby requiring them to be memorized.

Here are some suggestions that you can use to improve your spelling and vocabulary usage:

• **Make a running list of words that you find challenging.**

The way you use language is unique. Your reading, writing, and spelling skills have different strengths and weaknesses from everyone else. The way to become stronger is to tailor your studies to learning the specific words challenge you. As you read, circle the words that you do not understand, and take the time to look them up.

• **Subscribe to online vocabulary-building newsletters.**

For example, Merriam-Webster (www.merriam-webster.com) has "word of the day" as does Wordsmith (www.wordsmith.org).

• **Use new words in context: write two or three sentences with each new word.**

To learn a new word, you must practice it in context. By writing two or three sentences, you are applying the new word in a way that will make it easier to remember and use correctly.

- **As you learn a new word, check the correct pronunciation.**

  Break up the new word into syllables and use the dictionary guidelines for pronunciation. Ask a friend to pronounce the word for you; say the word out loud several times until you feel comfortable.

- **Use spelling rules that are easy to remember.**

  Use spelling rules that you find helpful. For example, the rule "use *i* before *e* except after *c* or when the sound is like *a* as in *neighbor*" is easy to remember and helpful. However, learning complex spelling rules that have a lot of exceptions may not be as helpful. Go to the Internet and Google "spelling rules." Glean what you need, and then move on.

- **Learn some of the Latin and Greek roots of words as well as prefixes and suffixes.**

  Learning roots, prefixes, and suffixes will help you figure out new words and gain a deeper understanding of the words you already know. A few are listed below.

A Sampling of Roots, Prefixes, and Suffixes

Root	Meaning	Origin
anthrop	man	Greek
biblio	book	Greek
cent	one hundred	Latin
equ	equal, fair	Latin
geo	earth	Greek
hydro	water	Greek
ortho	straight	Greek
psych	mind, soul, spirit	Greek
sci	to know	Latin
techn	art, skill	Greek
viv, vit	life	Latin

Prefix	Meaning	Example
a- or *an-*	not, without	amoral, apolitical
ab-	away from	abduction
ambi-	both	ambidextrous
anti-	against	antisocial
bene-	good	beneficial
bi-	two	biannual
contra-	against	contradict
de-	not	derail
dis-	not	disengage
ex-	out from	exhale
hyper-	over	hypertension, hyperactive
il-, im-, in-	not	illegal, impossible, indivisible
inter-	between	interstate
ir-	not	irreversible
macro-	large	macrocosm
micro-	small	microcosm
mis-	not	misconduct, misplace
mono-	one	monologue
post-	after	postpone
pre-	before	pretest
pseudo-	false	pseudonym
re-	again	repeat
semi-	half	semiannual
sub-	under	subversive
trans-	across	transport
un-	not	unable

Suffix	Meaning	Example
-able	able to	durable
-age	result of action	courage
-er	doer of	teacher
	more	greater

-ectomy	cutting	appendectomy
-ful	full of	peaceful
-ic, -tic, -ical	having to do with	dramatic, Biblical
-ism	the belief in	mysticism
-logy	the study of	psychology, biology
-ly or -y	like	friendly
-ment	state of	judgment
-ness	quality	kindness
-phobia	fear	claustrophobia
-ship	condition, status	ownership
-ous	full of	ridiculous

Practice

Instructions: Select five Greek or Latin roots. For each root, identify two words that were developed from it.

Recap

Improving your vocabulary improves your critical thinking skills as well as your writing skills. Practice new words in context: write two or three sentences with each new word so that you can use it with confidence.

Writing Workshop

Writing Practice

Instructions: In the Skills Workshop, you will find 5 lists of spelling words that were taken from the 100 most commonly misspelled words. Select one of those lists for this exercise.

Break into small groups of three or four. Allow ten minutes for each group to develop a paragraph using as many vocabulary words from the list as possible. Now determine which group used the most words in their paragraph. Make sure, however, that the paragraph makes sense!

Work through each list (one list per week). As a follow-up, write two sentences for each word to ensure that you can use it in context.

Skills Workshop

Worksheet 1. Similar Words

Instructions: Circle the word in parentheses to complete the sentence.

1. They have (to, too) many new projects and (to, too) little time.

2. You will be (appraised, apprised) of the situation before noon today.

3. Jackson (assured, ensured) me that you got the job.

4. If you feel (alright, all right) about it, ask for a raise.

5. (Your, you're) the right person to turn the situation around.

6. (Among, Between) the three of us, we have all the resources we need.

7. Try (and, to) see Leonard before you leave today.

8. Kevin said that he would (loan, lend) me his notes.

9. His remark was a real (complement, compliment).

10. I live (farther, further) from work (than, then) you do.

11. If you (could of, could have) spoken to Della, you'd understand.

12. Vera (past, passed) that trait on to her daughters (to, too).

13. How will that (affect, effect) you?

14. When you know the (affect, effect), let me know.

15. Carol (loaned, lent) me everything I needed for the trip.

16. The project lost (its, it's) appeal after Mike quit.

17. I (ensure, assure) all print materials will be of high quality.

18. After you (ensure, assure) me, (assure, ensure) the others also.

19. (There, They're, Their) boat has left the dock.

20. We are (farther, further) along (than, then) we realize.

21. Say (its, it's) time to go, and we will.

22. If the bank will (loan, lend) you enough funds, will you buy the car?

23. My (principle, principal) and interest are due on the 1st of the month.

23. That company does all training on (sight, site).

24. Did the officer (site, cite) you for the violation?

25. We all try to live by our (principals, principles).

Note: See page 446 for the key to the above exercise.

Worksheet 2. Similar Words

Instructions: Use each of the following words in a sentence.

1. its _____

2. their _____

3. than _____

4. adverse _____

5. too _____

6. assure _____

7. it's _____

8. effect _____

9. loan _____

10. further _____

11. they're _____

12. ensure _____

13. affect _____

14. then _____

15. all right _____

16. doesn't _____

17. don't _____

18. saw _____

19. seen _____

20. principle _____

Posttest

Instructions: Correct the words that are used incorrectly.

1. The affect of that decision is not yet known.
2. When you know principle on your loan, let me know.
3. Her advise was that you take the other part-time job.
4. Can you assure the quality of your work?
5. The dog chased it's tail, amusing several children.
6. They are a few issues that we need to discuss.
7. Is that are new computer?
8. You are farther along on the project than I am.
9. We meet everyday at 3 p.m.
10. Who's book is that?
11. Sue was taller then Mary last year.
12. Melanie ensured me that we would be finished by Friday
13. Its alright for you to contact the manager directly.
14. I'm not trying to infer that you were late on purpose.

Note: See page 447 for the key to the above exercise.

Spelling Lists 1 - 5

Each of the following 5 lists contains 10 of the 100 most commonly misspelled words. Master these words by using them in sentences.

Spelling List 1

1. acceptable   adj: satisfactory
2. believe   v: consider, accept as true
3. calendar   n: agenda, schedule
4. definitely   adv: absolutely, without doubt
5. existence   n: survival, subsistence, life
6. leisure   n: free time, relaxation
7. maintenance   n: preservation, looking after
8. neighbor   n: fellow citizen
9. privilege   n: honor, opportunity
10. separate   v: divide, break away; adj: unconnected, distinct

Spelling List 2

1. amateur   n: layperson, not professional

2. embarrass   v: humiliate, make self-conscious

3. conscience   n: sense of right and wrong

4. conscious   adj: aware, mindful, awake, deliberate

5. foreign   adj: overseas, unfamiliar, unrelated

6. inoculate   v: immunize, vaccinate

7. miniscule   adj: very small, tiny

8. precede   v: to go before, to lead

9. proceed   v: to go on, to carry on, to continue

10. relevant   adj: pertinent, applicable, important

Spelling List 3

1. accommodate   v: to house, to have capacity for

2. conscientious   adj: reliable, diligent, thorough

3. equipment   n: gear, tools, paraphernalia

4. hierarchy   n: rank order of things or people

5. jewelry   n: adornments

6. mischievous   adj: ill-behaved, bad, harmful

7. medieval   adj: pertaining to the Middle Ages

8. noticeable   adj: visible, evident, in plain sight

9. possession   n: ownership

10. questionnaire   n: survey, opinion poll, feedback form

Spelling List 4

1. acquire   v: to obtain, to attain
2. experience   n: knowledge, skill, familiarity; v: feel, live through
3. gauge   v: measure, estimate, judge
4. immediate   adj: urgent, high priority, instant
5. knowledge   n: information, expertise, skill, familiarity
6. license   n: authorization, permit, certificate
7. millennium   n: a thousand years
8. misspell   v: to spell incorrectly
9. occurrence   n: incident, happening, event
10. reference   n: mention, citation, note; v: to mention, to cite

Spelling List 5

1. argument   n: quarrel, disagreement
2. discipline   n: self-control, strictness, branch of learning
3. humorous   adj: funny, amusing, witty
4. ignorance   n: lack of knowledge, unawareness
5. intelligence   n: cleverness, aptitude, astuteness
6. kernel   n: core, essential part, seed
7. perseverance   n: insistence, resolve, determination
8. referred   v: recommended
9. schedule   n: agenda, timetable, plan
10. weird   adj: unusual, peculiar

14

The Colon,
the Dash, and the Ellipses

Since you have already mastered commas and semicolons, the minor marks of punctuation in this chapter should seem easy for you.

One reason that writing seems so difficult for many people is that they try to make a multitude of decisions all at once. The principles that you learn here allow you to make decisions about mechanics without effort, freeing your energies to create a writing style that is reader-friendly and clear.

The colon, the dash, and the ellipses enhance writing because they add variety and energy. Experiment incorporating these marks into your writing sparingly, but correctly, until you feel comfortable using them.

Let's start with the colon because it has unique and versatile functions.

The Colon

In general, the colon alerts readers that information will be illustrated, making the colon a strong mark of punctuation that commands attention. Use the colon for the following purposes:

1. After salutations of business letters and formal e-mail messages.

2. At the end of one sentence when the following sentence illustrates it.

3. At the end of a sentence to alert the reader that a list follows.

4. After words such as *Note* or *Caution*.

Each of these categories is explained below.

1. Colons after Salutations. The most common use of a colon is after the salutation in a business letter, which is the most formal type of written communication. Only when you write a letter to a personal friend should you relax that tradition, using a comma instead of a colon. Here are some examples of salutations using a colon:

Dear Mr. Jones: Dear Dr. Wilson: Dear Professor:

Dear Jorge: Dear Mia: Robert:

Notice that even when you use the recipient's first name, the colon is appropriate. You could also use the above salutations in an e-mail if the message were formal, such as an inquiry for a job. However, for the most part, business professionals use a comma after the salutation of an e-mail as in the following:

Dear Janet,   Jack,   Hi Carolyn,

The one mark of punctuation that you would *never* use for a salutation is the semicolon; however, some writers mistakenly use it, for example:

Incorrect: Dear Charles;

Correct: Dear Charles:

Correct: Dear Charles,

Now let's examine how to use the colon to add variety to your writing style.

2. Colons after Sentences. You have probably noticed that a colon is used to introduce lists, but have you noticed a colon sometimes occurs at the end of one sentence when the following sentence illustrates it?

Using a colon to illustrate a complete sentence is probably the colon's least common use, but possibly its most powerful use. This type of colon use adds a nice dimension to writing style, conveying the message in a slightly more emphatic way.

Here are some examples of one sentence introducing another:

The colon is a strong mark of punctuation: it draws the reader's attention.

Johnson Ecology accepted our proposal: we start on Monday.

In general, the first word of the independent clause following a colon should be in lower case. However, capitalize the first word if you are placing special emphasis on the second clause or the second clause is a formal rule, as shown below:[1]

Here is the principle that applies: Colons can be used in place of a period when the sentence that follows illustrates the one that precedes it.

Update your report by Friday: The accrediting commission's site visit is next week.

When you use a colon to illustrate a sentence, use it sparingly. While there is no hard and fast rule, limit yourself to using no more than one or two colons per page this way.

If you have never used a colon in this way, try it. Once you do, you may enjoy having this new and exciting punctuation alternative. Experiment by writing a sentence or two on the lines below to illustrate this principle.

_____

_____

3. Colons to Illustrate Lists. Using the colon to illustrate a list of words or phrases generally requires using words such as *these*, *here*, *the following*, or *as follows* within a complete sentence. Here are some examples:

These are the materials to bring to the meeting: your annual report and current data.

Bring the following identification: driver's license, social security card, and current utility bill.

Here are writing samples that you can use: Myers, Jones, and Riley.

However, do not use a colon after an incomplete sentence, for example:

Incorrect:	The items you need to bring are: a tent, a sleeping bag, and a flashlight.
Correct:	The items you need to bring are a tent, a sleeping bag, and a flashlight.
Incorrect:	This package includes: a stapler and 3-hole paper punch.
Correct:	This package includes a stapler and 3-hole paper punch.

Also notice that the colon can be used after the adverbial conjunction *for example* to alert the reader that an example follows.

4. Colons After *Note* or *Caution* Use a colon after a word of caution or instruction, for example:

Note: All meetings are cancelled on Friday.

Caution: Do not use the staircase.

If a complete sentence follows *Note* or *Caution*, capitalize the first word, as shown above. Space one or two times after the colon, but be consistent in the style you choose.

Practice 14.1

The Colon

Instructions: Place colons where needed in the following sentences.

Incorrect: The materials we need are: blankets, water, and cell phones.

Corrected: The materials we need are blankets, water, and cell phones.

1. I have some exciting news for you, Jeremy proposed on Friday.

2. Note, the office is closed on Monday for the 4th of July holiday.

3. The supplies we need are as follows; markers copy paper and staplers.

4. Giorgio said that we need: cereal, soy milk, and bananas.

5. Here is what you should do, complete the inventory list and then work on the schedule.

Note: See page 447 for the key to the above exercise.

The Dash

The dash is the most versatile mark of punctuation, at times replacing the comma, the semicolon, the period, and even the colon.

The dash adds energy, making information that follows one dash or that falls between two dashes stand out. Though you can use the dash in formal documents, you will find yourself using it most often in informal communications. However, do not overuse the dash. When overused, the dash gives the impression that the writer is "speaking" in a choppy and haphazard fashion. Limit yourself to no more than one or two dashes per page or e-mail message.

Here are some examples using the dash:

Bob called on Friday—he said he'd arrive by noon today.

Thanks—your package arrived right before our meeting.

Feranda Wilson—our new executive VP—will host the event.

Though the dash is different from the hyphen, the hyphen is used to create the dash. Here are two ways to create a dash using hyphens:

1. Use two hyphens without a space before, between, after them; some software will create an *em* dash, as illustrated in the sentences above.

2. Use two hyphens, but this time place a space before and after the hyphens to create an *en* dash, as follows:

   Marie Clair invited us to the opening – I am so pleased!

The *em* dash is the traditional choice. However, if you work for a company, check your company policy manual to see if the manual states a preference—some companies state a preference so that corporate communications remain consistent.

Once again, overusing dashes is similar to overusing colons or exclamation points. Writers enjoy using them, but readers tire of them easily. Thus, hold yourself back and use them sparingly. However, if you have never used a dash in your writing, try it. Dashes definitely add energy and are fun to use.

Practice 14.2

The Dash

Instructions: Place dashes where needed in the following sentences.

Incorrect: Mark scheduled the meeting, how could I refuse to go?

Corrected: Mark scheduled the meeting—how could I refuse to go?

1. Margie called on Friday George is home!

2. Mike's parents are visiting he invited me to have dinner with them.

3. Helen Jones the new CEO asked me to join her team.

4. Call if u need anything Im always here to support you.

5. Give as much as you can to that charity it's a good cause.

Note: See pages 447 - 448 for the key to the above exercise.

The Ellipses

Ellipses is the plural form for *ellipsis marks*. Ellipses indicate that information is missing, thereby removing an otherwise awkward gap.

In formal documents, ellipses allow writers to adapt quotations by leaving out less relevant information, making the main idea stand out. In informal documents, ellipses allow writers to jump from one idea to another without entirely completing their thoughts. Ellipses also allow the writer to convey a sense of uncertainty without coming right out and stating it.

- Ellipsis marks consist of three periods with a space before, between, and after each one, for example:

  This doesn't make sense to me . . . let me know what you think.

- Some software programs create ellipses when you space once, type three periods in a row, and then space once again, as follows:

   Vic was not pleased ... he will call back later.

Before using the unspaced ellipses described above, check to make sure that it is acceptable practice within the domain you are submitting your work, as the unspaced ellipses may not be acceptable.

Many writers are unsure of how to display ellipses and end up using two, four, or five periods; even worse, some writers vary the number of periods they use each time, not realizing that rules surround the use of ellipses.

The only time a fourth period would be used is when the missing information is at the end of the sentence in a formal quotation, for example:

   The topics taught include self-awareness, in the sense
   of recognizing feelings and building a vocabulary for
   them, and seeing the links between thoughts, feelings,
   and reactions . . . .[1]

Use ellipsis marks sparingly, but correctly, even for informal use.

Practice 14.3

The Ellipses

Instructions: Use ellipsis marks to show how to adjust the following quotations while retaining the key meaning of each quote; for example:

Original Quote by John F. Kennedy:

"The great enemy of the truth is very often not the lie—deliberate, contrived and dishonest, but the myth, persistent, persuasive, and unrealistic. Belief in myths allows the comfort of opinion without the discomfort of thought.[2]

Abbreviated Quote:

"The great enemy of the truth is very often not the lie . . . Belief in myths allows the comfort of opinion without the discomfort of thought."

1. Original Quote by Albert Einstein:

"The important thing is not to stop questioning. Curiosity has its own reason for existing. One cannot help but be in awe when he contemplates the mysteries of eternity, of life, of the marvelous structure of reality. It is enough if one tries merely to comprehend a little of this mystery every day. Never lose a holy curiosity." [3]

Abbreviated Quote:

_____

_____

_____

_____

2. Original Quote by Victor Frankl:

"Don't aim at success—the more you aim at it and make it a target, the more you are going to miss it. For success, like happiness, cannot be pursued; it must ensue, and it only does so as the unintended side-effect of one's dedication to a cause greater than oneself or as the by product of one's surrender to a person other than oneself. Happiness must happen, and the same holds true for success: you have to let it happen by not caring about it. I want you to listen to what your conscience commands you to do and go on to carry it out to the best of your knowledge. Then you will live to see that in the long run—in the long run, I say!—success will follow you precisely because you had _forgotten_ to think of it."[4]

Abbreviated Quote:

_____

_____

_____

_____

Note: See page 448 for suggested revisions to the above quotations.

Recap

Below is a summary of the colon, dash, and ellipses: three marks that can give your writing variety and flair as long as they are not overused.

> ➢ The colon illustrates information that follows it; here are some basic guidelines:
>
>> • Use the colon at the end of one sentence when the following sentence illustrates it.
>>
>> • Use the colon after a complete sentence that includes words such as *these* or *the following* to indicate that a list follows.
>>
>> • Use the colon after the words *Note* and *Caution*; if a complete sentence follows the colon, capitalize the first word of that sentence.
>
> ➢ The dash emphasizes information that falls between two dashes or after one dash; create a dash as follows:
>
>> • Use two hyphens without spaces before, between, or after them to create an *em* dash.
>>
>> • Use two hyphens with a space before (but not between) and after them to create an *en* dash.
>
> ➢ The ellipses fill gaps and allow the reader to express uncertainty; create ellipses as follows:
>
>> • Use three periods and include a space before, between, and after each period.
>>
>> • Use a fourth period at the end of sentence.

Writing Workshop

Activity A. Writing Practice

Instructions: Identify an historical figure whom you respect, and then log on to the Internet to find a long quotation by that person.

Search the following: "quotations by (insert the name)." Several quotation sites should become available. Select a quotation, and then use ellipsis marks to shorten your quote, making a key point of the original quotation stand out.

After you have worked with the quote, write about what the quote means to you.

Activity B. Journal

Instructions: Experiment using dashes, colons, and ellipses as you write your journals this week.

Go back to some of your earlier journal entries and notice how you used punctuation. Choose one entry from the first or second week that you started your journal; correct and revise the punctuation of that journal entry.

Write one journal this week that discusses how your thinking about punctuation has changed . . . or not changed.

Skills Workshop

Worksheet 1. Colons and Dashes

Instructions: Place colons and dashes where needed in the following sentences; *also correct other types of errors*. Answers may vary as these punctuation marks are often interchangeable. (*Note*: See pages 448 - 449 for the key to these exercises.)

Incorrect: Call if u need me, i will support u 100 percent in this venture.

Corrected: Call if you need me: I will support you 100 percent in this venture.

Corrected: Call if you need me—I will support you 100 percent in this venture.

1. Jeremy suggested several changes add more personnel, start offering carry out, and remain open on Sundays but I disagree with him on all points.

2. Heres what u need to look out for; their Eastern branch office does not have a sales manager.

3. If you ask for a lower price even one that is not unreasonable they will not know how to handle your request.

4. Caution, do not use this equipment in temperatures below freezing.

5. Note, Fri is a holiday and r offices will be closed.

6. Sean refused to share the plan he simply wouldnt answer my questions.

7. These are the people you should interview, Eddie Stone Fred Harris and Bill Janulewicz.

8. All of them especially Bill Janulewicz are extremely knowledgeable of our products.

9. Remain positive, you do not yet know how they will respond to your offer.

10. I received a call from McCracken's CEO, yes their CEO, to join the marketing team.

Worksheet 2. Colons, Dashes, and Ellipses

Instructions: Place colons, dashes, and ellipses where needed in the following sentences. Note: Your answers may vary as these marks of punctuation are sometimes interchangeable.

Incorrect: Think about it, the answer will become apparent.

Corrected: Think about it . . . the answer will become apparent.

Corrected: Think about it—the answer will become apparent.

1. Scot said that we shouldn't worry …..the product research team will meet tomorrow.

2. Note the following, more people need to travel today but fewer people enjoy it.

3. The Mercer group became involved of their own accord I didn't invite them.

4. Follow your passions u will create a career that you enjoy.

5. I couldn't understand what John said, "The biggest seller is."

6. Send your résumé directly to the CEO he is expecting to hear from u.

7. Toni and Joe bought the company they are ecstatic.

8. You know what I mean things just aren't working out.

9. Keep your spirits up you will have another opportunity soon.

10. Read between the lines watch the body language.

Editing Workshop

Instructions: Revise the e-mail below. Look for all types of errors, including text abbreviations, and feel free to do a lot of cutting.

Dear professor,
I apoloogise for my recent absences. i have been very sick with a sore throat and fever. Monday i tried to attend class but i didn't know where the class was. I e-mailed u but never recived a responce. Last wednesday i wasn't sure if we had class because of the comming holiday. Marc and Alicia r in one of my other classes but neither of them attended tusday so i was unable to ask them. When i didn't recieve a e-mail back from u i went to a doctor's appiontment on wednesday. Thankfully i am feeling much better. I will be in class tommrow. If it is in a room other then our regular room please let me know. Thank You,

Note: See page 450 for the suggested revision to the above exercise.

Endnotes

1. William A. Sabin, *The Gregg Reference Manual*, Tenth Edition, McGraw-Hill/Irwin, Burr Ridge, 2005, page 52.
2. Daniel Goleman, *Emotional Intelligence*, Bantam Books, New York, 1995, page 268.
3. The Quotations Page, www.quotationspage.com/quotes/J_F_Kennedy>, accessed on January 24, 2008.
4. The Quotations Page, <http://quotationspage.com/quotes/Albert_Einstein>, accessed on January 25, 2008.
5. Victor Frankl, *Man's Search for Meaning*, Beacon Press, Boston, 2006, page xiv-xv.

15

Capitalization and Number Usage

Capitalization decisions can be confusing. Some words and titles sound official, so they simply *must* be capitalized, right? However, you may be surprised to learn that most of the time those official-sounding words and titles are not capitalized: they are not proper nouns. Instead of wasting time and energy guessing, this chapter gives you the information that you need to make most capitalization decisions.

Then there is number usage. When you stop to decide whether to spell out a number in words or to use numerals, you waste time. Knowing a few basic number rules makes a big difference in how you use numbers in your writing.

Let's start with capitalization and then work on number usage.

CAPITALIZATION

Many writers are naïve about capitalization. Instead of respecting the basics and staying safe, they capitalize words almost randomly. However, it is an easy problem to solve. Let's start with the following:

When in doubt, do not capitalize.

In other words, unless you know for sure that a word should be capitalized, leave the word in lower case.

Here are the two major categories of words that should be capitalized:

- Proper nouns
- First words of sentences, poems, displayed lists, and so on

The challenge then becomes knowing which words are proper nouns and which are common nouns. Let's start by taking a look at the difference between the two and then identifying some of the most common types of capitalization errors.

Proper Nouns and Common Nouns

To avoid capitalizing common nouns, you must first learn the difference between common nouns and proper nouns. The chart below helps illuminate some of the differences:

Proper Noun	Common Noun
John Wilson	name, person, friend, business associate
Wilson Corporation	company, corporation, business
Southlake Mall	shopping, stores, shops
New York	state, city
Italy	country

Words derived from proper nouns become proper adjectives and are also capitalized:

Proper Noun	Derivative or Proper Adjective
England	English language
Spain	Spanish 101
Italy	Italian cookware
French	French class

Names are proper nouns, and that includes the names of people as well as the names of places and things, such as the following:[2]

Titles of literary and artistic works	Chicago Tribune, the Bible
Periods of time and historical events	Great Depression
Imaginative names and nicknames	Big Apple
Brand and trade names	IBM, 3M, Xerox copier
Points of the compass	the North, the South, the Southwest *(when they refer to specific geographic regions)*
Place names	Coliseum, Eiffel Tower
Organization names	National Business Education Association
Words derived from proper nouns	English, South American
Days of the week, months, and holidays	Thanksgiving, Christmas, Chanukah

Articles, Conjunctions, and Prepositions

Not every word of a title is capitalized, and the types words in question are articles, conjunctions, and prepositions. Here's what to look for:

Articles:	the, a, an
Conjunctions:	and, but, or, for, nor
Prepositions:	between, to, at, among, from, over, and so on

Here are rules about capitalizing articles, conjunctions, and prepositions:

1. Capitalize any of these words when it is the first word of a title or subtitle.

2. Capitalize prepositions only when they are the first or last word of a title or subtitle. (However, this preference varies among sources, with some sources saying to capitalize prepositions when they consist of four letters; others, when they consist of five or more letters.)

Here are some examples:

The University of Chicago

Pride and Prejudice

Writing from the Core

First Words

As you have already seen, the *first word* is given special designation. Make sure that you capitalize the first word of each of the following:[3]

Sentences

Poems

Direct quotations that are complete sentences

Independent questions within a sentence

Items displayed in a list or an outline

Salutations and complimentary closings

Also capitalize the first word of a complete sentence that follows a word of caution or instruction, such as *Note* or *Caution.*

Hyphenated Terms

At times, you will need to determine how to capitalize hyphenated words, such as e-mail, long-term, up-to-date, and so on. Here are some guidelines:

- Capitalize parts of the hyphenated word that are proper nouns:

    If I receive your information by mid-December, you will qualify for the training.

- Capitalize the first word of a hyphenated word when it is the first word of the sentence, for example:

    E-mail is the preferred mode of communication.

    Mid-January is when the quarterly reports are expected.

- Capitalize each word of a hyphenated term used in a title (except short prepositions and conjunctions, as previously noted), for example:

Up-to-Date Reports	Mid-July Conference
E-Mail Guidelines	Long-Term Outlook

Let's look at titles and terms associated with organizations, for which capitalization decisions can also be challenging.

Organizational Titles and Terms

Most people believe that their job title is a proper noun, but professional titles are *not* proper nouns. Here are some rules to follow:

- Capitalize a professional title when it precedes the name.

- Do not capitalize a professional title when it follows the name.

- Capitalize organizational terms in your own company (but not necessarily other companies), such as the names of departments and committees.

Here are some examples:

Incorrect: John Smith, Vice President, will be meeting with the Finance Department.

Correct: John Smith, vice president, will be meeting with the Finance Department.

Correct: Vice President John Smith will be meeting with the Finance Department.

You may capitalize organizational terms from other companies to show special importance. In addition, the titles of high government officials are capitalized, for example:

The President had a meeting in the West Wing of the White House.

Finally, let's examine two types of capitalization errors that are so pervasive that they merit special attention.

Two Common Capitalization Errors

You will have come a long way with capitalization if you stop capitalizing words randomly and follow the rules discussed above. However, the following two common types of errors fit into a special class of their own.

Error No. 1: Leaving the pronoun *I* in lower case.

The personal pronoun *I* is a proper noun and should always be represented in upper case. Partly due to text messaging, the problem of leaving the personal pronoun *I* in lower case has escalated, for example:

Incorrect: A friend asked me if i could help, so i said that i would.

Correct: A friend asked if I could help, so I said that I would.

Whenever you use the pronoun *I*, capitalize it; and that includes its use in e-mail messages.

Error No. 2: Using all UPPER CASE or all lower case.

Another type of error that occurs, especially with e-mail, is typing in either all lower case or all upper case. Neither version is correct, using all upper case has earned the reputation that the writer is shouting. The truth is, the writer is not necessarily shouting. Most of the time, when writers use all caps, it is because they are unsure about writing decisions; putting the message in all caps (inaccurately) seems to be an easy way out.

When writers use all lower case, it often reflects a tradition within certain professional niches. For example, some computer professionals communicate primarily with other technical professionals, and they write to each other almost exclusively in lower case.

When communicating to professionals outside of their inner circle, these technical professionals sometimes continue to leave their words in lower case. For these professionals, adjusting to their audience is the key: Distinguish who is within your circle and who is not and then adapt accordingly.

Global Communication and the Rules

Most professional communication is now global communication: global communication involves speaking English with and writing English to those for whom English is a second language.

Global communication makes following the rules, such as the ones discussed throughout this book, critical for clear communication. That is because people for whom English is a second language find deviations from the rules difficult to understand. Using a second language according to the standard rules is hard enough, and adapting to the idiosyncrasies that result from misuse of any language adds another layer of confusion.

The rules create standards so that everyone can understand the meaning of the message, reducing confusion and misunderstanding among all readers. Following the rules is an important element of adapting to your audience. In addition, by writing correctly, you enhance your ability to communicate across borders and continents.

Practice 15.1

Capitalization

Instructions: In the following paragraph, correct errors in capitalization.

Next year the President of my Company will provide a Financial Incentive for all employees, and i plan to participate in it. Jack Edwards, Vice President of Finance, will administer the plan. Everyone in my Department is looking forward to having the opportunity to save more. A Pamphlet entitled, "Financial Incentives For Long-term Savings" will describe the plan and be distributed next Week. If the Pamphlet has not arrived by friday, i will check with the Vice President's office to find out the details.

Note: See page 450 for the key to the above exercise.

NUMBER USAGE

Many writers, unaware of number rules, do not even stop to consider how to represent numbers. Other writers, aware that rules exist but unsure of the details, seek every possible way to represent numbers, thinking that they will be right at least some of the time.

The only way to break the confusion is to learn the rules; and unfortunately, the rules can seem complex at times. For example, the first number rule states the following:

**Write numbers under ten as words,
but write numbers above ten as figures.**

After this basic rule, every additional rule is some form of exception to it. In fact, *The Gregg Reference Manual* states that all numbers can be represented as figures—including those under ten—when the writer wants the numbers to stand out.

The number rules are not that difficult to learn, and your only other option is to guess, which creates more confusion for you than it creates for your readers. However, when you do guess, at least represent numbers consistently—do not go back and forth, representing a number as a word in one place and then as a numeral in the next. Let's get started with the basics.

Basic Number Rules

The following list of ten basic number rules provides a foundation for making most decisions about how to display numbers.[2]

Rule 1: Numbers 1 through 10

Spell out numbers 1 through 10 within written text (unless displaying the numbers for quick reference); use numerals for numbers above 10.

For example:	I have ten reports to complete.
	Our department recognized 12 employees for providing excellent client service.

Rule 2: Numbers Beginning a Sentence

Spell out numbers beginning a sentence (however, avoid starting a sentence with a number whenever possible). If you start a sentence with a number, all numbers in that sentence must be spelled out.

For example: Sixteen new chairs and twelve new desks have arrived for offices on the fourth floor.

Rule 3: Related Numbers

Use the same form for related numbers within a sentence, with figures trumping words. In other words, if some numbers should be written in words (numbers under 10) and they are mixed with numbers that are above 10, write all numbers in figures.

For example: Bob Anderson brought 12 new individual clients as well as 5 new corporate accounts to our firm.

Rule 4: Unrelated Numbers

When two unrelated numbers come together, write the shorter number in words and the longer number in figures.

For example: Order 7 two-piece organizational units for the employees my department.

Rule 5: Indefinite Numbers

Write indefinite numbers, such as thousands or hundreds, in words.

For example: You say that you have hundreds of problems, but in reality you could list them on one hand.

Thousands of people support you.

Rule 6: Ordinal Numbers

Write ordinal numbers such as *first*, *second*, or *third*, and so on, in words.

For example: Lorraine lives on the fourteenth floor of the building at 900 North Lake Shore Drive.

Rule 7: Large Numbers

Numbers in the millions or higher can be written as a combination of figures and words if the number can be expressed as a whole number or as a whole number plus a simple fraction or a decimal amount.

For example: Our company extended their $1.5 million loan until April.

Rule 8. Fractions and Mixed Numbers

Write fractions as words with a hyphen between the numerator and denominator; write mixed numbers as figures.

For example: Mix one-half of the dry ingredients before adding any liquid.

Increase the amount of tomatoes to 2½ cups.

Rule 9. Percentages

Use figures for percentages and spell out the word *percent* unless the percentage is part of a table or technical material. Use the word *percentage* rather than *percent* when no number appears with it.

For example: Chicago had a 10 percent decrease in crime last year.

That lower percentage pleased the mayor.

Rule 10. Weights and Measures

Use figures for weights, measures, and other types of dimensions.

For example: If you can lose 10 pounds, you are a better person than I am.

The new room needs a carpet that is 10 feet by 15 feet.

In addition to these ten basic rules, dates and time have special guidelines, which we will look at next.

Dates and Time

Dates and time are commonly used in e-mail messages as well as other formal types of communication. Here are some basic guidelines:

- Use figures for dates and time on everything except formal invitations.

- Use the abbreviations a.m. and p.m. or the word *o'clock*, but not both.

- Spell out the names of days and months; in other words, do not abbreviate.

- For time on the hour, you may omit the :00 (unless you want to emphasize time on the hour).

- Use the ordinal ending for dates only when the day *precedes* the month.

Here are some examples:

Incorrect:	The meeting is scheduled for Sept. 17th at 5 PM.
Correct:	The meeting is scheduled for September 17 at 5 p.m.
Incorrect:	Will you be available at 8:30 AM on the sixteenth of this month?
Correct:	Will you be available at 8:30 a.m. on the 16th of this month?

Now let's review how to represent addresses and phone numbers.

Addresses and Phone Numbers

As with dates, parts of addresses should not be abbreviated. So before reviewing the rules for addresses and phone numbers, here is a guideline:

When in doubt, spell it out.

Abbreviate parts of addresses when space is tight or when you are following a specific system of addressing. However, do not abbreviate simply for the convenience of it.

Here are some rules for displaying addresses:

- Spell out parts of addresses: Do not abbreviate points of the compass such as *North* or *South* or words such as *avenue*, *street*, or *apartment*.

- Spell out street names *One* through *Ten*.

- Use figures for all house numbers except the number *One*.

- Add ordinal endings only when points of the compass (North, South, East, and West) are not included, for example: 1400 59th Street.

- Use two-letter state abbreviations.

- Leave one or two spaces between the two-letter state abbreviation and the zip code.

Here are some examples:

Mr. Alistair Cromby
One West Washington Avenue
St. Clair, MN 56080

Dr. Michael Jules
1214 79th Place, Suite 290
Chesterton, IN 46383

Mrs. Lionel Hershey
141 Meadow Lane South
Seattle, WA 92026

Ms. Lorel Lindsey
Associate Director
The Fine Arts Studio
500 North State Street, Suite 311
Chicago, IL 60611-6043

In general, the broadest part of an address is on the last line (the name of the country or the name of the city and state), as shown above and below.

Mr. Lucas M. Matthews
72 O'Manda Road
Lake Olivia, VIC 3709
AUSTRALIA

Pierluigi e Sylvia D'Amici
Via Davide No. 1
00151 ROMA
I T A L I A

On the next page, you will find a list of the two-letter state abbreviations.

Two-Letter State Abbreviations

Alabama	AL	Montana	MT
Alaska	AK	Nebraska	NE
Arizona	AZ	Nevada	NV
Arkansas	AR	New Hampshire	NH
California	CA	New Jersey	NJ
Colorado	CO	New Mexico	NM
Connecticut	CT	New York	NY
Delaware	DE	North Carolina	NC
District of		North Dakota	ND
Columbia	DC	Ohio	OH
Florida	FL	Oklahoma	OK
Georgia	GA	Oregon	OR
Guam	GU	Pennsylvania	PA
Hawaii	HI	Puerto Rico	PR
Idaho	ID	Rhode Island	RI
Illinois	IL	South Carolina	SC
Indiana	IN	South Dakota	SD
Iowa	IA	Tennessee	TN
Kansas	KS	Texas	TX
Kentucky	KY	Utah	UT
Louisiana	LA	Vermont	VT
Maine	ME	Virgin Islands	VI
Maryland	MD	Virginia	VA
Massachusetts	MA	Washington	WA
Michigan	MI	West Virginia	WV
Minnesota	MN	Wisconsin	WI
Mississippi	MS	Wyoming	WY
Missouri	MO		

Display phone numbers by using a hyphen or period between parts.

Examples: You can reach me at 312-555-1212.

              I left the message at 502.555.1212.

Practice 15.2

Numbers

Instructions: Make corrections to the way numbers are displayed in the following sentences.

Incorrect: Reggie sent 10 copies of the report, but I received only 5.

Corrected: Reggie sent ten copies of the report, but I received only five.

1.   We r meeting on Jan. 5 at 10 AM at our offices on Lake St.

2.   Call me on Mon. at (407) 555-1212.

3.   Alex lists his address as 407 S. Maple St., Hobart, Ind. 46368.

4.   We received 100s of calls about the job opening but only five résumés.

5.   Purchase 12 laptops but only seven new printers for our department.

Note: See page 450 for the key to the above exercise.

Recap

Below is a summary of the rules and guidelines that you have learned in this chapter.

Capitalize the following:

> ➤ The personal pronoun *I*.
>
> ➤ Proper nouns and their derivatives, such as *England* and *English*.
>
> ➤ The first words of sentences, poems, displayed lists, and so on.
>
> ➤ Titles that precede a name, such as *President Gerry Smith*.
>
> ➤ The names of departments within your own organization.

Basic guidelines for representing numbers are as follows:

> ➤ Spell out numbers 1 through 10; use numbers if you want them to stand out.
>
> ➤ Use figures for numbers above 10.
>
> ➤ If numbers above and below 10 are in a sentence, use figures.
>
> ➤ Use numbers with the word *percent*, as in 25 percent.
>
> ➤ Use the word *percentage* (rather than *percent*) when used without a number.

For dates, time, and addresses, do the following:

> ➤ Do not abbreviate: *When in doubt, spell it out.*
>
> ➤ Omit the :00 for time on the hour.
>
> ➤ Use a.m. and p.m. or o'clock, but do not use both.
>
> ➤ Use two-letter state abbreviations.

Writing Workshop

Activity A. Writing Practice

Instructions: Write a Personal Mission Statement

While most companies have mission statements that reflect their core values and purpose, many individuals also write their own personal mission statement.

Personal mission statements help individuals become more aware of what is important in their lives. By writing your own personal mission statement, you focus on your goals and prioritize your actions. In the process, you enhance the likelihood that you will achieve them.

Use the prompts below to begin your personal mission statement.

The achievement in my life that I am most proud of is . . .

Each day I will try to be . . .

The things I value most in life are . . .

The most important of these is . . .

Each day I will contribute to others by . . .

In the future, I hope my successes will include . . .

To achieve these goals, I plan to . . .

The most important thing in the world to me is . . .

Your mission statement will change over time; so if this exercise gives you insight, you may consider repeating it in the future.

Activity B. Journal

Instructions:

What did you learn about yourself as a result of doing the above exercise?

Are you following the 2 x 4 approach: writing two pages, four times a week?

Skills Workshop

Worksheet 1. Number Usage and Capitalization

Instructions: The following sentences have errors in number usage and capitalization as well as other topics that you have covered in earlier chapters. (*Note*: See pages 451 - 452 for the key to the exercises below.)

Incorrect: Meet me in the lobby at 5;30 PM on Fri.

Corrected: Meet me in the lobby at 5:30 p.m. on Friday.

1.   The supply company delivered 5 copiers and 7 fax machines.

2.   Ian, our new company Auditor, scheduled the meeting for Fri. Sept. 10 at 9AM.

3.   Send the information to Lester Ostrom, 1213 W. Astor Pl., Chic., Ill. 60610.

4.   Did you request twelve catalogs or only two?

5.   The new budget for our computer purchase is $1,500,000 million.

6.   We received 100s of calls, not 1000s as Jeffrey said.

7.   Did you say i should meet you for lunch today at 12 o'clock PM or on Mon.?

8.   Austin Roberts, Accounting Manager, gave me the instructions on how to complete my Taxes.

9.   Vice president Tomas O'Rourke has a background in Law.

10. If the requirements call for 5 postings on 3 different days, allow yourself at least two hours a day to get the work done.

11. We had a ten percent decrease in our heating bill but a 50% increase in our water bill.

12. The closet is five ft. by eight ft.

13. If i can assist you with ½ of the mailing, let me know.

14. Eleven of the participants have arrived, but the remaining 12 are late.

15. Meet me on the 14th floor at 3:30 PM o'clock this afternoon.

Worksheet 2: Punctuation, Capitalization, and Number Usage

Instructions: Make corrections as needed in the following sentences.

Incorrect: On Mon. we will meet in the hawthorn room on the 4th floor on Wed. we will meet in the Concord Rm. on the fifth fl.

Corrected: On Monday, we will meet in the Hawthorn Room on the fourth floor; on Wednesday, we will meet in the Concord Room on the fifth floor.

1. Many colleges are offering online Degrees and you should learn more about the opportunities you have for finishing your degree.

2. Do your research only attend a fully accredited online College or University.

3. If ½ or more of the course offerings are online the college's commitment to online learning is strong.

4. A friend of mine received her Doctorate online as a result she increased her income and her job opportunities.

5. A decade ago few Colleges offered classes online now 100s of Colleges and Universities offer classes online.

6. Some of the advantages of online learning include the following; you can attend classes in the comfort of your own Home make use of special support services and tutorials and learn at your own pace.

7. Online learning occurs in countries around the world and 1000s of students learn in Virtual Classrooms every day.

8. Though class size varies many classes limit the number of participants to twenty students.

9. One of the results of online learning is improved Writing Skills good writing skills will benefit u throughout your career.

10. Finishing your education is what's important get your Degree online or attend college at a local University.

Editing Workshop

Instructions: Identify and correct the errors in the following e-mail message. You will find a variety of errors, including errors in capitalization and number usage as well as punctuation.

Dear Suzie;

THANK YOU for asking for more information about my work history. For 5 yrs. i worked for Rapid Communications as an Associate Manager in the Customer Service Dept. Here's info about how to contact my former boss Jake Roberts, Human Resources Director:

Mr Jake Roberts
Human Resources Dir.
Rapid Com.
14 N. Ogden Rd.
Burlington Iowa   52601

I look forward to hearing from u. You can reach me at (209) 555-1212 anytime between 9:00 AM and 5 o'clock PM Mon. thru Fri. until the end of Aug.

Best Regards,

Sylvia Marina

Note: See pages 452 - 453 for the suggested revision to this exercise.

Endnotes

1. William A. Sabin, *The Gregg Reference Manual*, Tenth Edition, McGraw-Hill/Irwin, 2005.

2. Dona Young, *Business English: Writing for the Global Workplace*, McGraw-Hill Higher Education, Burr Ridge, 2008, page 208.

3. *Ibid.*, pages 212-213.

16

Quotation Marks, Apostrophes, and Hyphens

Quotation marks, apostrophes, and hyphens are minor marks of punctuation, but they occur frequently: using them correctly improves the quality of writing and enhances its credibility.

QUOTATION MARKS

The primary reasons for using quotation marks are as follows:[1]

1. Inserting a direct quote of three or fewer lines within the body of a document.
2. Identifying technical terms or coined expressions that may be unfamiliar.
3. Using words humorously or ironically.
4. Showing a slang expression or an intentionally misused word.

However, do not use quotation marks to make a word stand out, for example:

That is a really "good" idea.

In the above example, your reader will assume that you really do not mean the idea is *good* because the reader may assume you were being sarcastic. To avoid overuse of quotation marks, follow this motto:

When in doubt, leave quotations out.

Quotation Marks with Periods and Commas

One of the reasons that quotation marks confuse writers is that there are two basic ways to display them: the **closed style** and the **open style**. Here is the major difference between the two:

- **Closed style:**

    Place quotation marks on the outside of commas and periods.

- **Open style:**

    Place quotation marks on the inside of commas and periods.

Here are a few examples:

Closed:	Bill's exact words were, "That dog can't hunt."
	The president said that he wanted "the data," but which data?
Open:	Reginald described the situation as "grim but not hopeless".
	Terry instructed me to put the package in the "boot of the car", so I did.

If you live in the United States, use the closed style; if you live in Great Britain, use the open style. (This book applies the **closed style**.)

Quotation Marks with Semicolons and Colons

For semicolons and colons, *always* place the quotation marks on the inside of the semicolon or colon, for example:

Senior management wants us to "go the extra mile"; however, everyone seems to be burnt out already.

Bryan said, "George's bid is overpriced": Is that correct?

According to policy, "Distribution of funds can be made only before the 15th of the month"; therefore, your funds will be sent in 10 days.

Quotation Marks with Questions and Exclamations

When using quotation marks with a question mark or an exclamation point, determine whether the question or exclamation is part of the quote or the entire sentence, for example:

> Did Margarite say, "Rose is getting married next month"?

> Fred asked, "How do you know?"

> Margarite said, "Rose is getting married next month!"

> I just won "the grand prize"!

Short Quotes and Long Quotes

Display short quotations (three lines or fewer) with quotation marks, leaving the quote in the body of the paragraph. However, for quotations four lines or longer, do not use quotation marks; instead set off the quote from the body of your writing by indenting it by five spaces on each side.

Here is an example of a short quote:

> According to Campbell, "Protein, the most sacred of all nutrients, is a vital component of our bodies and there are hundreds of thousands of different kinds."[2] Different kinds of proteins play different roles in health and nutrition, and some of these are discussed.

Quotation within a Quotation

When you need to display a quotation within a quotation, use the single quotation mark (') for the inner quotation and the double quotation mark (") for the outer quotation, for example:

> Bob said, "I'm not going to 'insult' George by inviting him to the meeting."

Complete the following exercise using the closed quotation style.

Practice 16.1

Quotation Marks

Instructions: Place closed quotation marks where needed in the following sentences. (*Note:* See page 453 for the key to the exercise below.)

Incorrect: Beth's exact words were, "I'll be in Boston next week".

Corrected: Beth's exact words were, "I'll be in Boston next week."

1. My answer to your request is an enthusiastic "yes".

2. If you think that's a "good idea", the so do I!.

3. The code was "307A", not "370A".

4. All he wrote was, "Our dog can hunt".

5. If you call that "good timing", I don't know how to respond.

APOSTROPHES

The apostrophe (') is used for contractions and possessives. Possessives are a bit more complicated than contractions, so let's review possessives first.

Possessives

When a noun shows possession of another noun, use the apostrophe to show ownership. Regular nouns are made possessive as follows:

- For a singular possessive noun, place the apostrophe before the s ('s).

- For a plural possessive noun, place the apostrophe after the s (s').

- If a noun ends in an s, add an apostrophe and s ('s) or simply an apostrophe (').

Singular Possessive	Plural Possessive
the cat's whiskers	the cats' toys
the dog's scarf	the dogs' bones
Mary's books	my friends' books

Here are a few examples of names and other nouns ending in *s* and showing possession:

> Francis' new job *or* Francis's new job
>
> Mr. Jones' office *or* Mr. Jones's office

When pronunciation would sound awkward with the extra syllable, do not add the *s* after the apostrophe, as follows:

> Los Angeles' weather
>
> the witnesses' replies

Irregular nouns are a bit tricky: place the apostrophe before the s ('s) for both singular and plural possession:

Singular Possessive	**Plural Possessive**
the child's coat	the children's toys
the woman's comment	the women's association
a man's advice	the men's sporting event

The easiest way to work with plural possessives—whether regular or irregular—is to make the noun plural first and then show the possession.

To show joint possession, place the apostrophe after the second name, for example:

> Janet and Bob's car

To show individual possession, place the apostrophe after each name, for example:

> Janet's and Bob's cars

Next, let's look at a category of possessives that often goes unnoticed, inanimate possessives.

Inanimate Possessives

Possessives are easier to spot when a person possesses an object, such as *Bob's car*. However, an inanimate object, such as *wind* or *newspaper* can also show possession, for example:

the wind's force   the newspaper's headline

To know if a word shows possession, flip the phrase around. If you need to use the word *of*, in all likelihood the word shows possession, for example:

the headline of the newspaper	the newspaper's headline
the force of the wind	the wind's force
the ending of the play	the play's ending
the work of the day	the day's work
the cover of the book	the book's cover
the fender of the car	the car's fender

Now let's look at another common use of apostrophes: contractions.

Contractions

Some words, primarily verbs, can be shortened by omitting a few letters and using the apostrophe in their place, for example:

Verb	Contraction
will not	won't
cannot	can't
did not	didn't
should not	shouldn't

Contractions are acceptable for e-mail; however, avoid using contractions for formal or academic writing. One contraction that creates a lot of problems for writers is "it's." *It's* is the contraction for *it is* or *it has*. The possessive pronoun *its* has no apostrophe.

Practice 16.2

Apostrophes: Possessives and Contractions

Instructions: Make corrections where needed in the following sentences.

Incorrect: Its all in a days work.

Corrected: It's all in a day's work.

1. My supervisors report wont be ready until next week.

2. The weather report says its going to rain later, but I dont believe it.

3. Though its Junes responsibility, its in Jacks best interest to complete the task.

4. Dr. Jones office isnt located down the hall; its next to Dr. Raines.

5. If you tell me its Tess project, i'll adjust my expectations.

Note: See page 453 for the key to the above exercise.

HYPHENS

Here are some of the primary uses of hyphens:

1. To divide words.
2. To form group modifiers.
3. To display fractions and numbers above twenty-one.
4. To form certain prefixes and suffixes.

Let's take a look at using hyphens for each of these uses.

Word Division

Because computers have eliminated the need to divide words at the end of lines, here is the most important current principle about word division:

When dividing words, divide only between syllables.

If you are unsure of a word's syllabication, look it up: *When in doubt, check it out*. However, avoid dividing words whenever possible.

Compound Modifiers

Using hyphens for compound modifiers merits attention. Compound modifiers are formed when two adjectives come together to modify a noun jointly, for example:

long-term project   two-word modifiers

first-quarter report   short-term earnings

second-class service   first-class accommodations

When the modifier follows the noun, do not use a hyphen. In fact, that is one way to check usage, for example:

meetings that are high powered   high-powered meetings

information that is up to date   up-to-date information

a woman who is well dressed   a well-dressed woman

Another way to test if you need a hyphen is to check one word at a time to see if the combination makes sense; for example, the *long-term report* is neither a *long report* nor a *term report*. Both words together form one unit of meaning, which adding the hyphen accomplishes.

When two or more compound modifiers occur in sequence, use a suspension hyphen at the end of the first modifier and follow it with a space:

The short- and long-term prognoses are both excellent.

The 30- and 60-day rates are available.

Now let's take a look at compound numbers.

Numbers

Compound numbers from twenty-one to ninety-nine are hyphenated. Here are a few examples:

thirty-three   forty-nine   seventy-three

So the next time that you write a check, display your compound numbers correctly!

Also display fractions standing alone as words, and use a hyphen:

one-half   two-thirds   one-quarter

You also need to use a hyphen with some prefixes; so let's take a brief look.

Prefixes

Rules about prefixes can be complicated, but here are a few points about common uses of hyphens with prefixes:

- Use a hyphen after the prefix *self*, for example:

  self-confidence   self-esteem   self-employed

- Use a hyphen after the prefix *re* when the same spelling could be confused with another word of the same spelling but with a different meaning: [2]

I re-sent the papers.	I resent your comment.
He will re-sign the contract.	I will resign immediately.
Sue will re-lease her car.	Sue will release her car.

- Use a hyphen after a prefix that is attached to a proper noun, as follows:

ex-President Carter	trans-Atlantic flight
pro-American policy	pre-Roman period

Work on the practice below, applying the principles you have just learned.

Practice 16.3

Hyphens

Instructions: Make corrections as needed in the following sentences to show correct use of hyphens.

Incorrect: The short term progress is good.

Corrected: The short-term progress is good.

1. Your first class treatment has impressed all of us.

2. The finance department approved one half of our budget.

3. The short and long term outlooks are quite different.

4. Twenty five people attended the conference.

5. Do you have funding for your 30 and 60 day payment schedules?

(*Note*: See page 454 for the key to the above exercise.)

Recap

Below is a summary how to use quotation marks, apostrophes, and hyphens.

> ➤ Use quotation marks with closed punctuation as follows:
>   - Place periods and commas inside of quotation marks.
>   - Place semicolons and colons outside of quotation marks.
>   - Place question marks and exclamation marks based on the meaning of the sentence.
> ➤ Use the apostrophe to show possession:
>   - With singular nouns, use an apostrophe plus *s*: *cat's meow*.
>   - With plural nouns, use an apostrophe after the *s*: *dogs' bones*.
>   - With inanimate objects, use an apostrophe, as in the *wind's force*.
>   - For joint ownership, place the apostrophe after the second noun: *Reggie and Grey's vacation*.
>   - To show individual ownership, place the apostrophe after each noun: *Janet Sue's and Dinkie's cars*.
> ➤ Use hyphens as follows:
>   - In group modifiers, such as *first-quarter report*.
>   - With numbers *twenty-one* through *ninety-nine*.
>   - For certain prefixes, such as *self-confident*.
>   - For words that would otherwise be confused, such as *re-sent*.

Writing Workshop

Activity A. Writing Practice

Instructions: What is listening?

Write a short paper on the topic of listening, defining what effective, active, and engaged listening is and what it is not. Before you begin to write, discuss the topic with a partner. Then mind map your response, and use major topics from your mind map to create a page map. Spend about a twenty minutes composing your response, and then another five minutes editing and revising your paper.

Activity B. Journal

Instructions: What do you value most in your life?

As a follow up to writing your personal mission statement, list the five things that you value most, such as education, secure finances, family, health, and so on. Before moving to the next step, force yourself to rank order your list.

Next, identify how much time and effort you are devoting to the things you value most. For example, if you value health, what are you doing (or not doing) to ensure good health. Finally, identify if there is an incongruence or inequality between what you value in life and how you spend your time and money. If you are not committing the time and money to the things and people that you value, what does this mean?

Skills Workshop

Worksheet 1. Quotations, Apostrophes, and Hyphens

Instructions: Use closed punctuation style as you place quotations as well as apostrophes and hyphens where needed in the following sentences. (*Note:* See pages 454 - 455 for the key to the following activities.)

Incorrect: Did you say that you would go "the extra mile?"

Corrected: Did you say that you would go "the extra mile"?

1. Margarets report is a first class example of what we need.

2. Bob asked, "may I receive a copy of the Barker proposal"?

3. If you can prove "that dog can hunt", well sign on to the "dotted line".

4. A one day workshop would help our part time staff.

5. After I rejected their "proposal", Mels response was "great".

6. Whats next on the agenda for our mid week meeting?

7. When I said "the games over", I was referring to Bills role.

8. A full time position is open in our accounting department.

9. A months worth of invoices are sitting on my desk.

10. You can use Jans office until the first floor conference room is free.

Worksheet 2. Review of Commas, Semicolons, Apostrophes, and Hyphens

Instructions: Place commas, semicolons, apostrophes, and hyphens (and anything else that is needed) in the following sentences, for example:

Incorrect: Janes answer was incomplete but no one pointed that out.

Corrected: Jane's answer was incomplete, but no one pointed that out.

1. Our brokers message got lost in the shuffle so I had to find his number on the Internet.

2. When I use the term "fixin to" it means that Im ready to go do something.

3. Do you have any favorite colloquial terms Sasha?

4. Call to see if their account executive is available, if hes not dont leave a message.

5. Lets go to the second hand shop to pick up supplies for our camping trip.

6. Mandy my new sales representative called about our "delay".

7. The short and long term projections will be available after 3 PM today.

8. Its been a long day already and one half of my work is yet to be done.

9. Enclose your check in the postage paid envelope and send it to us by Friday.

10. Sandros half baked idea was a hit at our departments meeting.

Editing Workshop

Instructions: Edit and revise the paragraph below. Look for all types of errors.

Trusts a important element of friendship. If you cant trust friends then whats really the point of being around them. Friends are they're to support you in everything that you do. They can tell you that they dont agree, but should always support you. Loyal and trustworthy friends are with you to the end and they should be treated just like family. If you learn and grow with someone, someone that you allow your feelings to open up and you can trust and beginning to share and enjoy things with. They are there threw the good times but they are there for the bad times also. A real friend understands what your going through even before you even tell them. A good friendship lasts for a very long time sometimes a life time.

Note: See page 455 for the suggested revision to this exercise.

Endnotes

1. Dona Young, *Business English: Writing for the Global Workplace*, McGraw-Hill Higher Education, Burr Ridge, 2008, p. 327.
2. T. Colin Campbell and Thomas M. Campbell II, *The China Study*, Bendella Books, Dallas, 2004, p. 29.
3. William A. Sabin, *The Gregg Reference Manual*, Tenth Edition, McGraw-Hill/Irwin, Burr Ridge, 2005, p. 2

Quick Guide to Academic Writing

Though all of the principles in this book relate to academic writing in a general way, academic writing merits specific discussion. This chapter and the next two chapters give you insight into how to adapt your writing as your academic career progresses.

Academic writing is a broad and varied topic: every discipline has its own culture, and writing at the undergraduate level differs somewhat from writing at the graduate level. However, in important aspects, academic writing is no different from other types of writing: you shape your writing for purpose and audience, applying conventions for consistency and ease of communication.

Academic writing involves research and citation. Therefore, the two chapters that follow this one are dedicated to those topics. The Quick Guide to Research gives you insight into how to interpret research to judge its credibility and scope, and the Quick Guide to Citation shows you how to apply conventions for various reference styles. These chapters give you a set of expectations and criteria on which to base your decisions. Use this information to make smooth and confident transitions as you progress through your academic writing experiences.

However, be aware that writing skills are a bit fickle: when you enter a new genre—that is, when you start writing in a new field—you are likely to feel as if you are a novice all over again. In other words, though you have built solid skills, you need to take time to adapt to different types of writing, regardless of how strong your current skills are.

Even though entering a new field or doing a new type of writing is somewhat like starting all over again, the learning curve is shorter: you will re-enter your comfort zone much more quickly the second (or third or fourth) time around.

Modes of Writing

Beginning academic writers practice their skills by writing essays, summaries, and analyses, which prepare the way for arguments and research papers. Before tackling an assignment, make sure that you understand the purpose of your assignment. Otherwise, you may write an exceptional paper, but one that does not meet your professor's criteria.

Writing in academic disciplines fills many purposes, such as writing to inform, to analyze events and processes, to propose solutions, to examine varied concepts or viewpoints, to narrate events, and to argue positions. Academic writing strives for clarity and follows a traditional format in which the writer:

- Offers a central idea through a clear introduction,

- Develops the idea through well-supported body paragraphs, and

- Provides resolution in a conclusion.

For the sake of analysis, most writing falls into one or more of the following three categories: **informative**, **expressive**, or **persuasive**. If your assignment calls for an argument (which is persuasive), and instead you write an exceptional summary (which is informative), your grade is not likely to reflect your efforts.

Informative writing analyzes data and summarizes information: facts, decisions, positions, questions, actions, and so on. Informative writing conveys complex ideas in an objective way.

Expressive writing is often creative and aims to reach the reader at a feeling or an emotional level. Forms of expressive writing include journals, memoirs, poems, songs, screenplays, novels, and short stories (fiction or nonfiction).

Academic writing generally refers to scholarly works: if you find yourself emoting in your papers or essays, edit out your feelings. In other words, in academia, the place for expressive writing is in your journals and blogs. (And a word of caution: be selective about what you post online, as your words may follow you throughout your career, costing you credibility and opportunity.)

Persuasive writing aims to influence the reader and, at times, argues a position: the writer attempts to bring the reader to agree with his or her position. Most advanced academic writing is persuasive and adheres to a traditional format in the form of an **argument**.

Argumentation has a formal structure that appeals to logic and reason. When writing an argument, use evidence to develop a position that leads logically to a conclusion.

However, every "story" has at least two sides; and at some point, a convincing argument must evaluate the strengths of the opposing view or views. Finally, the writer must provide evidence to show the opposition's weaknesses or flaws, revealing how the opposing view is inferior.

In contrast, some types of persuasive writing do not argue a point. Your aim may be to show only one side of a topic, convincing your reader to think the way that you do or persuading the reader to take action about an idea, product, or service. Persuasive writing uses reason, taps into the reader's emotions and, at times, broaches ethics.

In your academic career, you will write many essays, so let's take a look at how to develop a strategy to respond to essay questions.

Essay Questions

Essays prepare you for writing academic papers that will ultimately define your achievements.

For the best results, spend time before you start writing your response to develop a strategy: outline your response or do a mind map. You will not have time to write a draft and re-copy your answer; therefore, build in time to edit and proofread your essay. In fact, you will achieve the best results by practicing timed essays, adapting to the stress and adjusting your expectations.

The following key words indicate how to shape an effective response:

Analyze:	Break into parts and show how they relate to the whole.
Argue:	Give reasons for or against. Assess the strength of evidence on both sides, using specific examples and other criteria to back up your points.
Comment on:	Write about main issues but avoid personal opinion.

Compare:	Show the similarities and the differences. Is one more effective than the other?
Contrast:	Show only the differences. Are the differences significant? Is one preferable over the other?
Describe:	Write about a subject in detail, giving the main characteristics and features. Give enough detail so that your reader can develop a visual image.
Define:	Give the exact meaning of something.
Discuss:	Write about a subject in detail, giving reasons and examples.
Evaluate:	Assess and give your opinion about something: does it work or not? Is it important or not? Are there gaps? Use evidence to support your judgment.
Explore:	Examine thoroughly from various viewpoints.
Illustrate:	Give details, examples, and evidence.
Justify:	Give evidence—show why a conclusion was reached; answer objections.
Summarize:	Give the main points only; omit details and examples.

As you saw earlier in this book, conjunctions are transition words, and they signal the reader about how to interpret the words that follow them. Here are some words and phrases that signal transitions for your reader:

Compare:	in the same way, in a similar fashion, likewise, as well as
Contrast:	however, in contrast, on the other hand, on the contrary, conversely, otherwise, nevertheless, still, yet, instead, although, while, but, even though
Cause and Effect:	as a result, consequently, thus, therefore, for this reason, and so
Illustrate:	for example, for instance, hence, in general, thus, mostly, specifically, to illustrate

Show results:	fortunately, unfortunately, consequently, as usual, of course, in fact, even more important, above all
Summarize:	finally, in brief, in closing, in summary, as a result, thus, therefore, hence, in short
Sequence:	first, second, third, finally, meanwhile, in the meantime, to begin with
Show time:	currently, earlier, immediately, in the future, in the meantime, in the past, later, meanwhile, previously
Conclude:	finally, in conclusion, in summary

As you give your essay a final edit, add these and other words to show transitions, making it easier for your reader to follow your line of thought.

Another element of academic writing is viewpoint.

Viewpoint and Voice

As you recall, viewpoint relates to pronoun usage and emanates from one of the following points of view: first person, second person, or third person; singular or plural.

You may be comfortable writing in the first person (I, we) or second person (you); however, most academic writing occurs in the third person. For example, when you are summarizing an article, you are not speaking from *your* point of view; you are speaking from the *author's* point of view.

Let's say that you are writing a paper summarizing a theory by "George Alcott" about "neutrons." You will be writing from the third person singular point of view when you discuss "Alcott," and you will be writing from the third person plural point of view when you discuss "neutrons":

Alcott argues that neutrons exist . . .

Alcott further concludes . . .

He maintains . . .

Neutrons remain a viable . . .

When referring to the author of a study, book, or article, use that author's first and last name for the first reference, and then use only the author's last name for successive references. (And by the way, *never* refer to the author by first name only.)

Notice that you are not speaking directly to the reader, but instead you are speaking about the topic and what the author says. You are also not giving your personal feelings or beliefs about the topic. You are discussing points that you think that the reader will find of interest, which connects you to the reader in an indirect way, not in a direct way.

As a result, avoid using pronouns such as *I* and *you* in academic papers, unless you are writing the response as part of a summary-response essay. When you write the summary, stay in the third person viewpoint; however, when you write your response, feel free to use the first person singular *I* viewpoint.

If you find yourself speaking from a personal viewpoint in an academic paper, take special care to edit out your personal opinions unless, once again, your views are part of a response.

As a result of not speaking from a personal voice, writers commonly use passive voice, and passive voice is widely accepted in academic writing. This stand may sound somewhat contrary to what you learned in earlier chapters about avoiding passive voice. However, continue to do what you can to write in a clear and simple style, avoiding nominals whenever feasible.

Extensive use of passive writing can be found among scientific writing. However, even scientists are turning to a more concise, active style, relying on the passive voice to describe how an experiment was conducted, but otherwise applying the active voice.[1]

Be aware of the voice that you use: even with academic writing use simple constructions for readability, keeping your writing clear and to the point. Rest assured, you will still sound intelligent, and even esteemed professors appreciate receiving papers that are readable.

Verb Signals

As you edit, make special effort to use strong verbs to signal an author's position. Referring back to the previous example with "Alcott," (page 325), the last thing you would want to do is use "Alcott states" over and over again.

Here are some strong signal verbs to add variety to your writing:

admits	creates	organizes	remarks
argues	denies	observes	reports
asserts	emphasizes	persuades	solves
charges	expresses	points out	shows
claims	maintains	promotes	speculates
complains	finds	proposes	states
concedes	implies	proves	stresses
concludes	insists	refutes	suggests
conducts	interprets	reinforces	summarizes
contends	justifies	rejects	supports

Notice that the above verbs are listed in the third person singular, which is the *–s* form, the most common viewpoint of academic writing.

Verb Tenses

Verb tense is used slightly differently in academic writing than writing in real time. For example:

- You could be citing research that was conducted decades ago and still make a comment such as, "Alcott *concludes* . . . ."

- As you write a description of your paper, stay in the present tense: instead of saying "this paper will explore . . . ," instead say, "this paper explores . . . ."

In a literature review, if the discussion is of past events, stay within the chosen tense. Use past tense, such as "productivity increased" to describe the results. However, report *your* conclusions in the present tense, such as "the outcomes of the pilot indicate . . . ."

Here are some points to consider: [2]

- When emphasizing the findings of research, use the present tense; for example:

  o Jones shows . . .

- When emphasizing how the author conducted the research, use the past tense; for example:

  o Jones surveyed 20 participants . . .

- When contrasting research from different periods, use the past tense for older research and present tense for current research; for example:

  o Martin (2002) supported Jones' findings that training is a worthwhile investment for companies in transition.

- When describing situations that are conditional (which involve modals such as *would* or *could*), use the subjunctive mood; for example:

  o If the pilot *were* not conducted on site, the results *would* differ.

Use verbs to create smooth transitions among past, present, and future events. When you edit, screen your use of verb tense.

Basic Structure for Academic Papers

Academic papers follow the general format of introduction, body, and conclusion. In addition to papers, presentations follow a similar format.

Each part is described on the chart that follows.

Basic Structure for Academic Papers

INTRODUCTION

In your introduction, state your purpose, making it relevant to your audience.

- Give an overview of the topic.
- Connect your topic to your audience.
- Pose questions about your topic:

  What am I writing about and why?

  What is my general purpose . . . my specific purpose?

  What are my main points?

  Who are my readers?

  How can I shape my writing for my audience?

BODY

In the body of your paper, provide evidence. Focus on key points and give concrete examples; avoid generalizations not substantiated by fact.

- Break your topic into component parts.
- Provide evidence / examples / explanation.
- Cover all main points thoroughly.

CONCLUSION

In your conclusion, provide resolution for the problem that you are addressing. Answer the questions that you may have posed in the introduction, drawing conclusions for your reader.

Finally, make sure that your conclusion sounds fresh, glancing forward to next steps, if relevant.

If you use anything more complicated than introduction / body / conclusion as a framework, do not be obvious about it. For example, many students have successfully mastered the traditional 5-paragraph essay. This framework is an excellent tool; however, if you use it as a pattern for your essays, view it as "training wheels."

As a writer, you ultimately need to find your own stride and speak from your own voice. Most topics cannot be plugged into tidy frameworks and still express an authentic perspective. Writing at its best is messy; and when writers clean up their work as they edit and revise, they do not seek parallel structure at the level of idea, insight, or concept.

A tool that you can use to help structure your ideas is the *peer model* described below. Use the model in a loose fashion to stay focused on the elements that you need to provide for your readers.

The *PEER* Model

The **peer model** helps you look beyond "introduction, body, and conclusion," so that you focus on the purpose of each part. Use the model is a memory tool as well as a self-check to ensure that you have developed all relevant aspects of your essay or paper.

If you loosely apply the peer model as you compose, your content will be somewhat structured before you revise.

P	What is your **purpose**? What **points** are you making and why are they relevant?
E	What **evidence** demonstrates your main points? What are the facts and details?
E	What **explanation** or **examples** do your readers need to understand the evidence and its significance?
R	How can you **resolve** your thesis for your readers? What points do you need to **recap**? What are your conclusions and **recommendations**?

When you are composing, use these parts as side headings to rough out your ideas. When you are revising, evaluate whether you have developed your topic adequately with specific evidence and examples.

Now let's review some guidelines at how to shape an introductory paragraph for an academic paper.

Introductory Paragraph

The type of introductory paragraph that you write depends largely on the type of paper that you are writing. (In Chapter 1, you reviewed how to write a thesis or purpose statement; and in Chapter 3, you reviewed how to write cohesive and coherent paragraphs and use transitions.)

In an introductory paragraph, state your purpose and give an overview of your paper. In addition, you may wish to pose questions about your topic to awaken your reader's curiosity, use a quotation to draw interest, or include another sort of attention-getter to engage your reader.

When you are writing a summary of another writer's work, give a complete reference in the introductory paragraph. For example, include the author's first and last name, the name of the article or book, and its purpose. The following is one possible template to use:

> In Marcus Jones' article entitled "Facebook Addiction,"
> Smith argues (or asserts or reveals) that egocasting is
> more prevalent than authentic communication.

Your introductory paragraph is one of the most important paragraphs of your paper or essay: first impressions make a difference. If the reader is immediately engaged, he or she will look to confirm a good impression while reading the remainder of the work. However, the opposite is also true. An unfavorable initial impression leaves the reader looking to confirm his or her original reaction.

Many writers find writing an introduction a difficult way to start the process and instead work through the body and conclusion first. Without giving too much thought, you might not see the value of this approach.

However, since the introduction gives an overview of your paper, an introduction is naturally easier to write once you have developed your line of thought. By writing your introduction as a last step, you can incorporate the insight that you gained as you worked through the body and conclusion of your paper.

Latin Terms Apropos for Academic Writing

A few years back, Latin terms played a major role in academic citation. Even though Latin terms no longer play such a major role in citation, they are still used in academic writing.

The following are a few of the Latin terms that you will come across:

e.g.	*exempli gracia*: for example, for instance
et al.	*et allii*: and others
	When listing only one author for a work with multiple authors, use *et al.* to indicate other names were omitted.
etc.	*et cetera:* and the others; and other things
ibid.	*ibidem*: in the same place
	When citing the same source consecutively use *ibid.* directly under the citation which gives the author's name (or other identifying information).
i.e.	*id est*: that is; in other words
[sic]	so, thus, in this manner
	The term *sic* is placed within brackets to indicate the error which occurs in a text was made by the original author, not the current writer. (Brackets [ ] are also used around words added to another's quotation.)

Though academic writing may employ Latin terms, avoid using Latin abbreviations in other types of writing, such as business writing. In fact, substituting a term such as "among others" instead of using "etc." gives your writing a smoother style, even in academic writing.

Since professionals need to adapt their writing for various domains, let's look at the differences between academic writing and business writing.

Academic Writing vs. Business Writing

Whereas academic writing is highly formal, business writing is less formal, often labeled as professional writing.

In academic writing, process is critical. In fact, process is as important as product; and at times, more important: defining for readers how a study was conducted contributes to its credibility. In contrast, in business writing, data is almost always summarized as concisely as possible: the results are important, not the process. In business, the details about how a writer arrives at outcomes are considered background thinking that merits editing out.

Business writing is primarily informative, with an underlying persuasive element. At times, business writers aim to persuade their clients to think about their product or service in a specific way, especially in sales and marketing. However, business writing rarely uses argumentation—even when it comes to marketing.

Business writers apply visual persuasion to informative writing, using formatting, bullet points, and numbering to get their points across. Visual persuasion presents key ideas so that they are instantly visible, making it easy for a reader to understand the message. The easier a message is to understand, the easier it is for the reader to respond.

In contrast, academic writing does not necessarily incorporate visual persuasion. For example, American Psychological Association (APA) formatting requirements do not even allow special formatting features such as bolding.

In business writing, the context of the situation defines the problem and the "players." When you write in business, you are writing as one human being to another, connecting on a personal level. Readers expect you to speak from your own voice and even use niceties at times.

In academic writing, formality establishes a tone that contributes to the audience's ability to connect to the writing and the writer. The formality of academic writing gives readers shared expectations about quality and credibility. The formality of academic writing sets the tone that builds acceptance for your work.

Since business writing is less formal, feel free to use contractions in e-mail and business letters. However, for formal academic writing, avoid using contractions. As you can see, adapting to a genre aids you in shaping your writing to meet your readers' expectations.

Recap

Academic writing requires that you write about topics for their merit or someone else's requirement, and not necessarily your own interest. Therefore, in your academic career, you will write many essays and papers about topics that you do not find intrinsically interesting.

If you can embrace this requirement rather than resist it, writing becomes less stressful. In addition, by writing about a variety of topics, you become a much more versatile writer and thinker (and possibly a more well-rounded human being).

As you have seen, you can use many structural elements to ensure that your academic writing meets the requirements and expectations of your audience.

Here are some of the points stressed in this chapter:

➢ Understand your assignment before you start writing.

➢ Write in the third person singular and/or plural for most academic papers.

➢ Use verbs as signals.

➢ Use conjunctions and transition words to bring your reader's thinking along with yours.

➢ Follow a traditional format: present your central idea through a clear introduction, develop the idea through well-supported body paragraphs, and provide resolution in a conclusion.

➢ Allow time to edit your work, even when your writing is timed.

Skills Workshop

Instructions: Select an essay or paper that you wrote previous to reading this chapter, and analyze your paper for content and structure.

As an alternative or follow-up, exchange papers with a peer and complete the following analysis on each other's papers.

Content

What mode of writing was applied: informative, expressive, persuasive, or a combination? Please explain.

What was the original question? Did the paper answer that question effectively? Please explain.

Structure

What was effective about each part of the paper? What could the author do to improve each part?

- Introduction
- Body
- Conclusion

Style

Comment on the author's use of each of the following:

- Signal Verbs
- Point of View
- Transition Words

Format

Comment on the format of the document. Did the author follow basic formatting guidelines to produce a document that made good use of white space and other formatting features?

Endnotes

1. Marc E. Tischer, "Scientific Writing Booklet," Department of Biochemistry and Molecular Biophysics, University of Arizona, <www.biochem.arizona.edu/marc/sci-writing>, accessed July 2009.

2. *Concise Rules of APA Style*, American Psychological Association, Washington, DC, 2005, p. 9.

Quick Guide to Research

At a minimum, you cite research in the academic papers that you write. At some point in your career, you are also likely to conduct your own research. As you may already know, research should never be taken at face value: the more you understand research, the better prepared you are to interpret others' findings and to conduct your own.

Academic writing promotes intellectual reasoning validated by research while discrediting mere opinion, unsupported assumption, and over-reaching generalization. However, research comes in all shapes and sizes, and not all research is equal: research can become tainted for various reasons, including poor design, researcher bias, or any number of other intervening variables.

One of the most important qualities of scholarship is keeping an open mind. And all scholars—experienced and novice alike—are susceptible to mistaking theory for fact. "Facts" that were proven through research yesterday may not be facts today—as mankind extends its knowledge, some facts fall by the wayside. Therefore, even theories proven through the best research are true only to the extent that current knowledge confirms their accuracy. As Alfred North Whitehead once said, "Knowledge is like fish; it doesn't keep."

In addition, all theory has limits. At best, a proven theory illuminates only a small part of our total reality. In *The Republic*, the ancient Greek philosopher Plato argued that humans glimpse only shadows of reality; pure reality is evasive. So when discussing theories, never take them so seriously that you confuse them with a reality that may not yet be totally understood. All any theory can do—even an important one—is make one small part of reality more accessible than it was without the theory.

Another philosopher, Friedrich Nietzsche, is attributed to saying, "Insanity if repeating the same behavior but expecting a different result." In response, research enlightens mankind and intervenes in unproductive behavior, leading to educated choice: good research applied in the right way enriches life and helps alleviate human suffering.

There are two basic types of research: **quantitative** and **qualitative.** Here is a brief definition of each:

- **Quantitative research** collects numerical data to explain, predict, and/or control phenomena of interest.

- **Qualitative research** collects narrative data to gain insight into phenomena of interest.

Let's take a look at the qualities of each type of research, starting with quantitative research.

Quantitative Research

Quantitative research uses numbers to interpret and control phenomena. The phenomena in question could be anything of interest, such as a new product, a pharmaceutical drug, a method of training, and so on.

Quantitative research involves predictability: did an event happen by chance or does a causal relationship exist? To determine probability, research starts with a question, which when turned into a statement can become a *hypothesis*:

- A **hypothesis** is an explanation that can be tested.

For example, if the question is "Do customers prefer good service?" The hypothesis could read "Customers do prefer good service."

Researchers use probability theory (a branch of statistics) to test a hypothesis to determine if a causal relationship exists. According to probability theory, a researcher can prove the *unlikelihood* of an occurrence happening due to chance, but not the likelihood.

Therefore, to conduct research, a researcher needs to nullify the hypothesis, negating the positive statement. As a **null hypothesis**, our example would become "Customers do not prefer good service." If we surveyed 100 customers and they all preferred good service, we could reject our null hypothesis with a 100 percent level of probability.

When the probability level (usually preset at 95 or 99 percent) shows that our null hypothesis can be rejected, our hypothesis becomes acceptable: the higher the probability, the stronger the correlation. (You can find a statistical table that lists probability levels in any statistics book.)

To identify predictability, quantitative research often employs the **scientific method** to research designs that include a control group and an experimental group.

For example, let's say you were in a composition class in which the instructor wanted to test a new method for teaching writing skills. The researcher would write a hypothesis theorizing the expectations from the study. The hypothesis could be stated as follows:

Hypothesis: The experimental method improves writing skills.

Then the hypothesis would be turned into a null hypothesis stating that differences were *not* expected:

Null Hypothesis: The experimental method does not improve writing skills.

The experimental design would include at least two classes, with one class using the traditional method and the other class using the new or experimental method.

1. Both classes would take a **pretest** to measure current skill level.

2. Each class would follow a specified curriculum: one would learn by the experimental method; the other, the traditional method.

3. After a specified time, each class would take the **posttest**.

4. Pre- and posttest results would be tabulated and analyzed.

If the experimental group scored significantly higher, statistical tables would determine if the differences occurred due to chance or were a result of the treatment. (Of course, the research design would be more detailed than what is given here, but these are the basics.)

The sciences and medicine rigorously apply quantitative research, but education and the social sciences as well as business and economics also use quantitative research.

Qualitative Research

Qualitative research relates to gathering information, often through surveys and questionnaires.

This type of research is more common in business applications; through surveys and opinion polls, qualitative research identifies beliefs and opinions. Business uses qualitative research to adapt to the needs of clientele, make marketing decisions, and develop new products.

Qualitative research does not seek a cause-effect relationship but instead simply seeks to identify the current state of a specific topic. In the example above about writing skills improvement, the researcher could design a qualitative survey that asks students for their reactions to what they learned and how they learned. (For example, what improvements have you made in your writing?) Of course, this data could not be considered causal, as it would be purely subjective.

Business relies on qualitative research done through focus groups, questionnaires, and interviews. Many companies design products based on consumer opinion, and businesses change their policies based on customer reaction. Though qualitative research cannot be tested and rigidly scrutinized the way quantitative research can, qualitative research is valuable as long as its limits are respected.

Although researchers can also put qualitative research through "number crunching," the research designs are more simple in comparison to those that determine cause-effect relationships.

If qualitative research is repeated, it will not necessarily get the same results. For example, if a news organization runs a poll to see who voters support in an upcoming election, the results can change from week to week. Another example of qualitative research would be asking consumers the three to five most important factors they consider in buying a new car. This data could change based on geographic regions and economic conditions.

In other words, qualitative research is not necessarily reliable, so let's look at what *reliable* means as applied to research.

Reliability and Validity

The terms *reliability* and *validity* are basic to understanding the quality of research.

- **Reliability** refers to whether a researcher will find the same results again if an experiment is repeated.

- **Validity** refers to whether an experiment tests what it is supposed to test.

To understand reliability and validity, let's get back to the study about customer satisfaction. If a researcher found that the first sample of 100 customers preferred good service, the same test would be run two, three, or more times on other samples to see if the same results were received. If the results were replicated, they would be reliable.

To assess validity, questions on the survey would be tested to verify if the questions actually revealed customer satisfaction and good customer service.

Here are examples of how these two terms are used:

- Our research results are *reliable*: we are confident that you can test a larger population and get the same results.

- The questions on our survey have been tested extensively and have been proven to be *valid*.

- When research results are *reliable* and *valid*, they can be reproduced and used with confidence.

In addition to reliability and validity, another critical factor is credibility.

Credible Research

Regardless of the type of research, the primary goal of all research, quantitative or qualitative, is to obtain unbiased, objective results.

- Credible research does *not* take a position and then seek proof to confirm it.

- Credible research asks a question and then objectively evaluates evidence, with the data determining the conclusions.

The key to valid research starts with an open mind about a topic. A researcher may have a hunch or gut feeling (which may be the catalyst for the research); but to be valid, the research itself must remain objective to demonstrate unbiased outcomes.

Also, do not take "facts" proven through research at face value. To challenge research findings, examine if the research has been contaminated. Here are the types of questions to ask:

- Could intervening variables (people, things, or events) have interfered with the research, leading to inaccurate results?

- Were the samples (people surveyed or items examined) an accurate representation of the population being studied?

- Was the researcher biased in any way?

- Could a profit motive be involved? Who paid for the research?

Even theories proven through the best quantitative research are true only to the extent that current knowledge confirms their accuracy; they are not final truths.

As knowledge evolves, some proven theories fall to the wayside. Have you ever taken the results of research to be truthful and later found out the research was inaccurate or invalid?

Now let's take a look at how to collect research.

A Review of the Literature

The first part of any type of research relates to collecting what others have already discovered.

By reviewing the current literature, you are able to define the problem and put it in context. By identifying what others have discovered, you establish a credible base of evidence: the work of specialists provides a springboard for your thesis. You can move forward by extending established knowledge and by showing fallacies in views contrary to yours.

A thorough review of the literature includes all types of sources. A balanced search includes using hard copy sources (books and periodicals) as well as online sources found through credible Web sites and data bases.

Though the Internet has valuable resources, you do not have access to older research online, and not all online sources are credible. Think about it—anyone can say anything through a Web site without evidence to support views or information. The value of information relates to the credibility of the author or organization publishing it, but no authority screens information posted on the Web. The biggest issue related to a Web site's credibility is bias (which is the same issue that invalidates research findings).

Here are some ways that bias misleads:

- For financial profit, a site may present or highlight only select research (in other words, the site leaves out research that negates the site's position).

- The research presented may be shoddy, biased, contaminated, and thus invalid.

- The author may present opinions and beliefs but not evidence based on research.

- The site may represent a conflict of interest without making the conflict known.

Therefore, you cannot be sure that every site that you visit provides a balanced, accurate perspective on your topic. This skewed information can affect your views, especially if you were leaning in that direction already.

Here are some tips to ensure your online source is credible:

1. Look for impartial sites that are sponsored by large, credible organizations, such as the American Medical Association, the U.S. Bureau of Labor Statistics, and so on. (Small private organizations that you have never heard of may or may *not* be credible.)

2. Identify how long the site has been in operation; the longer, the better.

3. Identify how often the site is updated; some sites are posted and left unchanged for years.

4. Check to see if the site is linked to other sites you consider reputable.

5. Evaluate whether the site provides information to answer your questions accurately and objectively (as compared to trying to convince you to buy into their pitch).

Also consider the following:

1. Your library has already screened many sources through online subscriptions, data bases, and CD-ROMs. Use those sources *before* you put your topic into an outside search engine.

2. Since print materials are scrutinized heavily during the publishing process, consider online sources more seriously when they are validated by your print sources.

3. Finally, if you have a question, discuss your source with your local librarian. Librarians specialize in retrieving and evaluating all types of information and enjoy assisting eager researchers.

Though you may start your research online, use your online sampling as an entrée to books and periodicals which provide substance and balance. What your library does not carry in hard copy or online subscriptions, it may carry in the form of microfilm or microfiche. Libraries also request material for you through inter-library loan—one more reason to start your research early.

As you collect research on various topics, you may find yourself wishing to go beyond the literature to conduct your own qualitative research, so let's take a look at how to do just that.

Formal and Informal Qualitative Research

When you ask people questions about how they think or feel, you are conducting a primitive form of qualitative research. When you observe behavior and then use your findings to make decisions, you are also in the realm of qualitative research.

Qualitative research *describes* and *evaluates* to give a more detailed picture of the current state of a designated topic. Qualitative research appears every day in the news and in ordinary life.

Here are a few examples of qualitative research:

- A poll taken to determine who voters will support in the next election.

- A computer questionnaire giving three options for you to choose about a topic.

- A survey at your grocery store asking which hours you prefer to shop.

Some qualitative research does not involve a research design or have a mathematical dimension relating to probability, such as the survey taken at your local grocery store on shopping preference.

However, some qualitative research is painstakingly designed with statistics applied, such the poll taken to determine voter support. By doing a **random sampling**, a researcher can reduce bias and calculate a margin of error, producing results that would have a specified degree of accuracy within a given margin.

Of course, even the most meticulous design may not predict reality; for example, what if a significant event changes people's minds as the results are being tallied? Even without intervening incidents to change the results, qualitative research most aptly applies to a time and place and is not conducive to being applied outside of its realm.

The types of qualitative research that you are likely to use are **surveys**, **focus groups**, and **interviews**, which are discussed later in this chapter. These tools fall under a qualitative approach to research known as **action research**. You can use action research and its research tools on an ongoing basis; they ensure a more accurate, thorough depiction of the questions you are exploring.

Practice

1. Stop to consider the various qualitative research studies that you hear about daily.

2. Make a list of at least three qualitative research studies (opinion polls and surveys) which you have heard about or read about during the last month.

3. Did any of them give a margin of error? Do you remember what it was?

Action Research

Although action research is most often affiliated with education and the social sciences, businesses also use it effectively.

Whereas scientific research conducts experiments and then applies the results *after* they are proven, action research assists the researcher in collecting information to use in an immediate application. Thus, the researcher can take action *as* the improved understanding (or research) occurs.

According to L. R. Gay and Peter Airasian, *Educational Research, Competencies for Analysis and Applications*, action research is carried out in a *cyclical* manner:

> Initial information is reexamined and sharpened, reexamined and sharpened again, and the process continues until there is consensus or until additional cycles fail to generate significant new information. The four basic steps of scientific and disciplined inquiry guide the process of the action research:
>
> 1. Identifying a problem or question;
>
> 2. Conducting a meeting or brainstorming session to gain information about the problem or question;
>
> 3. Analyzing research data or information; and
>
> 4. Taking action to rectify the problem or illuminate the question.[1]

To use an analogy, action research is a way of testing the water by asking someone who is in the water as compared to assuming what the temperature might be by the way it looks. Action research provides feedback to assist in making decisions that lead to effective change. In addition, action research can involve both quantitative data (numbers, statistics) and qualitative data (feelings, beliefs, opinions).

In general, action research includes a "before" and an "after" with some remedy in between. In education, action research often consists of a pretest followed by a controlled remedy and then a posttest to measure change. The difference between the pretest scores and the posttest scores quantifies the degree to which the remedy (or practice) improved performance.

If the change were not quantifiable through a pretest/posttest design, participant attitudes could still be measured through a questionnaire. The results could be quantified by using a scale, for example 1 to 5, to gauge how much participants believed they improved. (One such measurement is a Likert scale, which is discussed later in this chapter.)

Of course, the results of action research are limited; a researcher could not necessarily use them to predict how other populations would respond. However, action research is an exciting way to make progress; everyone involved becomes more engaged.

Consider ways you can include action research to achieve better results in your personal and professional life. For example, if you wish to improve team communications, ask for feedback about what works well in getting a job done and what creates barriers to making progress. This informal "testing of the water" often makes a difference.

In preparation to reviewing qualitative tools such as surveys, focus groups, and interviews, let's first examine the kinds of questions to include in your design.

Open Questions vs. Closed Questions

Regardless of the type of survey you are constructing, questions need to be designed so that they solicit the information you seek. Two basic types are *open questions* and *closed questions*.

Closed questions provide simple options (such as *yes* or *no*) that a respondent can select as an answer. Other examples of closed questions are multiple-choice or true-false questions, such as "Prompt, efficient service gives a place of business more credibility. *True* or *False?*"

Open questions allow respondents more flexibility in answering. Respondents are not given specific choices and forced to select one or the other; they are given an open-ended question to which they reply in their own words. This type of question gives respondents an opportunity to put answers in their own words, such as "What difference does prompt, efficient service make in your buying decisions?"

These types of questions are markedly different from each other. Select the type of question based on the circumstances. If large numbers of people are to be surveyed, you can tabulate and compare results more efficiently using closed questions. With open questions, data is impossible to decipher in large numbers.

Of course, you can always design a questionnaire that has both types of questions. In fact, mixed questionnaires are common; for example, directions might include the following: "To any question that you answer *yes*, please explain."

Now let's look some of the instruments on which these questions are applied.

Surveys, Focus Groups, and Interviews

The most popular type of qualitative research relates to asking people their opinions about an issue or product.

Surveys, focus groups, and *interviews* represent important listening tools. As such, they have changed marketing dramatically over the decades. For example, at one time, a common approach was to manufacture a product and then *sell* consumers on why they should buy it. When consumers stopped buying, a company knew they had a problem. Now, the more common approach is to solicit input from consumers and then adapt the product as much as possible to consumer demands.

This approach is evident in various industries. For example, when consumers demand healthier foods, even fast food chains find a way to adapt. When consumers demand automobiles that have better mileage, the industry begins to produce them.

Turning from products and moving toward human endeavors, many companies use these tools to survey their employees. For example, rather than change employee benefits and then inform their employees, companies solicit input from their employees to find out what they need or want.

The two fields that manage this organizational role are human resource (HR) management and organizational development (OD). Human resource managers implement employee benefit packages, job appraisal procedures, and hiring processes. Organizational development professionals use qualitative tools for *planned organizational change.*

By staying attuned to employee needs and responding accordingly, HR and OD professionals can keep operations productive and employees satisfied. They use employee feedback to shape policies, procedures, benefits, training, and even management style. They help create a productive corporate culture by using qualitative tools to measure attitudes and behaviors. Depending on the purpose and the types of questions, information can be collected from individuals or small groups.

Survey Design

Surveys can be designed through a science of their own. In fact, because science is applied to developing certain types of surveys, many professionals avoid creating their own. They fear they will not construct one correctly, so they ignore the survey as a valid tool. That belief keeps many from an efficient, tailored option in collecting current information.

You can develop simple surveys without formal training. People generally like to share their opinions; it actually makes them feel more involved in the big picture. At times, surveys allow them to communicate grievances and let out steam; at other times, surveys give people an easy way to share their appreciation. At any rate, people feel more important when they feel that their views matter.

Determine what you would like to ask and then construct your survey. Keep your survey brief and focused; be honest about your reason for asking the information and how it will be used.

The limitation of surveys relates more to what you can do with the information than choosing questions to construct one. For example, research that you discover through surveys is *time sensitive*. What you learn today can change by tomorrow depending on circumstances. In addition, what you learn with one group may be invalid with another.

To design a survey, first figure out what is important to know verses what is not important. Setting priorities is a recurring issue; you can waste time by addressing unimportant issues that camouflage the real ones. At the onset, determine whether you will do a **paper survey**, an **online survey**, or use both methods.

1. Meet with colleagues to discuss the issues and brainstorm a list of questions.

2. Wait a day or two before you edit your list, but then edit it ruthlessly.

3. Keep your survey as simple as possible.

4. Depending on the topic, your survey may be more effective if respondents remain anonymous; make your decision based on how you will attain the most accurate results.

5. To ensure that the design meets your needs, run a pilot test of your survey to a small sample.

6. Set a time frame and then distribute the surveys.

7. Do not expect responses for all of the surveys that you distribute and expect some to be late.

8. Tally the results.

9. Report results in an unbiased, honest way (whether you like the results or not).

You can include an affective scale based on self-response, such as a Likert scale, which is discussed below. If so, you can run an average (mean) as well as other simple calculations, such as the mode (the most frequently appearing score) and a median (the score that falls at the center, with half of the scores coming before it and with half following it).

- **The Likert Scale:** An affective test that assesses feelings, values, and attitudes toward self, others, and environments. A Likert scale gives a range of numbers; for example, from 1 to 5.

Participants respond to a series of statements by indicating the degree to which they agree or disagree. Results are then tabulated numerically to assess responses.

This type of qualitative evaluation tool helps rank opinions. Though it may sound somewhat unscientific, these types of scales are even used in the medical field. For example, to discover how much pain a patient is in, a nurse may ask the patient to quantify the pain on a scale of 1 to 10. Pain medication is then prescribed based on the patient's assessment of his or her own discomfort.

Here is what a Likert Scale might look like:

	1	2	3	4	5
	Strongly Disagree	Disagree	Undecided	Agree	Strongly Agree
I attend help sessions	1	2	3	4	5
My grades improve	1	2	3	4	5

Other types of scales would be a **semantic differential scale** and a **rating scale**.

- A **semantic differential scale** gives a quantitative rating along a continuum.

The scale measures a respondent's attitude about a specific topic, such as how a person feels about a class or a project; it can even measure how someone is doing to break a habit, such as smoking.

Here are examples of how a semantic differential scale might be constructed:

Necessary ____ ____ ____ ____ ____ Unnecessary

Fair ____ ____ ____ ____ ____ Unfair

Better ____ ____ ____ ____ ____ Worse

- A **rating** scale gives respondents an opportunity to measure attitudes toward others.

Here is an example of a rating scale:

On a scale of 1 to 5, please indicate how often you are satisfied with our approach.

1	2	3	4	5
Never	Rarely	Sometimes	Often	Always

Experiment using the various tools you have available as you develop your own surveys. Using feedback to improve outcomes is an intelligent strategy to apply.

Online Surveys

Some companies specialize in online survey analysis. For a fee, these online survey sites assist you in creating your survey, giving you options for the various types of questions you will include.

The service distributes your survey, collects and tabulates the results (in real time), and then analyzes your data. These online services also provide you with graphs and charts, so you have statistical analysis along with visuals to represent your findings.

Log on to the Web and do a search for "online surveys." Go to a few of these sites and consider what they offer. If you ever need a professionally done survey, you may find this kind of tool a lifesaver.

Focus Groups

Companies often hire outside consultants to facilitate focus groups. Part of their reason for conducting formal focus groups is to solicit *honest, objective* feedback.

If the facilitator knows members in the group, the group also knows some of the facilitator's opinions; some members might try to please the facilitator and others might withhold information. Thus, a different set of psychological dynamics are set into motion than would exist with an outside facilitator.

However, even when an outside consultant conducts a focus group, some of the same psychological dynamics are at work. As a result, use discretion when interpreting the results of any focus group. In addition to using a trained facilitator, here are some tips in running a focus group:

1. Identify issues and brainstorm questions to ask.

2. Become clear on your purpose and what you would like to achieve.

3. Edit your list so that you do not collect too much detail.

4. Select a group large enough so that the group has diversity of thought but small enough so that everyone feels free to discuss issues openly. (An average number might be between 8 and 15 participants. Also, the only accurate way to recruit a focus group would be through random sampling of a defined population.)

5. Use open-ended questions and statements to solicit input.

6. Keep the tone of questions neutral.

> **Weak:** What do you think is wrong with the climate in the company?
>
> **Revised:** Describe the climate within the company.

7. Collect data.

8. Identify common themes.

Gathering responses manually rather than electronically has advantages. For example, rather than record responses, have an assistant key the responses into a computer. Assure the participants that their responses are anonymous. (If the session is recorded, the responses may be less reflective of true opinions and attitudes).

Report the information back without interpretation or bias. Consolidate *common themes* and reactions as you respect the importance of anonymity. If you betray a group's trust, you may lose your credibility; and your indiscretions may cause serious repercussions for participants.

Interviews

Individual interviews consume more time than other types of qualitative research and provide less generalized feedback; that is because the information relates to one individual and not a group.

An interview would be a good choice to use when working with a small population. For example, if there were a total of 20 people in an organization, individual interviews would be feasible and would give a total picture. In such a small organization, data gathered in a focus group could be less reliable because of close relationships. Individuals generally express more candor when their anonymity is guaranteed. To provide valid information in a large population, a random sample which applies statistical methods would be required.

However, interviews are used for many types of informal research, such as making hiring or promotional decisions as well as job performance appraisals. Another way to collect important information is to interview an expert in the field.

Researchers tally research from narrative answers and focus groups by looking for **common threads** or **consistent themes** among the responses: what information does everyone seem to hold in common?

The common threads are more objective data than individual responses and can more readily be applied to the larger population.

Demographics

When doing surveys, you are often interested in how a respondent thinks or feels (psychological qualities) about a selected topic. However, do social qualities play a role in responses? For example, do age, sex, income, race, religion, education, and marital status, among others, factor into the equation?

Demographics describe social characteristics and can be correlated to other factors you are researching. For instance, if you want to find out if your new product will be successful on the market, you might want to correlate age and income with respondents. Overall, you might find that 80 percent of the people you survey do not like your product, but 100 percent of those between the ages of 20 to 30 think it is great. Voila! You have found your market.

Recap

A serious gap exists between what people know through research and what they actually apply. For example, in the field of education, Dr. Ralph Tyler found that "It takes about 20 years . . . to apply in an average classroom what is discovered through research."[2]

You use research in an informal way when you make conscious decisions rather than basing your actions on guesses. In contrast, sometimes people do not really *decide*; they *react* or *act out of habit* rather than stop to think. Thinking leads to a more conscious decision; reflection reveals the pros and cons of a choice.

By actively using what you learn through research (not just intellectualizing information and then becoming passive), you can make important changes in your daily life. Over time, these changes will keep you focused, productive, and more satisfied with your behavior.

Research can become a part of your daily life by including it in the way that you think: more and more, you will be making decisions based on proven criteria rather than acting out of habit. You may even find that you have a passion for research—and that's a good path to follow. The world can use more incurable researchers!

As you write academic papers, choose topics that you can apply to expand your life, improving the quality of it.

Skills Workshop

Activity 1: Think Outside the Box

Instructions: Look at the following illustration—how many squares do you see?

Are there only 16? How about 21? Can you find 22 . . . 24 . . . 26?

Discuss this exercise with a peer. What insights do you have as a result of doing this exercise?

Activity 2: Develop a Survey

Situation 1: You are working in customer services for a large retail store. Your manager comes to you to find out the kinds of problems people are having. It seems your manager wants detailed information and numbers behind them.

Situation 2: You are working part-time for your college's learning resource center. Your manager has given you a special assignment to explore how college students use the Internet. Your first task is to design a short survey.

Instructions: Develop a survey that you can use.

1. What is the problem that you are trying to solve? What does it involve?

2. What kinds of questions and categories will you use on your survey?

3. Will you include both open and closed questions?

4. Will you include a Likert scale or other types of rating scales?

5. Will you ask for demographic data (for example, age, income, race, or other characteristics)?

Activity 3: The Practical Side of Action Research

The idea of conducting research may be daunting at first, but you are already doing it naturally in your daily life.

For instance, assume you need a haircut and your former hairstylist/barber has recently closed shop. You may start your informal research by asking a few people whose cut and style look good. Then you will narrow your choice based on restrictions of price and location.

To complete this activity, follow the instructions on the next page.

Instructions: Identify a practical question that you want to solve or a change you want to make in your personal or professional life. Now break it down into the following steps:

1. What is the problem you want to solve?

2. How can you state the problem in a question so that you can do informal research?

3. What data do you need to collect? What information do you need to gather?

4. What sources can you use?

5. How do you know your sources are credible?

6. What conclusions are you able to draw from your data and information?

7. Do your conclusions represent complete and final answers?

Endnotes

1. L. R. Gay and Peter Airasian, *Educational Research: Competencies for Analysis and Applications*, Merrill Prentice Hall, Upper Saddle River, NJ, 2003, pages 265 - 271.

2. Dona Young, "General Education: Developing a Common Understanding," master's paper, The University of Chicago, 1988: quoted from an interview by Dona Young with Ralph W. Tyler, Chicago, August 4, 1986.

Quick Guide to Citation

Citation involves details, and details can be challenging. However, citing your research not only validates your findings, citation also provides information so that others can find your source and read it in its entirety.

There are multiple systems for citation in all fields, and the person or organization commissioning your work will determine the documentation system that you need to use.

Here are three common citation systems:

- American Psychological Association (APA)
- Modern Language Association (MLA)
- The Chicago Manual of Style (CMS)

Other documentation systems are used as well. If you study medicine or the physical sciences, you may be asked to use the Council of Biology Editors (CBE). On the other hand, if you use the *Chicago Manual of Style* as your reference source, you will find two sets of guidelines: one for fine arts and humanities (academic), the other for social and physical sciences.

Sometimes citation preferences vary from professor to professor; at other times, the same reference system is used throughout a university. Before you turn in any work, check to make sure you are using the correct referencing style.

Before looking at citation styles, let's look at plagiarism, a topic that goes hand in hand with citing sources.

Plagiarism

Citation is one antidote to plagiarism; another antidote to plagiarism is commitment to learning. Citation allows you to use another's words or ideas to add richness to your work, and citation adds credibility to your line of thought.

If you use someone's work without giving proper credit, you must ask yourself "why?" Plagiarism robs the plagiarist more than anyone else, even if the crime is never discovered. Students plagiarize for various reasons, such as fear and anxiety along with poor writing skills. The "catch 22" is that plagiarism feeds the dynamic that keeps students from developing their writing skills, robbing potential as it pulls down confidence and self-esteem.

When novice writers cut and paste another's words into their work, they are giving themselves a message that is loud and clear: *I'm not good enough. Good writing and insightful thinking are out of reach for me.* The irony is that good writing is not out of reach for anyone who actually does the work.

Writing effectively has never been more important than it is today: technology has fueled the importance of writing and, at the same time, made plagiarism that much easier to accomplish. Teachers can spot plagiarism easily, becoming familiar with a student's vocabulary, spelling, grammar, and syntax through only one writing sample. To identify plagiarism, teachers also use online subscription services. With only a sentence or two, the real source can be immediately identified. In fact, many instructors screen for plagiarism *before* they even read a paper.

Students need to learn how to write effectively when they have the chance, not waste their educational experiences on cutting and pasting. Though every writer must grow through the pain and uncertainty on the road to building skills and confidence, the payoff is incredible.

Place process above product—focus more on what you are learning than your final grade. In the "real world," grades are not nearly as important as the ability to solve problems. In fact, the last time you are likely to be asked your GPA is *before* you secure your first job. After that point, your career is about your skills and accomplishments. Without effective writing skills, you significantly limit your opportunities: ask and you will find the help that you need to improve your writing skills.

What to Credit

Not all information needs to be documented. For example, information that is considered common knowledge (something generally known to everyone) or facts available from a wide variety of sources. According to *The New St. Martin's Handbook*, here is a list of information that needs to be documented:[1]

1. Direct quotations and paraphrase.
2. Facts that are not widely known or assertions that are arguable.
3. Judgments, opinions, and claims of others.
4. Statistics, charts, tables, and graphs from any source.
5. Help provided by friends, instructors, or others.

The two most common types of references are direct quotations and paraphrase.

- **Direct quotes:** Set off someone else's exact words; for short quotes, use quotation marks; for quotes of four or more lines, indent margins at least ½ inch on either side.

In the academic world, tradition demands bringing in authority to support a position; outside sources add credibility. However, even with academic writing, use quotations selectively. Just as quotes in exactly the right places can enhance your work, too many quotes or unnecessary ones distract your reader. Aim for flow and be selective.

- **Paraphrase:** Cite your source when you put someone else's ideas in your own words.

What paraphrasing is not: making a few changes in word order, leaving out a word or two, or substituting similar words.

Novice writers have difficulty with paraphrasing. True paraphrasing occurs when you read material, digest it, write about the concepts in your own words, and credit the original author.

Working Bibliography

As you collect and use what others have discovered, citing your sources is a critical piece in validating your position. However, citing research can be challenging because it involves details.

Though each system of documentation has slight variations from the others, they all contain similar information. To save yourself time and frustration, compile a **working bibliography** (use note cards, a small notebook, or a special file on your computer) as you collect your research.

Here is the kind of information you need to collect:

For Books:

- Author, title, and page number
- Publisher, location, and year of publication

For Periodicals:

- Author, title of article
- Journal, date of publication

For Web sites:

- Author (if known) and title
- Uniform Resource Locator (URL) network address, which includes path and file names and which are enclosed in angle brackets
- Date Web site was established (if available, it is found at the bottom of the home page)
- Date on which you accessed the information
- Date the source was published in print (if previously published)

Because electronic sources are ever changing, print a hard copy of the material you are referencing or download the accessed information.

Your citations may be the last piece of information you compile for your work. Keep a working bibliography so that you can cite your sources properly and without undue frustration.

Elements of Citation Systems

All citation systems require that sources be referenced both in the text and at the end of the work. Both references together provide the reader with complete information through cross-referencing.

APA   In-text Citation, References

CMS   Footnotes, Endnotes, Bibliography

MLA   In-text Citation (author and page number enclosed in parentheses), Works Cited, Works Consulted

If you are writing a document in which you want to comment or provide parenthetical information related indirectly to your text, CMS allows that through footnotes and endnotes.

For footnotes, use a superscript (raised number) at the end of the sentences in which the reference occurs; place the information at the bottom of the page. For endnotes, display references on a separate page at the end of each chapter or at the end of the work. Indent the first line of footnotes and endnotes; single space footnotes and endnotes and provide an extra space between references.[2]

For all citation methods, you may cite one book several times in your manuscript; however, you only need to include identifying information about the book (author, publisher, and date) one time in your bibliography, works cited, or reference list.

For a bibliography (CMS), you can list sources that you do not actually cite in your work. However, if you are using the MLA system, keep your *works cited* and *works consulted* on separate pages. If you are using APA style, list only references on your reference page that you cite in your work.

The following pages contain a summary of major points from MLA and APA styles; later in the chapter, you will find a summary of major points from APA style written in that style along with an example taken from a paper written in APA style. Also, later in this chapter, you will find an example of a works cited page. You can also find exceptional resources online to assist you with the various citation systems.[3]

MLA

For in-text parenthetical citations in MLA style, use the author's last name and the page number of the citation.

Parts	Manuscript (no title page: put title on page 1) Works Cited page
Reference Page	Works Cited
Authors/editors	Spell out names; if more than three, list first of the names along with *et al*.
Titles	Follow standard capitalization guidelines (capitalize the first letter of all words except articles and prepositions)
Publisher	Shorten name and list only city
Dates	Place at the end of the citation

Format:

- Double space entire document
- On page 1, center title and place the following heading in upper left corner (double-spaced):
    - Your name
    - Your instructor's name
    - Course title
    - Date
- After page 1, display author's name and page number in upper-right corner of each page.
- On the Works Cited page:
    - Center the title *Works Cited*.
    - Alphabetize by author's last name, putting last name first.
    - Spell out the first and last name of authors.
    - Put the first line of each entry flush at the left margin; indent second lines.
    - Underscore titles or enclose in quotation marks.

APA

For in-text parenthetical citations in APA style, use the author's last name and the year of publication (separating name and year with a comma).

Parts	Title page (title of paper and by line)
	Abstract (between 150 and 250 words)
	Introduction, methods, results, and discussion
	Reference page
Reference Page	References
Authors/editors	use last name and first initial; list all authors
Titles	capitalize first word only; italicize
Publisher	use full name; list state abbreviations when city is lesser known

Format:

- Double space entire document
- Insert a page header and running head:
    - Insert page header: upper right-hand corner of each page
    - Use one to three words of the title, 5 blank spaces, and page number
    - Insert "running head" the title page only and follow it with a colon and an abbreviated title of the paper using 50 characters of less; display the abbreviated title in all caps
- Center the title and by line on the upper half of the title page; use up to two lines for the title
- Begin numbering on the title page
- Use 1-inch margins; use Times New Roman or Courier, 12-point
- Use up to 5 levels of headings for transitions in content
- Do not use special features such as bolding or bullet points
- Use visuals such as tables and graphs on separate pages from text
- Space one time after punctuation, including periods
- Do not justify right margin
- On the reference page:
    - Alphabetize by last name of authors; use last name and first initial; list all authors
    - Do not indent the first line of an entry; indent second and subsequent lines
    - Italicize titles of books and journals

Quick Guide to APA Style

The American Psychological Association (APA) is widely used in the social sciences as a guide to formatting and referencing. APA (American Psychological Association, 2005) requires in-text parenthetical references.

The following is a brief discussion (Stevens, 2009) of how to present some common elements in APA style.

General Guidelines

Your paper will include four main parts: the title page, abstract, body, and references.

On the upper half of the title page, double space and center, on different lines, the title of your paper, your name, and the name of your university. Use up to two lines for the title of the paper.

Following the title page, write an abstract of your paper in one paragraph between 150 and 250 words. Double space the abstract, along with the body and reference page.

Formatting

For your entire document, use 1-inch margins at the top, bottom, right, and left of each page. Use 12-point Times Roman or 12-point Courier font, and double space the entire paper, including title page and reference page. Indent each paragraph 5 spaces, but do not use right justification.

Number all of the pages, starting with the title page. Create a header that includes the first 2 or 3 words of your title, leaving 5 spaces before the page number. Type the page header in upper- and lower-case letters. By the way, APA does not allow any bold or bullets in papers.

Headings and Subheadings

For most papers, you will need only one or two levels of headings. However, APA guidelines (Purdue University Online Writing Lab, 2009) provide five levels of headings

Level 1:
                    Center and Use Standard Capitalization

Level 2:
                Center and Italicize with Standard Capitalization

Level 3:

Flush-Left and Italicize with Standard Capitalization

Level 4:

Indent and italicize. Capitalize only first words and words after colons. End the level 4 heading with a period, and follow immediately with text.

Level 5:
                    CENTER IN ALL CAPS

Here is a recap of the headings, displayed according to their specifications:

LEVEL 5 HEADING

Level 1 Heading

Level 2 Heading

Level 3 Heading

Level 4 heading. Start your text here.

Here is a breakdown of the headings you would use based on the number of levels of headings that you would need:

One level of heading: level 1

Two levels: levels 1 and 3

Three levels: levels 1, 3, and 4

Four levels: levels 1, 2, 3, and 4

Five levels: levels 5, 1, 2, 3, and 4

In-Text Citations

Use in-text citations to identify your sources, crediting authors whether you quote them directly or you put their ideas and research in your own words. For indirect references, cite the author's last name and the publication year; for direct quotes, include the page number. Put this information in parentheses at the end of the quotation. However, if you

368 *Writing from the Core*

use the author's name in your text, do not repeat the author's name in the parentheses.

For signal verbs, APA style recommends using the past tense (such as, "stated") or present perfect tense (such as, "has stated"), for example: Tyler (1988) stated, "All students can learn what the schools teach if they can find an interest in it" (p. 45).

For a citation that has only one author, list the author's last name and the year of the publication. If you are giving an exact quote, also list the page number, as shown above. For a citation with two authors, list both authors for all citations; for example: Winger and Ginther (1992) developed a new method.

For citations with three to five authors, list all authors for the first citation, as follows: Ginther, Tyler, and Winger (2001) supported their findings with research.

For the second citation of the same work, cite the first author's surname and add *et al.* (the Latin abbreviation for *and others*). Put the year of publication in parentheses; for example: Ginther et al. (2001) broke down the groups based on level of experience.

Reference List

Place the reference list at the end of the paper on a separate page. Begin the page with the word "References" centered at the top. Double space and do not indent the first line; however, indent the second and subsequent lines 5 spaces.

List only those works that you cite in the text (*Concise Rules of APA Style*, 2005). Arrange the citations in alphabetical order by surname.

Each kind of reference requires specific information in a specific form, so refer directly to the rule that discusses the type of source you are citing.

References

American Psychological Association. (2005). *Concise rules of APA style.* Washington, DC: American Psychological Association.

Purdue University Online Writing Lab (OWL) July 22, 2009. *APA formatting and style guide.* Retrieved August 3, 2009, from http://owl.english.purdue.edu/owl/.

Stevens, A. (2009). *Some guidelines from the publication manual of the american psychological association.* Gary, Indiana: Indiana University Northwest.

Student Paper in APA Style

Running head: PHYS ED ROLE IN PREVENTING CHILDHOOD OBESITY

Physical Education's Role in

Preventing Childhood Obesity

John C. Young

St. Xavier University

Abstract

Childhood obesity is a serious health issue that is becoming more prevalent in today's youth. Though other factors are involved, research (Neufeld, 2004) shows that the best way to prevent obesity is through proper nutrition and exercise. This research will clarify physical education's role in preventing future cases of childhood obesity and intervening to help those children who have already been diagnosed.

Physical Education and Childhood Obesity

Childhood obesity is a worldwide epidemic and quickly becoming a serious health issue. The Center for Disease Control (2007) reports that in the year 2000, twice as many children were obese as compared to 1970. The first step in solving a problem is accepting that the problem exists.

According to Larimore, Flynt, and Haliday (2001), "A shocking 40 percent of our 8000 pediatric patients at South End Community Health Center are clinically obese. On a recent Friday, 75 percent of children I saw were obese" (p. 58). Only after we understand this problem can we develop effective solutions to reverse this trend.

What Defines Obesity in Children?

The definition of obesity in children varies based on who you ask. According to the Center of Disease Control (2007) some use a Body Mass Index (BMI) with obesity for males being defined as 30 percent heavier than the average weight for persons the same height. A Swedish research study (Berg, 2005) that followed the lives of 735 men over the course of a lifetime found that concluded that BMI did not accurately predict risk for these individuals because it did not provide an accurate measurement of body fat percentage.

Though sources vary on how to define obesity, research (Neufield, 2004) shows that the best way to prevent obesity is through proper nutrition and exercise.

References

Berg, F. (2005) *Underage and overweight.* New York:

   Hatherleigh Press.

Center for Disease Control. (2007). BMI-Body Mass Index.

   Retrieved November 2007 from http://www.cdc.gov.

Larimore, W., Flynt, S., & Halliday, S. (2001). *Super sized*

   kids. New York: Warner Books.

Neufeld, N. (2004). *Kid shape.* Nashville: Rutledge Hill

   Press.

Works Cited Page

When using MLA referencing style, your reference page will be titled *Works Cited*. Arrange entries alphabetically by the author's last name; numbering is not necessary.

Below is an example of references displayed on a worked cited page. Notice that titles of books and periodicals are underscored rather than italicized, as they are in APA style.

WORKS CITED[4]

Colvin, Geoffrey. "Stop Blaming Bangalore for Our Jobs Problem." Fortune 19 Apr. 2004: 68.

Cooper, James C. "The Price of Efficiency." Business Week 22 Mar. 2004: 38-42.

Dobbs, Lou. "The Jobless Recovery." Money Apr. 2004: 45-46.

Dolan, Kerry A., and Robyn Meredith. "The Outsourcing Debate: A Tale of Two Cities." Forbes 12 Apr. 2004: 94-102.

Gottheil, Fred M. Principles of Economics. Australia: South-Western, 2002.

Hagel III, John. "Offshoring Goes on the Offensive." McKinsey Quarterly 2 (2004): 82-92. Business Source Elite. EBSCOhost. 11 May 2004 <http://web1.epnet.com>.

Kleiman, Carol. "Outsourcing: A Matter of Many Sides." Chicago Tribune 11 Mar. 2004. 13 Apr. 2004 <http://infoweb.newsbank.com>.

Mintz, Steven. "The Ethical Dilemmas of Outsourcing." CPA Journal 74.3 (2004): 6-9. 13 Apr. 2004 <http://www.nysscpa.org/cpajournal/2004/nv1.htm>.

Nussbaum, Bruce. "Where Are the Jobs?" Business Week 22 Mar. 2004: 36-37.

Rosencrance, Linda. "Offshore Moves Can Bring Benefits, but Not Without Pain." Computerworld 19 Apr. 2004. 11 May 2004 <http://www.computerworld.com/ printthis/ 2004/0,4814, 922.html>.

Sowell, Thomas. "Outsourcing." 16 Mar. 2004. Townhall.com 6 Apr. 2004 <http://www.townhall.com/columnists/thomassowell/ts200406.shtml>.

Since academic writing differs significantly from the kind of writing you will do in the business world, let's take a brief look at how business handles intellectual property.

How to Credit in Business

Formal credit is not the only type of credit that counts. Giving colleagues informal credit for their ideas also makes a difference. Those who acknowledge others build better rapport and receive more respect in a team environment than those who take credit for other's ideas.

In business, information is not tracked as it is in the academic world. Most writing involves solving current problems, conveying immediate information, and developing informal proposals for action. As a result, most writing on the job involves no citation.

In all situations, including the work environment, credit other people for their ideas. Generally, it is the idea and action you take that counts, not the "who said what, when, where, and how." However, attaching names to ideas builds trust.

To protect intellectual property, businesses and individuals make use of trademarks, patents, copyrights, and incorporation.

Individuals and businesses can register names, ideas, designs, logos, slogans and complete works with the Federal government for trade marks, patents or copyrights; with state governments for incorporation. Thus, when business does keep track of ownership, it does so in a legal way. This type of branding protects ownership of information deemed integral to doing business.

When you start your own business, meet with an attorney to learn your options or go online and do your research. In fact, you can do much of the legwork yourself by contacting the secretary of state in the state in which you reside.

Recap

A key element of citation is detail—just like writing, the more that you practice, the better you become.

Each one of the citation systems discussed in this chapter has entire books published to explain them. This chapter was an entrée to get you started. As you go forward, you can find a wealth of information online, including sites that will put your references in correct format for each style and do it free of charge: now go do your research . . . *and have fun*!

Skills Workshop

Instructions:

Select a paper that you have previously written and change the format and citation style to a different system than the one you originally used.

In other words, if you originally wrote your paper in MLA style, change it to CMS or APA style.

Endnotes

1. Andrea Lundsford and Robert Connors, *The New St. Martin's Handbook*, Bedford/St. Martin's, Boston 2001, pp. 495-497.

2. Citation Chicago Style, <http://www.unc.edu/depts/wcweb/handouts/chicago.html>, accessed July 15, 2009.

3. Purdue University Online Writing Lab, <http://owl.english.purdue.edu/owl/>, accessed July 2009.

4. Courtesy of Lynita Perry, DeVry University.

Quick Guide to
Job Survival Tools

Charles Darwin once said, "It is not the strongest of the species that survive, nor the most intelligent, but the ones most responsive to change."

Regardless of your achievements, looking for a job can make you question everything you have ever achieved. That is because the job search process is different from other activities and projects. You are not just using your talents to solve a problem: you have become the *central theme* of the project. Like it or not, *you* are focal point, and the job itself is secondary.

Verbalizing your job survival skills equates to marketing yourself; to do that, you first need to identify your unique qualities so that you establish your **job search profile**. Your job search profile provides base information for your résumé and prepares you for interviewing.

Career Portfolio

You may feel more confident using your skills than talking about them—that is why you need to develop your career portfolio. Everything you put in your job-search toolbox will eventually come together as your career portfolio.

Your portfolio can be as simple or as thorough as you choose. Start with a three-ring binder; if you chose one with a zipper or other closure, you will be sure not to lose business cards or loose items. Use tabs to organize the various parts.

Here are some suggestions about what to include in your portfolio:

- **Purpose Statement**. Write a purpose statement that captures your life's mission. A purpose statement can enhance your job search as it gives you clarity in making career decisions; a purpose statement also assists you in intertwining your professional career goals with your personal objectives.

- **Résumé**. Prepare your traditional and scannable résumés. As you go on interviews, tailor your résumé for each that you apply for. In the meantime, prepare a generic résumé that you can adapt as needed. You may even want to prepare a curriculum vitae (CV) just in case you apply to an international corporation.

- **Work Samples**. Select a few exhibits of your best work from classes or previous jobs: a letter, a report, a paper, and so on. A sample of your work demonstrates your skill and commitment to quality.

- **Reference Letters**. Ask for letters now, before you need them. Having reference letters in your portfolio gives you more confidence in your job search. Ask your references to use the salutation "To whom it may concern."

- **Networking contacts**. Select a notebook that has a secure pocket for business cards. This feature will keep you organized and function as a reminder of who your contacts are and with whom to follow up.

- **Business Card**. Design your own job-search card with your name, address, phone number and a few vital points about your skills.

Bring your portfolio with you on job interviews. Your portfolio will speak for you by demonstrating your motivation and organizational skills.

Also keep an electronic file of everything that you collect so that you can transform your hard copy into an **e-portfolio**. (Of course, you can start with an e-portfolio, rather than a hard copy portfolio.)

Let's get started by assisting you in getting in touch with your skills, qualities, and experience.

Skills, *Not* Titles or Degrees

Have you ever been asked this question: *What do you want to be when you . . . ?* Most of us fumble with this question until we can answer it with a job title: teacher, accountant, mechanic, doctor, nurse, lawyer, engineer, and so on. But titles and majors are *labels*, and they do not accurately capture who you are or what you are capable of doing.

Because shifts in the job market are now common, job titles and college majors limit a job seeker's opportunities. New job titles are created every day as traditional titles are eliminated. People who have had a certain "title" all of their lives may now find that that they must relocate, retrain, or repackage themselves to earn a living.

Though a title will not follow you throughout your career, your skills, talents, and achievements will. You will begin your job search by identifying your skills and how they transfer to *any* business environment.

Transferable Skills

Defining marketable skills is a challenge, especially when you think that you do not have any. Approach this task with an open mind. By being flexible, you will have access to more opportunities.

Some of your skills have come from interests or hobbies, and you may not even be aware of what you have learned. Let's start to develop your job search profile by exploring these basic areas:

- People Skills
- Knowledge and Experience
- Personal Qualities

People Skills

How do you work with people? Consider formal and informal experiences at school, at your place of worship, with volunteer groups, on part- and full-time jobs, in sports activities, and in associations.

Here are some terms to open up your thinking; go through the list slowly and notice your impressions as well as the specific experiences that come to mind.

Selling	Giving Feedback	Receiving Feedback
Working on Teams	Supervising	Working Independently
Marketing	Expressing Humor	Listening Actively
Leading	Organizing Projects	Organizing Events
Delegating	Counseling	Care Giving
Advising	Negotiating	Mediating
Entertaining	Serving	Phoning/Soliciting
Cleaning	Being Compassion	Fixing
Training	Evaluating	Facilitating

Identify three of the terms listed above that seem to stand out among the others and that describe you. For each term, recall an experience in which you used your people skills successfully, for example:

Giving Feedback: When I worked on a team project, I gave objective feedback even though it was difficult. Some team members did not agree with me, and I needed to defend my position until they understood my point. As a result, we ended up with a stronger team and a better project.

Serving: I work part-time at the local diner and take pride in assisting our customers in whatever way I can. Sometimes they can't make up their minds, and I'm honest about the best things to order.

For each of the three terms you choose, give an example of how you used your people skills successfully.

For each of your three terms, give a specific example of an experience that demonstrates it. Use the space below to start.

1. _____

2. _____

3. _____

Knowledge Base

In which subjects or areas have you developed knowledge that you can apply? In addition to formal learning, consider hobbies and interests. Read through the list below and circle the terms that apply to you.

Writing (composing, editing, revising) / Communication / Languages (speaking, writing, translating, interpreting) / Global Communication / Business / Management / Accounting / Math / Statistics / Budgeting / Calculus / Science / Physics / Biology / Medicine / Pharmaceuticals / Music / Instruments / Voice / Theater / Film Making / Art / Archeology / Anthropology / Law / Criminal / Civil / Police Science Political Science / History / Social Sciences / Psychology / Sociology / Social Work / Counseling /Physical Sciences / Sports / Nutrition / Cosmetology / Physical Therapy / Organizational Development / Human Resource Development / Fundraising /Child Care / Early Child Development / Elementary or Secondary Education / Graphic Arts / Graphic Design / Interior Design, and so on.

Select your top three areas and reflect on your experience in each area, thinking of an example of how you use the skill or talent.

For example:

- I feel confident with my **writing** skills. I can compose, edit, and revise e-mail messages, letters, and reports.

- I like working with **numbers**. I make a budget, follow it, and balance my checking account online; I also have good **computer skills**.

- **Nutrition** and **sports** have always been major interests. I **coach** my friends when we're at the gym and they've seen good results.

What other subjects or major areas can you identify? If need be, take out your college catalog and list specific classes and assignments that were particularly meaningful.

Can you come up with three or more subjects in which you feel especially competent? Identify the subject and write a sentence describing your experience or competence with it.

1._____

2._____

3._____

Job Duties

Job duties consist of tasks that you perform on the job. What kinds of job duties can you perform? Consider all of the classes that you have taken as well as job experience, paid or volunteer. Also consider your hobbies and interests; these activities are important to employers.

Which tasks can you perform well? Which tasks do you enjoy? Use the list of nouns and verbs that follow to generate a list of tasks that you enjoy.

Computers / CAD / Keyboarding / Drafting / PowerPoint / Web Design
Automotives / Machinery / Repair / Design / Paint / Draw / Sketch
Sculpt / Construct / Build / Maintain / Restore / Analyze / Solve Problems
Trouble Shoot / Survey / Landscape / Gather Information / Organize and
File / Spreadsheets / Tables / Graphs / Letters / E-mail / Memos / Agendas
Minutes / Reports / Proposals / Set Goals / Canvass / Meet Quotas / Read
Write / Edit / Work with Children / Counsel / Wait Tables / Caddy Greet
and Receive / Clean Houses, Cars, or Offices / Play Music / Compose
Cashier / Style Hair / Drive / Walk Dogs / Care for Children / Coach
Groom Horses / Manage / Supervise

What other tasks relate to your experience?

_____

Give examples of successful experiences, for example:

- During my free time, I enjoy walking dogs. I posted an announcement in my neighborhood, and now I get several jobs a month. The dogs are fun to work with and their owners are grateful that I can help them out in a bind.

- My mother is a member of an organization that helps raise funds for the disease lupus. I helped the director by taking minutes at one of their meetings and then organized and filed papers in their office. I even made some calls to solicit money for fundraising. Every part of it was fun because I was helping people.

- My phone work is good. I enjoy making follow-up calls to tell people about a meeting or to let them know what we did at a meeting that they missed.

Can you give examples of three tasks that you do well and enjoy? (An example may include more than one task, as in the second example above, which involves taking minutes, organizing and filing papers, and making phone calls.)

1. _____

2. _____

3. _____

In addition to the specific tasks that you performed, also describe what you learned about yourself and others from performing these tasks, for example:

- When I volunteered at the lupus organization, I acted friendly and confident, even though I didn't feel secure at first. I was also patient with clients on the phone. When I made a mistake, I took responsibility for it and corrected it quickly.

- When I posted the sign for my dog-walking business, I showed initiative and courage. I didn't know if I'd get any business and was very excited when people started to call.

This exercise is difficult because most people are used to doing a task rather than analyzing what they learned from it. Select three of your tasks or work experiences and record what you learned about your skills and attitudes.

The unfamiliar is challenging for everyone . . . until it becomes *familiar*. Reviewing tasks you do well will build your confidence, remind you of your competence, and put your job search into perspective.

You are spending your time well by identifying specific tasks that you are good at and that you enjoy.

1. _____

2. _____

3. _____

Personal Qualities

You are unique whether or not you realize it. What are your personal qualities that shape you into who you are? Which of the following qualities describe you?

reliable	dependable	motivated	self-starter
persistent	optimistic	self-reliant	strong
independent	capable	fast learner	supportive
eager	focused	purposeful	task oriented
disciplined	friendly	persuasive	artistic
committed	easy going	encouraging	flexible
balanced	open minded	accepting	prompt
courteous	patient	dedicated	supportive
loyal	adaptable	credible	ethical
competent	kind	helpful	determined
confident	decisive	creative	enthusiastic
honest	responsible	self-learner	passionate

Close your eyes and reflect for a moment. What adjectives come to mind when you think of yourself? _____

Write three of your positive qualities below, and give examples of times when you displayed them to get a job done or help someone.

1. _____

2. _____

3. _____

Now that you have established several good qualities, you can list an area or two that you wish to improve; call them your *growing edges* if you wish.

Prospective employers will ask about your weaknesses, you need to be ready with an honest answer. Human Resource (HR) professionals interview hundreds of applicants and can see through insincere answers.

If you are honest yet optimistic about your weaknesses, you will actually score points. You see, we all have weaknesses, whether we like to admit it or not.

State your weakness in a positive way. For example:

Don't Say: I'm late getting my work done all the time, and I need to get control of my schedule.

Say: Sometimes I get so involved in solving a problem that I lose track of time. I'm working on structuring my time so that my schedule is more balanced. Overall, it feels as if I have more time and more control over my time.

Don't Say: When I work on a project, I'm a perfectionist. Because I want everything perfect, I worry about it and then put things off till the last minute; sometimes I miss deadlines.

Say: I'm a bit of a perfectionist. Rather than working on a project to get it perfect, my goal now is to achieve good quality, which is a more realistic aim. I am getting better at producing good work and then moving on to other projects. My schedule is getting more balanced and I'm achieving better results.

Others' Perceptions

When you are on a job interview, one of the questions that you may be asked is "how do others perceive you?" This exercise prepares you for that question.

Ask three people who know you well to describe your skills and attitudes. Choose people who are positive and supportive. Let them know that you are doing research for your job search profile. If they are willing, you would appreciate receiving feedback in writing via e-mail or a short note. Getting feedback in writing will help you build your career portfolio.

Here are some questions you can ask:

- What are three adjectives that you would use to describe me?

- What are some tasks that you have seen me do well?

- In your eyes, what achievements have I made?

- Do you consider me a team player? . . . a leader? . . . a self-starter?

- What do you think are my growing edges or areas in which I can improve?

You may be surprised at how positively others perceive you. If you feel uncomfortable when you hear good things about yourself, simply say "thank you" and move on. The same advice is true if you hear negative things. Keep an open mind, and use the feedback to develop objectives for self-growth.

Take a few moments to reflect on the input that you received and record it, especially if it is all verbal. Otherwise, you are likely to lose the essence of the valuable information that you receive.

COACHING TIP

What is your track record?

When you go on an interview, be prepared with an example that demonstrates one of your achievements.

For example, perhaps you are the first person in your family to graduate from college or maybe you recently won an award. These types of notable experiences give prospective employers insight into your personality and interests as well as how you apply your skills.

Of course, use some discretion in choosing which achievements to cite. A prospective employer does not want to hear about personal milestones such as engagements or weddings; and no matter how cute your children are, save those stories for your friends and relatives.

Work Experience

Make a list of all paid or volunteer jobs you have had; along side your experience, identify the time frame. Instead of exact dates, you can list the month and year from when you started until you left. For example:

Market Store, Part-time Cashier

January to March, 1999	7 weeks
July to August, 1999	6 weeks
December, 1999	3 weeks
Total	about 4 months

Though you are concerned with dates, you also want to have an idea of the amount of time on the job. Quantify your experiences in terms of years and months or even weeks.

After you tally the specifics, you can list your experience as follows:

Market Store, Part-time Cashier

January to December, 1999   4 months

Now take a moment to record the jobs you have held and tally your job experience in months and years.

Job 1.   **Company/Title**   **Dates**   **Time**_____

Job 2.   **Title/Company**   **Dates**   **Time**_____

Total time: _____

For each position, write a sentence or two that demonstrates the skills that you applied. Write active sentences using strong verbs, and avoid filler verbs and phrases, such as "I learned how to" or "I gained experience doing," as shown in the examples that follow.

Don't Say:	While working as a cashier at Market Store, *I learned how to communicate* with all types of clients.
Say:	While working as a cashier at Market Store, *I communicated* effectively with all of our clients.
Don't Say:	While I volunteered at Benevolent Hospital, *I gained experience from assisting some of the* nurses distribute medication.
Say:	While volunteering on the children's ward at Benevolent Hospital, *I assisted* nurses distribute medicine to children.
Don't Say:	As an apprentice at the Car Exchange, *I was able to learn how* to make minor repairs.
Say:	As an apprentice at the Car Exchange, *I assisted* in minor repairs such as changing oil, changing brake fluid, and assessing transmissions.

You have now summarized important information to use on your résumés and for job interviews.

Business Cards

To aid you with your job search, create a business card. Select a few accomplishments and list them as bullet points on your card:

James Franklin	**312.555.1212**
	jbf@email.com

B.A., Journalism, Philadelphia College
- Three years of editorial experience
- Creative, Dedicated, and Motivated
- Excellent GPA and References

References are available upon request.

Your new business card is a useful tool for networking; your card provides your contact information and reminds associates of your skills.

Once you create your card, either take your card to a local printer or buy a few pieces of high quality, hard-stock paper and print your own cards. Use a good quality paper cutter—the type you would find at an art supply store—so that your cards look professional.

Networking

Networking may be *the best* way to make new contacts and secure a job.

- Connect with people who have similar interests or who can support you in your objectives.

Your network can include everyone you know through peers, past or current jobs, organizations (such as your place of worship), friends of your family, club memberships, associations, volunteer groups, and so on.

Networking builds your reputation and credibility within your field—networking is about staying active and involved.

- **Build your network *before* you need it.**

Many people make the mistake of looking for ways to build a network *after* they already need it. Start your networking now and network on an ongoing basis so that you make contacts, remain visible, and get the support you need.

- **View networking as a communication exchange, not a one-sided dialog.**

Before you call on someone to network, articulate why the meeting would be *mutually* beneficial. Look for common interests, experiences, or shared acquaintances.

- **Reciprocate favors: when you ask people in your network for help, also ask what you can do for them in return.**

As well as finding mutual interests, ask those with whom you come into contact how you can help them. You may find that an opportunity that did not work out for you is perfect for someone else.

- **Use professional organizations as career opportunities**.

Professional organizations within your field provide a steady stream of new people with whom you can network; these types of experiences can also enhance your managerial and leadership skills.

- **Continue to network within your organization.**

Networking is associated with contacts outside your workplace; however, also network *within* your organization to promote your visibility.

Volunteer to serve on task forces, participate in focus groups, and attend company activities. Find new friends in the company cafeteria. Treat everyone at your organization with respect, including the support staff (such as mailroom and cleaning personnel).

Job-Search Letters

Letters are important tools for initiating, developing, and following up with contacts and job prospects. Even though everyone seems to be using e-mail for everything, a hard-copy letter still makes a strong impression.

Here are two types of letters that are part of the job search process:

1. Cover Letter
2. Thank-you Letter

Tailor every letter that you write to the specific position that you are going after and the company that you are sending it to. In addition, some companies prefer that all application letters and résumés be submitted online; other companies prefer to receive hard copies. Check each company's preference as you engage in your job search.

If you send your application letter and résumé electronically, send them to yourself first so that you can print them out to make sure that they print as nicely as they look on the screen.

Let's review how to get the information you need to customize your letter.

Cover Letters

Send a cover letter whether you send you résumé through the mail or online. State why you would be right for the job and highlight your accomplishments. While your letter may not get you the job, a poorly written letter will keep you from getting in the door to apply.

Here are some guidelines that relate to job-search letters.

- **Know the name and title of the person to whom you are writing.** Do not address a letter to "Dear Sir" or "Dear Madam." Go to the company Web site or make a phone call to find out the addressee's name and its correct spelling;

- **Find out the company preference for receiving résumés is online or through the mail.** If you submit an application letter and résumé online, e-mail it to yourself first and print out your file to make sure it looks professional.

- **Stress what you can offer the organization.** Rather than focus on what you are looking for in a position, instead stress how your skills can benefit the organization.

- **Develop a plan for follow-up.** Take charge: do not expect others to contact you after they receive your information.

- **Aim for perfection: your written communication creates a strong first impression.** A letter of application presents high stakes—treat it seriously.

- **Write in a simple, clear, and concise way.** Write in the active voice, use the *you viewpoint*, and be concise.

A strong cover letter has an opening to capture the reader's attention but also identifies the job for which you are applying.

Example: The opportunity listed in Sunday's Chicago Tribune for a marketing associate is a great fit with my background and qualifications; my résumé is enclosed.

Example: Our mutual colleague Jennifer Lopez suggested that I have the talent and qualifications that you are looking for in a marketing associate. My enclosed résumé highlights some of that experience.

In the next paragraph, explain your special skills by listing some of your major accomplishments or qualifications that are relevant to the position you are seeking.

Example: As a recent graduate of Best University, I have knowledge of computer systems and accounting software. My grade point average of 3.8 demonstrates only part of my achievements. My degree in marketing includes a three-month internship. As an intern, I supported three vice presidents who trusted me with clients and managing their portfolios.

In the last part of your cover letter, request an interview. State that you will call within a specific time frame to establish a mutually agreeable time to meet.

Example: I'd appreciate the opportunity to meet with you to discuss how my background can benefit your corporation. I will contact you the week of June 12 to arrange a time that we can meet.

Thus, the first paragraph identifies the job, the second paragraph explains your special skills, and the third paragraph is the call to action.

Be sure to follow up with your commitment to call. If the party is not available, ask if there is another time that would be convenient for you to call back. Leave your name and number, but do not feel slighted if you do not get a callback: the responsibility for communication is on your shoulders.

Follow-Up Letters and Thank-You Notes

Two of the most powerful tools in your job search toolkit are a follow-up e-mail and a handwritten thank-you note.

A thank-you note that is handwritten may have the most impact. Your note will make your new networking associate feel good for rearranging a schedule to meet with you or for making a call or two on your behalf. The next time your name comes up, that person is likely to react positively.

If you choose to write a formal thank-you letter, you have another opportunity to sell yourself. Your letter allows you to restate your skills and accomplishments. Write a letter that is simple, friendly, and genuine.

Do not use a boiler-plate, *one size fits all* message. Customize each letter, e-mail message, and handwritten note by specifically referring to something you discussed. (Avoid using software to generate letters and résumés; however, if you do, at least customize your final product— remember, you are not the only person who bought the software!)

Get a business card from each of your contacts so that sending a note or e-mail takes less effort. Surprisingly, no matter how good the results are when letters are sent, few thank-you letters are actually written. Make a decision right now to upgrade that statistic.

The Résumé

Human resource executives and hiring managers typically receive hundreds of résumés for every job opening. What will make your résumé stand out among others?

To start, your résumé should not exceed two pages. If you can highlight your experience effectively in one page, that is even better. Being brief is critical.

Whatever you do, do not use flamboyant fonts or fancy paper; use conservative fonts (such as Times New Roman or Arial) and crisp, white heavy-weight bond paper.

Concentrate on substance, style, and consistency: your résumé should reflect your values and achievements. Even though you may start the process by using a résumé template from your computer software, make sure you *individualize* your résumé before you sent it out, customizing it for the specific job that you are applying for.

Take a moment to review the sample cover letter on the next page.

Rosalie Lindsey
1212 Arquilla Lane
Winter Haven, FL 35319

January 6, 2009

Ms. Eileen Karuso
Human Resource Manager
Toye and Bhee Corporation
8100 South Nashville
Tallahassee, FL 35316

Dear Ms. Karuso:

Thank you for the time that you spent discussing opportunities at Toye and Bhee Corporation.

My résumé and business card are enclosed. As you can see, I've worn a number of hats in the publishing field—writing, editing and managing—almost all in the areas of marketing and advertising.

I will follow up with you soon to find out if there is a convenient time for us to meet.

Sincerely,

Rosalie Lindsey
Enclosures

Chronological Formatting

The chronological format is a traditional format that gets good results.

- The **chronological format** lists your education, positions, and accomplishments in order, starting with the most recent and working backward in order of occurrence.

Using chronological formatting, the first job listed would be your most recent; the last job listed would be your first job.

This format has the advantage of being the more traditional; readers find it easy to evaluate your background quickly and to see a history of steady promotions or increased responsibility.

To produce a clean, crisp résumé, do the following:

- Be concise; prioritize information and include only the most important details.

- Be specific about your accomplishments; quantify your achievements when possible.

- Apply parallel structure (represent words in a consistent form).

- Edit ruthlessly then proofread to perfection.

- State your educational and professional background honestly.

- Keep your résumé to one page if you can, two pages if you cannot.

Write your résumé to answer questions before they arise. Use your cover letter to fill in gaps of unemployment that might appear on your résumé.

Realize that employers assume you are telling the truth until they find out otherwise. When employers check specific details, they usually do so only after they have already decided to hire you.

PAT VINCENT

**109 Ogden Avenue
Downers Grove, IL 60515
(630) 555-1212 (H) • (630) 555-1212 (C)
*pv@email.com***

SUMMARY

Dedicated administrative professional with extensive experience in office and facilities management, meeting planning, and computer applications. Good organizer who can lead, train, and motivate others.

EXPERIENCE

Executive Assistant   **June 2005 to Present**
Duneland Doctors, Valparaiso, IN

- Scheduling and maintaining calendar, appointments, files, and travel.

- Contacting attorneys, doctors, and patients.

- Renewing State and Federal licenses.

- Coordinating building issues, such as furniture, office machines moves and ordering office supplies.

- Composing correspondence and completing monthly reports.

EDUCATION

B.A., Business Management, Best College

A.A., Communications, Ivy Tech

SKILLS

Windows, Word, Excel, PowerPoint, WordPerfect, Lotus Notes, Harvard Graphics, AIM, Calendar Creator Plus, Pegasus, Outlook E-mail, Internet (Orbitz & Expedia)

References available upon request.

Quick Guide to Job Survival Tools 401

Scannable Formatting

A good electronic résumé should provide the same information as a good traditional résumé, including an inventory of skills and accomplishments.

Here are a few more tips for your e- résumé:

- Use a maximum of 65 characters per line.

- Omit italics and underlines.

- Include a key-word summary at the top of the page which highlights your experience or duties you have performed.

- Adhere to parallel structure and end verbs in their *ing* form, for example, "answering phone and e-mail messages," "interviewing prospective clients."

The key word summary allows organizations to pull up résumé that fit the position they are looking to fill.

Because applying for a job online involves little more than the push of a button, many employers have reported receiving thousands of résumés for jobs listed online. Unless the job advertisement calls for "apply by e-mail only," the best approach is to respond with a traditional résumé and cover letter.

Electronic résumés are sent through e-mail, attached as part of online applications or posted on the Internet within personal Web pages. On your electronic résumé, include a *key word summary.*

- The **key word summary** should appear at the top of the page after your name and contact information and consist of 20 to 30 words and phrases that relate to your education and experience.

Emphasize your knowledge, experience, and skills that are likely to attract prospective employers.

On a traditional résumé, describe your work experience in verb phrases that begin with strong action verbs (such as managed, supervised, processed). However, on an e- résumé, key word summaries usually consist of noun and adjective phrases. Some examples might be "fluent in Spanish," "team-oriented," or "strong communication skills."

Sample Scannable Résumé

PAT VINCENT
109 Ogden Avenue, Downers Grove, IL 60615
E-mail: pv@email.com
630-555-1212

KEYWORDS

graphic arts, digital arts, communication and writing skills, leadership
ability, Office 2007, Flash MX, Dreamweaver MX, JavaScript, analytic,
willing to travel, high school graduate

OBJECTIVE

A position in which I can use my digital art skills, business communication
skills, and leadership skills to grow within an organization that has an
environmental mission.

EDUCATION

Best College, Chicago, Illinois
BA—degree in progress
Major: Communications
Minor: Information Science
Related courses: psychology, journalism, political science

South Side High School, Downers Grove, Illinois
Graduated 2006

WORK EXPERIENCE

Computer Lab Assistant, 2007-Present
Best College
Assisting students in logging on to computers, using programs, and
finding missing files; fixing printer problems.

ACTIVITIES

President of Spanish Club, Best College

Whereas traditional résumés contain tabs and headers such as *Education* and *Work Experience* highlighted with bolding or italics, e-résumés lack these tabs and highlighting. Because e-mail programs usually have difficulty reading tabs and highlighting, remove both to ensure that your recipient receives your résumé in tact.

To change your traditional résumé into an electronic one, follow these steps:

1. Remove all highlighting: bolding, underlining, and italics.

2. Eliminate bullets, and replace them with dashes, small o's, or asterisks.

3. Move all your text to the left.

4. Remove returns except for those separating major sections.

5. Use all capitals for headers.

6. Provide an additional line or two of spacing between sections.

7. Save the file in ASCII or Rich-Text Format

To send your electronic résumé, start with a subject line that states the title of the job for which you are applying, such as "Graphic Arts Applicant." Then copy and paste your cover letter followed by your résumé within an e-mail.

Check first before sending your traditionally-formatted résumé as an attachment. Employers are reluctant to open attachments from applicants whom they do not know. In your cover letter, refer to the résumé that follows. Then copy and paste your letter into the e-mail first and follow it with your résumé.

Quick Skills Pitch: Elevator Speech

By developing a quick pitch of your skills, you will be ready for any networking event or even the impromptu meeting of a potential employer.

Think of the quick pitch as an "elevator speech": a short monologue that provides vital information, keeping the listener's attention and peaking their interest. Create an actual script that you memorize—but be sure to sound natural when you use it.

Here is an example of a quick skills pitch:

> Hi. My name is Reggie Vincent. I'm a recent graduate of Best College with a degree in communications. As well as specializing in effective communication systems, I am a good team player with strong leadership qualities. Would you be interested in receiving my résumé, or do you have any jobs that I might apply for?

Your *elevator speech* should take no more than *ten seconds*. Give the listener enough honest information that highlights key reasons how you could contribute to his or her company.

Before you end your conversation, get the contact information and find out how you should send your information: electronic copy or hard copy.

Recap

Finding a job is itself a job. Commit to preparing your career portfolio as well as preparing your mindset toward success.

You have worked hard to build your skills. And while searching for a job might feel daunting, the best response is to take action and stay active until you achieve your dreams. As Leonardo daVinci once said, "Inaction weakens the vigors of the mind . . . action strengthens the essence of creation."

Get into action and you may be surprised how much progress you make.

Skills Workshop

Instructions: Prepare your career portfolio in hard copy format and electronic format.

Here is a check list to help you get started:

_____ Write your career objective or personal mission statement

_____ Create a personal business card

_____ Collect samples of your written work

_____ Compose a sample cover letter

_____ Prepare your résumés: chronological and scannable

_____ Ask two to three contacts for a letter of reference

_____ Prepare a list of networking opportunities

_____ Buy heavy-weight bond paper and envelopes for résumés and letters

What else would you like to add to your portfolio?

_____

Keys to Activities

Chapter 1

Part A: Grammar

1. The attendant asked Joe and **you** for the information.

2. Keep the meeting between Charles and **me** confidential.

3. **She** and her manager brought the equipment we needed.

4. Sylvia is the account representative **who** made the sale.

5. If you have more time than **I (do)**, complete the project . . .

6. Ms. Adamchek insisted the account be given to you and **me**.

7. If you need a new client, call Jim or **me** for referrals.

8. **He** and his entire team went to lunch at Yogi's.

9. If Bob, **you**, and Jim were on my team, we would win.

10. They assigned the project before Reggie and **you** could respond.

11. The new budget will be **frozen** until further notice.

12. Their customer **enclosed** the check with the application.

13. Has your supervisor ever **spoken** about that policy?

14. If Martin **were** you, he would have made the same decision.

15. If the game had **gone** better, we could have won conference.

16. Ms. Donata **did** a good job as a presenter.

17. After the team has **gone** to the conference, the answers will be clear.

18. You should **have** sent the invoice directly to the distributor.

19. Our budget **doesn't** have an unlimited amount of funds.

20. Martin, along with his team, **is** going to the meeting.

21. Alice felt **bad** about the situation and wanted a change.

22. Next week is the **busiest** or **most busy** time of our entire year.

23. To get the job, you need to take their policies more **seriously**.

24. Your team performed **well** on the evaluation.

25. Don't give **anyone** the information about our project.

Part B: Punctuation

1. They listed the product on August 15, 2007, in their online catalog.

2. Rose, Bob, and Charley agreed to the new contract.

3. Before you send in your application, get the exact address.

4. Our old location was closed last April; therefore, you should have been using our new address.

5. Juan Marquez, human resources director, will be in Denver, Colorado, on August 10.

6. Fortunately, my résumé is up-to-date and ready to mail.

7. Ms. Patlan, please assist me with this issue when you have time.

8. The applicant's portfolio arrived on September 4, and we promptly scheduled an appointment.

9. Ken finished the project; however, the company sent him another one.

10. My project ended two weeks ago; all reviews were excellent.

11. Any merger, therefore, requires trust from all parties involved.

12. Mrs. Fleming, thank you for supporting our charitable projects.

Part C: Word Usage

Instructions:

For the following sentences, make corrections in word usage as needed.

1. Your **principal** and interest have remained the same for two years.

2. A company won't change **its** policy just because you don't like it.

3. Mike **assured** his team that he would finish the project promptly.

4. The changes will **affect** everyone in our branch office.

5. If the bank will **lend** you the capital that you need, you are lucky.

Chapter 2

Practice 2.1: Sentence Core

1. The <u>order</u> <u>contained</u> too many unnecessary products.

2. <u>I</u> <u>thanked</u> the new engineer for fixing the electrical problem.

3. (I) <u>Thank</u> you for asking that question.

4. Our new <u>program</u> <u>will begin</u> in one month.

5. (You) <u>Examine</u> the order carefully before sending it out.

Practice 2.2: Redundant Subjects

1. My <u>friends</u> (or <u>associates</u>) <u>tell</u> me now is a good time to buy gold.

2. The <u>details</u> (or <u>specifics</u>) about the project <u>were</u> fascinating.

3. <u>Visitors</u> (or <u>guests</u>) <u>should sign in</u> at the front desk. ("sign in" is a verb phrase)

4. My <u>goals</u> (or <u>objectives</u>) <u>reflect</u> my dreams.

5. The <u>results</u> (or <u>outcomes</u>) <u>reflect</u> our success.

Practice 2.3: Redundant Verbs

1. **Milton's <u>decision</u> (<u>uncovers</u> or) <u>reveals</u> his true motives.**

2. Mark's <u>actions</u> ~~surprised me and~~ <u>caught</u> me off guard.

3. <u>We</u> ~~started the project and~~ <u>worked</u> on (the project) for two hours.

4. <u>I</u> ~~understand and~~ <u>appreciate</u> your commitment to our mission.

5. <u>Melanie</u> ~~greeted us and~~ <u>welcomed</u> us to the banquet.

Practice 2.4: Parallel Phrases

List 1:

1. Order supplies   or Ordering supplies

2. Schedule appointment   or Scheduling appointment

3. Renew certificate   or Renewing certificate

List 2:

1. Coordinate schedules   or Coordinating schedules
2. Distribute supplies   or Distributing supplies
3. Phone clients   or Phoning clients

List 3:

1. Train staff   or Training staff
2. Develop policy   or Developing policy
3. Reconcile profit and loss   or Reconciling profit and loss

Practice 2.5: Sentence Fragments – Answers will vary.

1. Making the right decision at the right time *felt good.*
2. *We could all go to lunch* because he finished the project earlier than anyone expected.
3. After I made the decision to reclaim my spot on the team, *I was happy.*
4. To show interest in a project that no longer had merit *does not make sense.*
5. *Our goal was* going slower than planned but staying under budget.

Practice 2.6: Real Subjects and Strong Verbs

1. Customer service needs to fill five orders.
2. An electrical problem on the fifth floor caused the outage.
3. Randy will revise the document today.
4. A new report arrived earlier today.
5. You can decide tomorrow.

Practice 2.7: Information Flow--Answers may vary.

1. *Consumers* are not buying too many unnecessary and costly items at this time.

2. *Many consumers* are choosing to spend their money on good used items at a reduced price.

3. *A change in consumer attitudes* is partly due to the rapidly increasing cost of gasoline.

4. *For your next paper, consider the topic* of outsourcing jobs to third-world countries.

5. *As you complete your report,* please consider the cost as well as the time required to make the revisions.

Skills Workshop

Worksheet 1: Removing Redundancy

1. We ~~appreciate and~~ value your efforts on the project.

2. The instructions ~~and directions~~ were clear, but our task was confusing ~~and puzzling~~ at times.

3. We hope ~~and trust~~ that you are interested in working on another project.

4. If you ~~need and~~ want a part-time job, I know someone for you to contact.

5. Your ~~first and~~ initial contact with him should be professional ~~and positive~~.

6. If you prepare for the interview ~~and are ready~~, you will make a good ~~and lasting~~ impression.

7. If this job ~~is good for you and~~ works out, you can refer ~~and recommend~~ your friends ~~also~~.

8. My friends will arrive ~~and be here~~ shortly.

9. Everyone will ~~notice and~~ appreciate the help that you give them.

10. (You) ~~Make a note and~~ mark your calendar for April 15; attend this event with a friend ~~or associate~~.

11. ~~First and foremost,~~ we ~~thank you for~~ appreciate your business.

12. (You) <u>Make</u> sure that the materials ~~are here and that they~~ have arrived in time for the meeting.

Editing Workshop – Chapter 2

Dear Mr. Jones,

I am interested in applying for the job you that you posted with our college placement office.

My résumé is attached. After you review it, I am sure that you will find that I have the skills that you are seeking for this position.

You can reach me at 219-555-1212, or you can send me an e-mail at roger@e-mail.com.

I look forward to speaking with you about this position.

Best regards,

Roger Di Nicolo

Cell:312-555-1212

Phone: 219-555-1212

Chapter 3

Practice 3.1: Paragraphs and Information Flow—answers may vary.

> Good writing is about composing and editing. As you compose, allow yourself to write freely and make mistakes. When you edit, identify the mistakes that you have made and correct them. Once you understand how to manage the writing process, good writing becomes much easier to produce.

Practice 3.2: Pronoun Point of View and Consistency

1. I usually work late on Thursdays because *I* can get a lot done at the end of the week. When *I* work late, I usually see other people

working late also. Having *my* boss notice that *I am* putting in extra time always makes me feel good.

2. Good nutrition leads to good health. When *you* eat well, you are likely to feel better. *You may* not find it easy to eat in a healthful way, though. *You may* prefer to eat fast food at the end of the day when you are tired.

   Or: Good nutrition leads to good health. When *I* eat well, *I* feel better. *I* do not find it easy to eat in a healthful way, though. I usually prefer to eat fast food at the end of the day when *I am* are tired.

Practice 3.2

The construction for the 9th floor conference room was extended two more weeks. *However, w*e were not informed until Friday. *As a result,* our meetings for the following week needed to be reassigned to different *rooms, but none* were available. *Fortunately,* Jane Simmons agreed to let us use her office*, and s*everal serious conflicts were avoided.

Skills Workshop

Worksheet 1: Conjunctions as Transitions—Answers may vary.

How does your revised message compare with the following? Do not expect your message to be the same—what improvements did you make?

Tom,

In your last message, you requested 10 sets of materials. *Although* I do have some materials to send you, I will *also* have a meeting with my staff next week. *Therefore*, I cannot send you all of the materials that I have available, *or* I would not have enough for my meeting.

Since I do not have enough binders, I can send you only 7 complete sets. *However*, you can have as many revised policy manuals and new product flyers as you need. *Thus*, you will only need to purchase 3 binders from your office supplier.

Editing Workshop – Chapter 3

When you proofread, check a manuscript for errors in grammar and spelling and correcting them. Also look for errors in punctuation, capitalization, and number usage. Identify and correct run-on sentences and incomplete thoughts. By proofreading your document and correcting its errors, your document becomes more professional and credible.

Chapter 4

Practice 4.1

Rule 2: Conjunction (CONJ)

1. <u>Mark Mallory</u> <u>is</u> the new district manager, and <u>he</u> <u>starts</u> on Monday. CONJ

2. <u>Mark</u> <u>will be</u> an inspiration to our staff and an excellent spokesperson for our product. (no commas)

3. <u>You</u> <u>can leave</u> him a message, but <u>he</u> <u>will</u> not <u>be</u> able to reply until next week. CONJ

4. The <u>office</u> in St. Louis also <u>has</u> a new manager, and her <u>name</u> <u>is</u> Alicia Rivera. CONJ

5. <u>You</u> <u>can mail</u> your information now and <u>expect</u> a reply within the next two weeks. (no commas)

Practice 4.2

Rule 3: Series (SER)

1. <u>We</u> <u>were</u> <u>assigned</u> Conference Rooms A and B on the first floor. (no commas)

2. (<u>You</u>) <u>Make</u> sure that you bring your laptop, cell phone, and client list to the meeting. SER

3. <u>You</u> <u>should</u> <u>arrange</u> the meeting, call your manager, and submit your proposal. SER

4. <u>Mitchell</u>, <u>Helen</u>, and <u>Sally</u> <u>conducted</u> the workshop on culinary science. SER

5. <u>They</u> <u>gave</u> a workshop for Elaine, Arlene, Donald, and Joanne on preparing, cutting, and storing vegetables. SER

Practice 4.3
Rule 4: Introductory (INTRO)

1. Because the <u>letter</u> <u>arrived</u> late, <u>we</u> <u>were</u> not able to respond on time. INTRO

2. However, <u>we</u> <u>were</u> <u>given</u> an extension. INTRO

3. Although the extra <u>time</u> <u>helped</u> us, <u>we</u> still <u>felt</u> pressured for time. INTRO

4. To get another extension, <u>George</u> <u>called</u> their office. INTRO

5. Fortunately, the office <u>manager</u> <u>was</u> agreeable to our request. INTRO

Practice 4.4
Rule 5: Nonrestrictive (NR)

1. Our <u>manager</u> *who specializes in project grants* <u>will</u> <u>assist</u> you with this issue. (restrictive: no commas)

2. <u>Tomas Phillips</u>, *who works only on weekends,* <u>will</u> <u>call</u> you soon. NR

3. The <u>paralegal</u> *who researched this lawsuit* <u>is</u> not available. (restrictive: no commas)

4. <u>Nick Richards,</u> *who is in a meeting until 3 p.m.,* <u>can</u> <u>answer</u> your question. NR

5. Your new <u>contract</u>, *which we mailed yesterday,* should <u>arrive</u> by Friday. NR

Practice 4.5
Rule 6: Parenthetical (PAR)

1. <u>Customer service</u>, I believe, <u>can</u> best <u>assist</u> you with this issue. PAR
2. <u>T. J.</u>, therefore, <u>will</u> <u>work</u> this weekend in my place. PAR
3. Our <u>invoice</u>, unfortunately, <u>was</u> <u>submitted</u> incorrectly. PAR
4. The new <u>contract</u>, in my opinion, <u>meets</u> specifications. PAR
5. <u>Brown Company</u>, of course, <u>recommended</u> us to a vendor. PAR

Practice 4.6
Rule 7: Direct Address (DA)

1. (<u>You</u>) <u>Give</u> your report to the auditor by Friday, Marcel. DA
2. Jason, <u>do you have</u> tickets for the game? DA
3. Doctor, <u>I</u> <u>would</u> <u>like</u> to know the results of my tests. DA
4. <u>Would</u> <u>you</u> <u>like</u> to attend the banquet, Alice? DA
5. (I) <u>Thank</u> you for inviting me, George. DA

Practice 4.7
Rule 8: Appositive (AP)

1. <u>Jacob Seinfeld</u>, our associate director, <u>decided</u> to hire Williams. AP
2. My lab <u>partner</u>, Carol Glasco, <u>applied</u> for a job here. AP
3. <u>Jim Martinez</u>, the registrar, <u>approved</u> your request. AP
4. The <u>department chair</u>, Dr. George Schmidt, <u>did</u> not <u>receive</u> your transcript. AP
5. The <u>director</u> <u>asked</u> Claire, my sister, to join us for dinner. AP

Practice 4.8

Rule 9: Addresses and Dates (AD)

1. (<u>You</u>) <u>Send</u> your application by Friday, December 15, to my assistant. AD

2. <u>San Antonio</u>, Texas, <u>has</u> a River Walk and Conference Center. AD

3. <u>Would</u> <u>you</u> <u>prefer</u> to meet in Myrtle, Minnesota, or Des Moines, Iowa? AD

4. <u>Springfield</u>, Massachusetts, <u>continues</u> to be my selection. AD

5. <u>We</u> <u>arrived</u> in Chicago, Illinois, on March 15, 2009, to prepare for the event. AD

Practice 4.9

Rule 10: Word Omitted (WO)

1. The <u>president</u> <u>shared</u> two intriguing, confidential reports. WO

2. The <u>crew</u> <u>scheduled</u> filming on Tuesday at 5 p.m., on Wednesday at 6 p.m. WO

3. The <u>problem</u> <u>is</u>, some of the results are not yet known. WO

4. (<u>You</u>) <u>Leave</u> the materials with Alicia at the Westin, with Marcia at the Hilton. WO

5. <u>Silvana</u> <u>presented</u> a short, exciting PowerPoint on Italy. WO

Practice 4.10

Rule 11: Direct Quotation (DQ)

1. Patrick shouted "Get back!" before we had a chance to see the falling debris. DQ

2. According to Tyler, "All children can learn if they find an interest in what is taught." DQ

3. My father warned me, "When you choose an insurance company, find one with good customer service." DQ

4. Sharon encouraged me by yelling "Go for the gold!" as I was starting the race. DQ

5. Lenny said to me, "Good luck on your exam," before I left this morning. DQ (OR: no commas because it is a short quote)

Practice 4.11

Rule 12: Contrasting Expression or Afterthought (CEA)

1. <u>You will find</u> the manuscript in John's office, not in Bob's. CEA

2. <u>Marcus secured</u> the contract, but only after negotiating for hours. CEA

3. (<u>You</u>) <u>Chair</u> the budget committee, if you prefer. CEA

4. <u>Lester</u>, rather than Dan, <u>received</u> the award. CEA

5. (<u>You</u>) <u>Work</u> to achieve your dreams, not to run away from your fears. CEA

Worksheet 1: Conjunction (CONJ), Series (SER), Direct Address (DA)

1. <u>I completed</u> my report, and <u>Alice sent</u> it to Wanda. CONJ

2. <u>Wanda received</u> the report, but <u>she did</u> not yet <u>file</u> it with the department. CONJ

3. (<u>I</u>) <u>Thank</u> you for letting me know about your concern, Marsha. DA

4. <u>Wanda will appreciate</u> your telling her about the missing information for John Wilson, Bill Jones, and Mark Kramer. SER

5. (<u>You</u>) <u>Give</u> Wanda the information today, and <u>you will save</u> her some time. CONJ

6. The <u>report</u> often <u>needs</u> to be adjusted, and <u>Wanda</u> kindly <u>helps</u> us with it. CONJ

7. Marsha, <u>you are</u> wonderful to assist us with the extra work in our department. DA

8. (You) <u>Call</u> Marcus, Mary, and Phil about the schedules. SER

9. You <u>can ask</u> for additional time, but <u>you</u> <u>may</u> not <u>receive</u> it. CONJ

10. The training <u>room</u> <u>needs</u> new chairs, tables, and flip charts. SER

11. (You) <u>Go</u> to the mail room to get the catalog for ordering supplies, Mallory. DA

12. The <u>accounting department</u> <u>issues</u> guidelines for expenses, and <u>someone</u> in that department <u>can assist</u> you with your expense account. CONJ

Worksheet 2: Introductory (INTRO), Appositive (AP), Direct Address (DA)

1. While <u>I</u> <u>waited</u> for a bus, <u>I</u> <u>completed</u> the report. INTRO

2. However, the <u>report</u> <u>may need</u> some major revisions. INTRO

3. (You) <u>Give</u> me your honest opinion, Mike. DA

4. <u>Mr. Sisco</u>, our new office manager, <u>will use</u> the report to make important decisions. AP

5. If <u>I</u> <u>had known</u> how important the report would be, <u>I</u> <u>would</u> not <u>have agreed</u> to do it. INTRO

6. However, <u>I</u> <u>felt</u> pressured to agree to do it because everyone has too much work. INTRO

7. You <u>can ask</u> Susan, our sales representative, for a second opinion. AP

8. When <u>I</u> <u>started</u> this job, <u>I</u> <u>had</u> no idea about the long work hours. INTRO

9. However, <u>I</u> <u>would have taken</u> it anyway because of its wonderful opportunities. INTRO

10. After <u>you</u> <u>work</u> here for a while, <u>you</u> <u>will appreciate</u> your fellow workers. INTRO

Worksheet 3: Conjunction (CONJ), Addresses and Dates (AD), Nonrestrictive (NR) , Parenthetical (PAR)

1. Mr. Gates started a computer company, and Miller decided to invest in it. CONJ
2. Miller, however, did not realize the potential at that time. PAR
3. The company, which is quite successful, has satellites around the world. NR
4. He revealed that March 27, 2008, will be the official kick-off date. AD
5. (You) Arrive to the interview on time, and you will make a good impression. CONJ
6. We have, as a result, chosen another vendor. PAR
7. The time management seminar was excellent, and its cost was reasonable. CONJ
8. Your paper, unfortunately, did not meet the standards. PAR
9. Our management team assessed the damages, and they recommended changes. CONJ
10. On September 4, 2011, we will arrive in Denver, Colorado, for a meeting. AD / AD

Worksheet 4: Introductory (INTRO), Series (SER), Words Omitted (WO), Contrasting Expression or Afterthought (CEA)

1. If you choose to attend the event, (you) let us know by the end of the day. INTRO
2. (You) Bring a guest to the luncheon, if you prefer. CEA
3. If you need extra tickets, (you) ask Elizabeth. INTRO
4. After the awards, they will serve a meal of fish potatoes and broccoli. INTRO

5. (You) <u>Resume</u> the program at the north branch, not at the south branch. CEA

6. Although the <u>offer</u> still <u>stands</u>, our <u>deadline</u> quickly <u>approaches</u>. INTRO

7. Before <u>they</u> <u>rescind</u> their offer, (<u>you</u>) <u>give</u> them an answer. INTRO

8. After <u>you</u> <u>review</u> the contract, (<u>you</u>) <u>let</u> us know what you think. INTRO

9. The <u>contract</u> <u>can be changed</u>, but only on our terms. CEA

10. Your <u>feedback</u> <u>should include</u> items to add, delete, or change. SER

11. The <u>fact</u> <u>is</u>, your input will assist us in many ways. WO

12. (You) <u>Begin</u> the year with a detailed, comprehensive plan. WO

Editing Workshop – Chapter 4

Dear Mrs. Adams:

We have an opening for an intern in our accounting department. Therefore, please post the attached job order in your placement department.

Anyone interested in applying for the position (delete comma) can contact Mary Jones, our human resource recruiter. Mary (delete comma) is expecting to hear from your students, and she will interview (delete comma) any students who apply. She is planning to conduct interviews (delete comma) on Wednesday, June 5, and Thursday, June 13.

You have always been so helpful, Mrs. Adams, in encouraging students with great skills to apply for positions at our company. As a result, we contact you first when we have (delete comma) an opening.

All the best,

Georgia Smith

All Pro Temporaries

Chapter 5

Practice 5.1

Rule 1: Semicolon No Conjunction (NC)

1. <u>Keri</u> <u>will</u> not <u>approve</u> our expense account; <u>she</u> <u>needs</u> more documentation.

2. (<u>You</u>) <u>Ask</u> Bryan for the report; <u>he</u> <u>said</u> that it was completed yesterday.

3. (<u>You</u>) <u>Arrive</u> on time to tomorrow's meeting; (<u>you</u>) <u>bring</u> both of your reports.

4. A <u>laptop</u> <u>was</u> <u>left</u> in the conference room; <u>Johnny</u> <u>claimed</u> it as his.

5. (<u>You</u>) <u>Recognize</u> your mistakes; (<u>you</u>) <u>offer</u> apologies as needed.

Practice 5.2

Rule 2: Semicolon Bridge (BR)

1. <u>Carol</u> <u>suggested</u> the topic; fortunately, <u>Carlos</u> <u>agreed</u>.

2. The project management <u>team</u> <u>offered</u> assistance; however, their <u>time</u> <u>was</u> limited.

3. <u>Ken</u> <u>compiled</u> the data; therefore, <u>Mary</u> <u>crunched</u> it.

4. The <u>numbers</u> <u>turned out</u>* well; as a result, our new <u>budget</u> <u>was</u> <u>accepted</u>.

5. <u>Roger</u> <u>ran</u> in the marathon; unfortunately, <u>he</u> <u>was</u> unable to finish.

* "Turned out" is a verb phrase.

Practice 5.3

Rule 3: Semicolon Because of Commas (BC)

1. (<u>You</u>) Please <u>include</u> Rupert Adams, CEO; Madeline Story, COO; and Mark Coleman, executive president.

2. By next week I will have traveled to St. Louis, Missouri; Chicago, Illinois; and Burlington, Iowa.

3. Mike applied for jobs in Honolulu, Hawaii; Sacramento, California; and Santa Fe, New Mexico.

4. Your application was received yesterday; but when I reviewed it, information was missing.

5. You can resubmit your application today; and since my office will review it, you can call me tomorrow for the results.

Skills Workshop

Worksheet 1: Semicolon No Conjunction (NC) and Comma Conjunction (CONJ)

1. The Green Tree reception was elegant; it was a black tie event. NC

2. I arrived early to the event, and everyone seemed very friendly. CONJ

3. The group expressed concern about the environment; they all wanted to see immediate and substantial change. NC

4. The keynote speaker shared new data about climate change; everyone listened attentively to the entire speech. NC

5. Mark suggested that we join the group, so he inquired about the requirements for membership. CONJ

6. Membership required participation at various levels; both of us were already overextended. NC

7. The group's mission appealed to me, and I was excited about getting involved. CONJ

8. Mark thought it over for a while, yet he was still not ready to commit. CONJ

9. The environmental movement grows every year, but more help is urgently needed. CONJ

10. Mark finally <u>agreed</u> to join the group; my <u>excitement</u> <u>tipped</u> him in the right direction. NC

11. Their first <u>meeting</u> <u>is</u> next week, and <u>we</u> both <u>plan</u> to go to it. CONJ

12. I <u>will volunteer</u> for the same project that Mark works on; <u>working</u> together <u>is</u> fun. NC

Worksheet 2: Semicolon Bridge (BR) and Comma Parenthetical (PAR)

1. <u>Keeping up with technology</u> <u>can</u>, however, <u>enhance</u> your career. PAR

2. Different <u>generations</u> <u>have</u> different sorts of issues with technology; for example, younger <u>people</u> <u>have</u> an easier time learning new technology. BR

3. Today's young <u>people</u> <u>used</u> computers throughout their schooling; consequently, <u>they</u> <u>find</u> technology a natural part of their world. BR

4. Older <u>generations</u>, however, <u>did</u>n't <u>have</u> access to technology in school. PAR

5. <u>They</u> <u>needed</u> to learn how to use computers and software on the job; as a result, <u>many</u> <u>considered</u> themselves "technologically illiterate." BR

6. It <u>is</u> never too late, though, to learn how to use a computer. PAR

7. <u>Taking classes</u> at a local college <u>can</u> sometimes <u>be</u> inconvenient; however, <u>you</u> <u>can research</u> training opportunities online. BR

8. Online <u>classes</u> <u>make</u> learning convenient; for example, <u>you</u> <u>can learn</u> while you are in your own home office. BR

9. Most <u>companies</u> <u>offer</u> in-house training; fortunately, their <u>employees</u> <u>stay</u> at the cutting edge of technology. BR

10. <u>Getting a job</u> at a major corporation, therefore, <u>helps ensure</u> that you will keep your skills up-to-date. PAR

11. (<u>You</u>) <u>Take</u> advantage of all opportunities to build your skills; for example, (<u>you</u>) <u>keep</u> an eye on your college and company newsletters. BR

12. Computer <u>classes</u> and other sorts of career <u>classes</u> <u>are offered</u>; however, only the most <u>motivated</u> <u>enroll</u> in them. BR

Editing Workshop – Chapter 5

Dear Ms. Allison:

Thank you (delete comma) for your résumé and cover letter. Your qualifications are excellent; however, we have no full-time positions available at the present time.

We will, however, have openings later in the year, and I will certainly hold your résumé until that time. In the meantime, I can offer you a position as a part-time floater.

A floater, in case you are wondering, shifts from task to task quickly (delete comma) and must adapt to different environments. This position (delete comma) might be perfect for you as a new college graduate; you will be able to sample many types of projects. If you would like to discuss this option further, please call me.

I hope, Ms. Allison, that you will consider being a floater; we are sure to have full-time positions open within the next six months.

Best regards,

Margaret Parson

Chapter 6

Practice 6.2: Regular Verbs in Past Time

1. The coach misplaced the roster before the game began.

2. My counselor suggested that I submit my résumé.

3. Bart received the award for most valuable player.

4. Last week no one on our team wanted the schedule to change.

5. When Jonika suggested that we meet after school, everyone was pleased.

Practice 6.3: Irregular Verbs in Past Time

1. We had already seen that movie last week. (Or: We already saw . . .)

2. The professor said that you wrote a good paper.

3. I brought my lunch today so I don't need to buy one.

4. Bob lent me $5 so that I could go to the game.

5. The assistant has taken all the papers to the office.

Practice 6.4: The –S Form

1. The coach says that we need to practice for one more hour.

2. Our team finishes in first place every year.

3. Taylor has chosen the players for both teams.

4. The coach has enough good players already.

5. If the group listens carefully, they will learn the information.

Practice 6.5: Verb Tense and Consistency

1. The note is not clear and needs to be changed.

2. My boss said that I arrived late to work every day this week

3. The new computers arrived today, so then I had to install them.

4. Yesterday my counselor told me I needed to take an extra elective.

5. Last week my teacher told me that I had to redo the paper.

Practice 6.6: Active Voice

1. My math instructor gave me the assignment.
2. My Uncle John purchased the car for me.
3. The entire team chose the new soccer jersey.
4. The Art Council will plan the annual art exhibit.
5. Please pay your invoice by the beginning of the month.

Practice 6.7: Parallel Structure

1. My professor asked me to submit a new paper and (to) hand it in on Friday.
2. My friends and I plan to visit a cathedral and (to) see the ancient ruins in Rome.
3. Everyone focused on showing good team spirit and winning the game.
4. Your attitude will go a long way toward achieving success and getting what you want in life.
5. I received the new soccer jerseys, and now I must pass them out.

Practice 6.8: Subjunctive Mood

1. The president insisted that Melba **attend** the reception.
2. Jacob wishes that he **were** on this year's team.
3. If Dan **were** your team captain, would you support him?
4. My mother said that it is imperative that my sister **complete** her college education.
5. If I **were** you, I would run for office.

Skills Workshop

Worksheet 1: Verbs in Past Time

When I **gave** my manager notice that I was resigning, she **asked** me for a formal letter of resignation. However, I had never **written** that kind of letter, so I didn't know how to get started. One of my friends **said** that she would help me, so I felt **relieved**. Last Saturday, it **seemed** that we **worked** all day on that letter until we finally **came** up with a professional version. By the time that I **finished** the letter, I **had decided** not to quit my job. I sure hope that my change of mind goes over well with my manager!

Worksheet 2: Third Person Singular: the -S Form

1. Melissa **doesn't** have the correct information.
2. Her friend Jeanne **has** given her misleading advice.
3. When she **asks** me, I always tell her the truth.
4. The economy **has** not done well this year.
5. Willis **doesn't** know anyone to ask to join our team.
6. If you are looking for a job, Jerrod **knows** the right people to contact.
7. The professor **passes** out reports at the beginning of every class.
8. My paper **has** not yet been completed.
9. The library **closes** at noon but reopens at 1 p.m.
10. Though my manager **doesn't** belong to that organization, she should.

Worksheet 3:   Subjunctive Mood: Present and Past

The athletic department announced the swim team will have its first meeting on Friday. If I **were** you, I would go. The captain said that if you want to be considered for the team, it is imperative that **you be** on time. In fact, I wish that I **were** as talented in sports as you are. If I **were**, I would try out for more than one sport.

Worksheet 4: Verb Tense, Agreement, and Consistency

1. Bob should not have **gone** to the luncheon on Friday.

2. Our receptionist **doesn't** give that information to anyone.

3. The new president had **spoken** at the annual event.

4. Randle **lent** me the material for the team project.

5. You should have **written** a draft first.

6. The phone must have **rung** 20 times while we were in the lecture hall.

7. I should have **brought** another copy of my paper.

8. Who has **drunk** the last glass of milk?

9. We were **frozen** before the game even began.

10. You should have easily **seen** the error in the report.

11. Everyone in the room was **taken** by surprise.

12. It felt as if we had **swum** with sharks.

13. My heart **sank** when she gave the news.

14. The budget is **frozen** until next quarter.

15. Bob was displeased that he **was** not able to complete the project.

Chapter 7

Practice 7.1: Subjects and Objects

1. If you can't reach anyone else, feel free to call **me**.

2. The director told Catie and **me** to try the scene again.

3. Fred and **she** collected for the local food drive.

4. His manager and **he** have two more reports to complete.

5. That decision was made by Jim and **me**.

Practice 7.2: Pronouns Following Between and Than

1. Between you and **me**, who has more time?

2. Beatrice sings better than **I do**.

3. The decision is between Bob and **you**.

4. The Blue Jays are more competitive than **we are**.

5. You can split the work between Margaret and **me** so that it gets done on time.

Practice 7.3: Pronoun and Antecedent Agreement

1. When **tellers do** not relate well to their customers, they need more training.

2. **Servers** go beyond **their** job description when they prepare carry-out orders for customers.

3. A pilot has a challenging job because **he or she** works long hours under difficult conditions. **(Or: pilots have . . . they work)**

4. When **students do** not turn in their work, **they** should expect penalties.

5. **Writers need** to submit **their** work in a timely manner.

Practice 7.4: Point of View and Consistency

1. I enjoy jogging because exercise keeps **me** fit.

2. You should follow the guidelines until **you** finish the project. (Or change both pronouns to **we**.)

3. As long as **I** stay motivated, I won't mind finishing the project.

4. **You** should strive to get the best education possible so you can have a satisfying career.

5. Sue and Mary worked on the project together, and **Sue** will present it at the next conference. (Or **Mary**)

Practice 7.5: Relative Pronouns: Who, Whom, and That

1. **Who** wrote the monthly report?

2. **Whom** are you going to the meeting with?

3. Is Jim the person **who** spoke with you?

4. The doctor **who** saw you yesterday is not available.

5. Every person **who** arrives late will be turned away.

Practice 7.6: Demonstrative Pronouns

1. The manuals are on **that** table in the corner.

2. Anderson asked for **those (or these)** pamphlets, not the ones you are sending.

3. Are **those** your clients you are referring to?

4. **That** is a good reason to give them the project.

5. Jacob asked that we solve **these** problems before it's too late.

Practice 7.7: Indefinite Pronouns

1. Either one of the programs **works** perfectly.

2. Everyone who finished the project **is** free to go.

3. None of the employees **send** e-mail on Saturday.

4. Some of the assignments **need** to be distributed before noon today.

5. Everything **runs** much better when we are all on time.

Skills Workshop

Worksheet 1: Pronoun Case

1. John and **I** completed the project yesterday.

2. Barbara was more competent than **he was**.   (Implied verb?)

3. Why were the materials delivered to **her** and Bob?

4. Between you and **me**, we have enough expertise.

5. The supervisor required Bob and **me** to attend the seminar.

6. You can ask George or **me** for the updated report.

7. They are more competent to do the job than **we are**.

8. The attorney asked that the case be divided among you, Alice, and **me**.

9. She asked who would do the report, my secretary or **I would**.

10. Margaret is taller than **I am**.

11. Bill likes Sue better than **"he likes me" or "I like Sue."**

12. The professor told my associate and **me** to complete our report.

13. The information was sent to **her and me**.

14. George and **I** watched the game before **he and I** left.

15. Upon recommendation, he gave the project to Jim and **me**.

16. Bob has more time than **I do**.

17. The project will be split between John and **me**.

18. She asked Phyllis and **me** to attend the board meeting.

19. The problem should remain between Bob and **you**.

20. I am going to make **myself** an excellent dinner.

Worksheet 2: Pronoun and Antecedent Agreement

1. When **patients ask** for more medicine, you must tell them to check with their doctor.

2. I like to eat lunch before the afternoon because it is better for **my** health.

3. When **a person** works hard at a task, he/she usually gets good results. (or people . . . they)

4. I usually work late on Thursdays because **I** can get a lot done at the end of the week.

5. Bob said that **his** department is exceptionally productive when **he** least **expects** it.

6. If you listen carefully, **you** can hear inconsistencies in their response.

7. When **you graduate** from college, your first worry usually is finding a job.

8. For many graduates, however, **their** first worry is credit card debt.

9. Many banks offer credit cards to college students knowing that **they** are least likely to pay off all of **their** debt.

10. In this way, creditors can make quite a bit of money off the interest it charges **them**.

11. College students are hurt in many ways by **their** credit card debt.

12. College students should consider the post-graduation monthly cost of their student loans before **they** accept a credit card offer.

Editing Workshop – Chapter 7

By sending a thank-you note after your interview, **you have** another opportunity to make a good impression. By taking the time to send a note to the person **who** interviewed you, you will be letting **that person (or the interviewer)** know that **you are** sincerely interested in the position.

You will also be letting **the interviewer** know that you are a candidate **who** is different from other candidates. By mentioning something that **you** and **he or she** discussed during the interview, you will show that **you were** paying attention.

The format of the note is also important, and **it** should be written with care. Use the business card that the interviewer gave **you** to address the note so that you get important details correct.

Chapter 8

Practice 8.1: Modifiers and Verbs

1. Drive **slowly** so that you do not get in an accident.
2. George feels **bad** about the situation.
3. The trainer spoke too **loudly**, and our group was offended.
4. The music sounds **good** to all of us.
5. The entire group felt **bad** about the change in management.

Practice 8.2: Comparative and Superlative Modifiers

1. Use your editing skills to make this letter **better** than it was before.
2. Toni made the **silliest (or most silly)** comment at the board meeting on Tuesday.
3. I was the **hungriest (most hungry)** person in the room but the last to be served.
4. Of all the people at this college, I live the **farthest** from campus.
5. Our committee is **further** along on this project than I could have imagined.

Practice 8.3: Implied Words in Comparisons

1. Roger's office is nicer than our **manager's office**.
2. My office has more windows than **yours (your office)**.
3. Reggie learned to use the software sooner than **I did**.
4. The executives ordered their lunches before **we did**.
5. However, our desserts were much tastier than **theirs (their desserts)**.

Practice 8.4: Modifiers and Their Placement

1. The report *on policy change* is due in September.
2. Major issues *relating to dress policy* must be addressed at the fall meeting.
3. Filling out the forms, *the applicant* made a mistake.
4. The letter *giving details about the incident* was sent out yesterday.
5. *As I answered the phone,* my feet slipped right out from under me.

Practice 8.5: More on Correct Placement

1. I received *only* three copies of the report.
2. Louis bought *almost* all of the new software in the catalog.

3. During the meeting, we finished *nearly* all of the doughnuts and coffee cake.

4. Congratulations, Jerry, you have *nearly* ten years on the job!

5. We will need to purchase *only* one computer for the research team.

Practice 8.6: Double Negatives

1. The receptionist wouldn't give us **any** information over the phone.

2. Martha didn't have **any** intention of helping us with the proposal.

3. Sylvestri **could** barely wait to tell us his answer.

4. The contractors will not start construction **regardless** of what we offer them.

5. The accountants won't give us **anything** for the charity deduction.

Skills Workshop

Worksheet 1: Adverbs and Adjectives—the Basics

1. You did **well** on your latest report.

2. Her new computer crashes more frequently than **yours**.

3. Riki felt **bad** about firing Sue.

4. You will be able to go **faster** if you take the train than if you walk.

5. Our bookstore finds the **latest** technology available.

6. Your team works more diligently than **any other team.**

7. I **can** hardly wait until summer break. (Or **I can't wait** . . .)

8. The **least** of your worries is how many vacation days you have left.

9. The middle managers have requested **better** working conditions.

10. Why didn't the client have **any** way of getting to the open house?

11. Leaving the corporate world was one of the **hardest** decisions I've ever had to make.

12. The client seemed **happier** after we waived the initial fees.

Worksheet 2: Place Modifiers Correctly

1. All of our managers attended the conference *on international trade* in Tulsa.
2. Give the information *about the revised plan* to Doris.
3. The account *for new car loans* was lost to our competitor.
4. Mr. Jordan is man *with the briefcase in his hand* talking to your manager.
5. You will find the new forms *for joint accounts* in the supply closet.
6. The driver *in the black sedan* left 20 minutes ago.
7. The group *meeting in Room 202* would like to have lunch served at noon.
8. You can pick up the proposal *for new business* from the development office today.
9. The official title for the new position *in our New Jersey office* is development director.
10. File the papers *for incorporation* early in the day to meet the deadline.

Worksheet 3: Dangling Modifiers

1. Following the account closely, the new sales representative still made a mistake.
2. Applying a service fee, the bank overdrew the account.
3. To achieve the best results, our team developed a plan.
4. Leaving in frustration, our team leader cancelled the meeting.
5. To open an account, (you) fill out the forms.

Editing Workshop – Chapter 8

One of the ~~most~~ greatest lessons you can ever learn is to never say *anything* negative about people you work with. It can ~~like really~~ cause you problems if the person ~~like~~ ever finds out what you said about *him or her*. Even if you feel *bad* about what you said, you can't ~~never~~ take your words back. Until you learn this lesson *well*, you are not likely to ~~never~~ change. Be *kind* to people, and you will reap the ~~most~~ best results.

Chapter 9

Practice 9.1: Active Voice

1. Sean's manager asked him to lead the diversity team.
2. Phelps' coach gave him another chance by his coach to swim in the relay.
3. Our department hosted the holiday event last year.
4. Our president implemented a new policy on reimbursement for travel expenses.
5. The mayor cancelled the program due to lack of interest.

Practice 9.2: Passive Voice, the Tactful Voice

1. Meyers made an error in invoicing on your account last week. (passive is more tactful)
2. If you wanted to avoid an overdraft, you should have deposited your check before 4 p.m. (passive is more tactful)
3. You should have enclosed your receipt with your return item. (passive is more tactful)
4. We sent your order to the wrong address and apologize for our mistake. (active)
5. You needed to pay your invoice by the first of the month to avoid penalties. (passive is more tactful)

Practice 9.3: Nominals

1. Management implemented the dress policy in August.

2. Jane suggested that all new hires start on the first day of the month.

3. Our broker gave us information about that stock.

4. We discussed the new account at our last team meeting.

5. Our president announced the merger before the deal was final.

Skills Workshop

Worksheet 1: Active Voice

1. One of the sales representatives must have canceled your order.

2. To reinstate the order, you must submit a new order form.

3. If we receive the form today, we can fill your order today.

4. You should have sent your check by Monday to avoid this situation.

5. Every company values the loyalty of its customers.

6. Your publisher sent me a copy of your book.

7. Our staff enjoyed your book.

8. Our staff requested that you present a workshop.

9. Most of our staff would attend the event.

10. Our human resource department will arrange a book signing.

11. If you agreed, our attorney could draw up a contract.

12. In addition to providing a motivating event for our staff, you and your publisher will build good public relations.

Worksheet 2: Active Voice and Nominals

1. The customer returned the package unopened.

2. Customer service issued a full refund.

3. Bill's coach recommended him for the job.

4. Everyone from Bill's team encouraged him.

5. When he accepted the job, no one was surprised.

6. Dr. Wyatt will perform a short surgical procedure.

7. A surgical nurse will assist Dr. Wyatt.

8. An author from London wrote the novel on wizardry.

9. Several publishing companies rejected the novel.

10. Many publishers expressed regret because they had not given the book more thoughtful attention.

11. After a year, the author turned the novel into a film script.

12. People who read the book acclaimed it.

Editing Workshop – Chapter 9

Dear Helen:

Every five years, our data processing unit updates their records on all active accounts. The procedure is simple. We send a current data sheet to clients and then ask them to change any information that is no longer current; your form is enclosed.

- As you review your account information, please initial any changes that you make.

- After you are certain your information is correct, sign the bottom of the form and return it in the enclosed self-addressed envelope.

We value your business and appreciate your prompt attention to this update.

Sincerely,

Mitchell Szewczyk

Account Executive

Chapter 10

Practice 10.1: Clauses

1. My manager asked me to attend the annual meeting, and he suggested arriving early on Friday.

2. My family will join me in Florida, and my assistant will make reservations for them.

3. Though I gave input, my manager planned my schedule.

4. If I can adjust my schedule, I will take time off for some fun with my family.

5. My boss approved the extra time, so now I must change my travel arrangements.

Practice 10.2: Tenses

1. The message was not clear and needed to be changed.

2. My boss said that their account was closed for some time now.

3. The new computers arrived today, so then I had to install them.

4. Yesterday my co-worker told me that I was supposed to attend the budget meeting.

5. First Mary said that she wanted the position then she said that she didn't.

Practice 10.3: Lists

- Create High Performance Teams
- Develop Effective Communication Skills
- Coach Effective Job Performance
- Resolve Conflict
- Recruit and Retain Managers
- Value Personality Differences in the Workplace
- Assess Climate Change Efforts

Practice 10.4: Correlative Conjunctions

1. My boss not only asked me to complete the report but also to present it at the meeting.

2. Milly both applied both for the job and got it.
3. Our team neither focused on winning the game nor showed good team spirit.
4. The solution not only makes sense but also saves time.
5. My new car neither has a warranty nor runs well.

Skills Workshop: Parallel Structure

1. Getting too many phone calls distracts me and causes me to make mistakes.
2. Mathew's job duties are writing quarterly reports and editing the company newsletter.
3. The director gave her employees two options: attending the meeting or completing the report.
4. The applicants are similar in that both have good qualifications and extensive experience.
5. The director suggested that our committee focus on novel solutions, seek outside advice, and remain open to our options.
6. Please suggest research studies that are informative, interesting, and thought-provoking.
7. Weekly meetings help your staff stay current with department goals, develop innovative solutions, keep everyone updated.
8. Either John will complete the report on time or he will not.
9. We discussed the project over lunch and agreed to go forward with it.
10. To improve how I manage my time, my supervisor advised me to structure my time, stay focused on one task at a time, and consolidate similar projects.

Editing Workshop – Chapter 10

At the Leadership Workshop, you will achieve the following:

- Understand state-of-the-art leadership qualities
- Develop strategies to improve productivity
- Identify and applying best practices for training programs
- Create a personal network for problem solving
- Gain insights into the processes that create effective teams
- Acquire tools for managing training programs

Chapter 11

Practice 11.1: Cut Redundant Modifiers

1. We trust that you find our services worthwhile.
2. Our new design makes our laptop even better than it was before.
3. The outcome of this project depends on all employees doing their best.
4. Before you finish this step, please review the items in your shopping cart.
5. We want you to be certain that you have not ordered multiple items that are alike.

Practice 11.2: Remove Redundancy / Outdated Expressions

1. The papers that you requested are attached.
2. You have our confidence, and we value our business partnership.
3. As we discussed, the new policy should be reviewed this week.
4. You can eliminate any questions by sending your agenda in advance of the meeting.
5. Thank you for your support and assistance. (or simply "support")

Practice 11.3: Use Simple Language

1. We use that product, and the marketing department is aware of our choice.

2. After to the merger, we tried to compromise as much as possible.

3. As you requested, we are omitting that information.

4. If the merger depends on our use of their facilities, we should try to change locations.

5. If you are aware of their objections, try to make respective changes.

Practice 11.4: Modify Correctly

1. In my opinion, you should feel certain what the facts are before you sign the contract.

2. Can you confirm that that they might back out of their agreement?

3. I would like for you to speak to the person who knows much about this topic.

Skills Workshop: Using Simple Language

1. The decision to use that product was made by our advertising department. (Or: Our advertising department decided . . .)

2. After they became involved, we made little progress.

3. As you suggested, I have told my supervisor about our competitor using our coupons.

4. Would you please fill me in on the new manager's background?

5. As you requested, my assistant is sending you several brochures and flyers. (Or: Regarding your request, . . .)

6. If a power outage occurs, the generator will keep our file server running.

7. Welcome to our company. Or: The marketing department welcomes you.

8. Was the committee aware of the Jones Company's history of defaulting on loans?

9. If the merger is depends on our using their software, we should try to make the change.

10. Always do your best, especially when you know the challenges.

11. We use the best materials in our new product line.

12. The end of the project will occur in June. Or: The project will end in June.

Editing Workshop – Chapter 11

Jaclyn,

I should be able to help with Carrie's cell phone problem, but I need more information.

1. Where is Carrie currently located?

2. What kind of cell phone does she have? Specifically, which brand?

3. Where is Carrie trying to call?

4. When Carrie's cell phone last worked, where was she?

Once I get this information, I can start the process.

Hope you are having a great day—talk to you soon.

Matteo

Chapter 12

Editing Workshop – Chapter 12

Jesse,

The dates for the training sessions in Washington, D.C., are April 12, June 7, and September 27.

Here is what we need for the training:

1. Two flip charts, markers, and name tents.
2. U-shaped room.
3. Set-ups for 15 participants.

For breakfast, I have ordered muffins and coffee; for lunch, sandwiches, chips, soft drinks, and cookies.

I have prepared the invoices, and participants should receive them by next week.

Should I contact participants before the training?

Best regards,

Diana

Chapter 13

Key to Pretest

1. Will that decision ~~effect~~ **affect** you in a positive way?
2. The ~~principle~~ **principal** on my loan is due on the 1st of each month.
3. My ~~advise~~ **advice** is for you to get a job before you buy that new car.
4. Please ~~ensure~~ **assure** my manager that I will return in one-half hour.
5. ~~Its~~ **It's** been a challenging day, but things are getting better.
6. ~~Their~~ **There** are a few issues that we need to discuss.
7. The agency gave ~~are~~ **our** report a new title.
8. Pat lives ~~further~~ **farther** from work than I do.
9. You can have a meeting ~~everyday~~ **every day**, if you prefer.
10. ~~Whose~~ **Who's** going to the ballgame?
11. I enjoy movies more ~~then~~ **than** I enjoy plays.
12. Megan ~~assured~~ **ensured** that the project would be successful.
13. It's ~~alright~~ **all right** for you to contact the manager directly.

14. I didn't mean to ~~infer~~ **imply** that you were late on purpose.
15. Try ~~and~~ **to** be on time for the next meeting.

Worksheet 1. Similar Words

1. They have **too** many new projects and **too** little time.
2. You will be **apprised** of the situation before noon today.
3. Jackson **assured** me that you got the job.
4. If you feel **all right** about it, ask for a raise.
5. **You're (you are)** the right person to turn the situation around.
6. **Among** the three of us, we have all the resources we need.
7. Try **to** see Leonard before you leave today.
8. Kevin said that he would **lend** me his notes.
9. His remark was a real **compliment**.
10. I live **farther** from work **than** you do.
11. If you **could have** spoken to Della, you'd understand.
12. Vera **passed** that trait on to her daughters **too**.
13. How will that **affect** you?
14. When you know the **effect**, let me know.
15. Carol **lent** me everything I needed for the trip.
16. The project lost **its** appeal after Mike quit.
17. I **ensure** all print materials will be of high quality.
18. After you **assure** me, **assure** the others also.
19. **Their** boat has left the dock.
20. We are **further** along **than** we realize.
21. Say **it's** time to go, and we will.
22. If the bank will **lend** you enough funds, will you buy the car?
23. My **principal** and interest are due on the 1st of the month.
23. That company does all training on **site**.
24. Did the officer **cite** you for the violation?
25. We all try to live by our **principles**.

Posttest – Similar Words

1. The **effect** of that decision is not yet known.
2. When you know **principal** on your loan, let me know.
3. Her **advice** was that you take the other part-time job.
4. Can you **ensure** the quality of your work?
5. The dog chased **its** tail, amusing several children.
6. **There** are a few issues that we need to discuss.
7. Is that **our** new computer?
8. You are **further** along on the project than I am.
9. We meet **every day** at 3 p.m.
10. **Whose** book is that?
11. Sue was taller **than** Mary last year.
12. Melanie **assured** me that we would be finished by Friday
13. **It's all right** for you to contact the manager directly.
14. I'm not trying to **imply** that you were late on purpose.

Chapter 14

Practice 14.1: The Colon

1. I have some exciting news for you: Jeremy proposed on Friday.
2. Note: The office is closed on Monday to honor the Martin Luther King holiday.
3. The supplies we need are as follows: markers, copy paper, and staplers.
4. Giorgio said that we need cereal, soy milk, and bananas.
5. Here is what you should do: complete the inventory list and then work on the schedule. (Or: Complete . . .)

Practice 14.2: The Dash

1. Margie called on Friday—George is home!

2. Mike's parents are in town—he invited me to have dinner with them.

3. Helen Jones—the new CEO—asked me to join her team.

4. Call if you need anything—I'm always here to support you.

5. Give as much as you can to that charity—it's a good cause.

Practice 14.3: The Ellipses—Answers may vary.

1. **Abbreviated Albert Einstein Quote:** "The important thing is not to stop questioning . . . Never lose a holy curiosity."

2. **Abbreviated Victor Frankl Quote:** "Don't aim at success—the more you aim at it and make it a target, the more you are going to miss it . . . success will follow you precisely because you had *forgotten* to think to it."

Skills Workshop

Worksheet 1: Colons and Dashes

1. Jeremy suggested several changes: add more personnel, start offering carry out, and remain open on Sundays—but I disagree with him on all points.

2. Here's what you need to look out for: their Eastern branch office does not have a sales manager. (Or use a dash instead of a colon.)

3. If you ask for a lower price—even one that is not unreasonable—they will not know how to handle your request.

4. Caution: Do not use this equipment in temperatures below freezing.

5. Note: Friday is a holiday, and our offices will be closed.

6. Sean refused to share the plan—he simply wouldn't answer my questions. (Or use a colon or semicolon instead of a dash.)

7. These are the people you should interview: Eddie Stone, Fred Harris, and Bill Janulewicz.

8. All of them—especially Bill Janulewicz—are extremely knowledgeable of our products.

9. Remain positive: you do not yet know how they will respond to your offer.

10. I received a call from McCracken's CEO—yes their CEO—to join the marketing team.

Worksheet 2. Colons, Dashes, and Ellipses—answers may vary.

1. Scot said that we shouldn't worry . . . the product research team will meet tomorrow.

2. Note the following: more people need to travel today but fewer people enjoy it.

3. The Mercer group became involved of their own accord—I didn't invite them.

4. Follow your passions: you will create a career that you enjoy.

5. I couldn't understand what John said: "The biggest seller is . . ."

6. Send your résumé directly to the CEO: he is expecting to hear from you.

7. Toni and Joe bought the company—they are ecstatic.

8. You know what I mean . . . things just aren't working out.

9. Keep your spirits up—you will have another opportunity soon.

10. Read between the lines . . . watch the body language.

Note: For the above sentences, you could substitute a variety of punctuation marks and still be correct.

Editing Workshop – Chapter 14

Dear Professor,

I apologize for my recent absences. I have been very sick with a sore throat and fever.

Thankfully I am feeling much better, and I will be in class tomorrow. If it is in a room other then our regular room please let me know. Also, please let me know if you would like to see my doctor's note.

Thank you,

Chapter 15

Practice 15.1: Capitalization

Next year the president of my company will provide a financial incentive for all employees, and I plan to participate in it. Jack Edwards, vice president of finance, will administer the plan. Everyone in my department is looking forward to having the opportunity to save more. A pamphlet entitled, "Financial Incentives for Long-term Savings," will describe the plan and be distributed next week. If the pamphlet has not arrived by Friday, I will check with the vice president's office to find out the details.

Practice 15.2: Numbers

1. We are meeting on January 5 at 10 a.m. at our offices on Lake Street.

2. Call me on Monday at 407-555-1212.

3. Alex lists his address as 407 South Maple Street, Hobart, IN 46368.

4. We received hundreds of calls about the job opening but only five résumés.

5. Purchase 12 laptops but only 7 new printers for our department.

Skills Workshop

Worksheet 1: Number Usage and Capitalization

1. The supply company delivered five copiers and seven fax machines.
2. Ian, our new company auditor, scheduled the meeting for Friday, September 10 at 9 a.m.
3. Send the information to Lester Ostrom, 1213 West Astor Place, Chicago, IL 60610.
4. Did you request 12 catalogs or only 2?
5. The new budget for our computer purchase is $1.5 million.
6. We received hundreds of calls, not thousands as Jeffrey said.
7. Did you say I should meet you for lunch today at 12 o'clock or on Monday?
8. Austin Roberts, accounting manager, gave me the instructions on how to complete my taxes.
9. Vice President Tomas O'Rourke has a background in law.
10. If the requirements call for five postings on three different days, allow yourself at least two hours a day to get the work done.
11. We had a 10 percent decrease in our heating bill but a 50 percent increase in our water bill.
12. The closet is 5 feet by 8 feet.
13. If I can assist you with one-half of the mailing, let me know.
14. Eleven of the participants have arrived, but the remaining twelve are late.
15. Meet me on the fourteenth floor at 3:30 p.m. this afternoon.

Worksheet 2: Punctuation, Capitalization, and Number Usage

1. Many colleges are offering online degrees, and you should learn more about the opportunities you have for finishing your degree.

2. Do your research: attend only a fully accredited online college or university.

3. If one-half or more of the course offerings are online, the college's commitment to online learning is strong.

4. A friend of mine received her doctorate online; as a result, she increased her income and her job opportunities.

5. A decade ago, few colleges offered classes online; now hundreds of colleges and universities offer classes online.

6. Some of the advantages of online learning include the following: you can attend classes in the comfort of your own home, make use of special support services and tutorials, and learn at your own pace.

7. Online learning occurs in countries around the world, and thousands of students learn in virtual classrooms every day.

8. Though class size varies, many classes limit the number of participants to 20 students.

9. One of the results of online learning is improved writing skills: good writing skills will benefit you throughout your career.

10. Finishing your education is what's important; get your degree online or attend college at a local university.

Editing Workshop – Chapter 15

Dear Suzie,

Thank you for asking for more information about my work history. For five years, I worked for Rapid Communications as an associate manager in the Customer Service Department.

Here's information about how to contact my former boss, Jake Roberts, human resources director:

Mr. Jake Roberts
Human Resources Director
Rapid Communications
14 North Ogden Road
Burlington, IA 52601

I look forward to hearing from you. You can reach me at 209-555-1212 anytime between 9 a.m. and 5 p.m. Monday through Friday until the end of August.

Best regards,

Sylvia Marina

Chapter 16

Practice 16.1: Quotation Marks

1. My answer to your request is an enthusiastic "yes."

2. If you think that's a "good idea," so do I.

3. The code was "307A," not "370A."

4. All he wrote was, "Our dog can hunt."

5. If you call that "good timing," I don't know how to respond.

Practice 16.2: Apostrophes: Possessives and Contractions

1. My supervisor's report won't be ready until next week.

2. The weather report says it's going to rain later, but I don't believe it.

3. Though it's June's responsibility, it's in Jack's best interest to complete the task.

4. Dr. Jones's (or Dr. Jones') office isn't located down the hall; it's to Dr. Raines' (office).

5. If you tell me it's Tess's (Tess') project, I'll adjust my expectations.

Practice 16.3: Hyphens

1. Your first-class treatment has impressed all of us.

2. The finance department approved one-half of our budget.

3. The short- and long-term outlooks are quite different.

4. Twenty-five people attended the conference.

5. Do you have sufficient funding for your 30- and 60-day payment schedules?

Skills Workshop

Worksheet 1: Quotations, Apostrophes, and Hyphens

1. Margaret's report is a first-class example of what we need.

2. Bob asked, "May I receive a copy of the Barker proposal?"

3. If you can prove "that dog can hunt," we'll sign on to the "dotted line."

4. A one-day workshop would help our part-time staff.

5. After I rejected their "proposal," Mel's response was "great."

6. What's next on the agenda for our mid-week meeting?

7. When I said "the game's over," I was referring to Bill's role.

8. A full-time position is open in our accounting department.

9. A month's worth of invoices are sitting on my desk.

10. You can use Jan's office until the first floor conference room is free.

Worksheet 2: Review of Commas, Semicolons, Apostrophes, and Hyphens

1. Our broker's message got lost in the shuffle, so I had to find his number on the Internet.

2. When I use the term "fixin' to," it means that I'm ready to go do something.

3. Do you have any favorite colloquial terms, Sasha?
4. Call to see if their account executive is available; if he's not, don't leave a message.
5. Let's go to the second-hand shop to pick up supplies for our camping trip.
6. Mandy, my new sales representative called about our "delay."
7. The short- and long-term projections will be available after 3 p.m. today.
8. It's been a long day already, and one-half of my work is yet to be done.
9. Enclose your check in the postage-paid envelope, and send it to us by Friday.
10. Sandro's half baked idea was a hit at our department's meeting.

Editing Workshop – Chapter 16

Trust is an important element of friendship. If you can't trust friends, then what's the point of being around them? Friends are there to support you in everything that you do. They can tell you that they don't agree, but they should always support you.

Loyal and trustworthy friends are with you to the end, and you should treat them like family. If you grow with your friends and allow your feelings to open up, you can share and enjoy things with them. Friends are there through the good times, but they are there for the bad times also. Real friends understand what you are going through even before you tell them.

A good friendship lasts for a very long time—sometimes a lifetime.

INDEX

Made in the USA
Charleston, SC
02 June 2010